the definitive guide to
BETTING
ON HORSES

D0808871

RACING POST
expert series

the definitive guide to

BETTING
ON HORSES

edited by nick pulford

Raceform

Published in 2004 by Raceform Ltd,
Compton, Newbury, Berkshire, RG20 6NL.
Raceform Ltd is a wholly-owned subsidiary of Trinity-Mirror plc.

A catalogue record for this book is available from the British Library.

ISBN 1-904137-35-9

Designed by Robin Gibson and Fiona Pike
Printed by CPD, Wales

CONTENTS

Introduction by Nick Pulford 9

FINDING YOUR WINNER

PART ONE **ASSESSING ABILITY**
1 The Essentials by Nick Pulford 11
2 Off the Mark by Paul Curtis 24
3 Speed's All You Need by Nick Mordin.................32
4 Tools of the Trade by Nick Pulford.............................38

PART TWO **ASSESSING POTENTIAL**
5 Introduction by Nick Pulford 43
6 Race Analysis by Graham Dench 44
7 Breeding Matters by Rachel Pagones 50
8 Reading the Signs by Gerald Delamere 58

PART THREE **THE KEY VARIABLES**
9 The Essentials by Nick Pulford 64
10 Beauty in the Bias by Graham Wheldon.................82
11 Stay with the Pace by James Willoughby 104

PART FOUR **RACE TYPES**
12 The Essentials by Nick Pulford 109
13 A Useful Performer by Paul Curtis 110
14 One Jump Ahead by Steve Mason.................126
15 Glittering Prizes by Tom Segal 134

CHOOSING YOUR BET

PART FIVE **BETTING OFF-COURSE**
16 The Essentials by Nick Pulford 148
17 Bets to Consider by Richard Birch 174

PART SIX **BETTING ON-COURSE**
18 The Essentials by Nick Pulford 180

PART SEVEN **NEW MEDIA**
19 Introduction by Nick Pulford 191
20 Exchange of Views by Nick Pulford 192
21 Spread the Risk by Nick Pulford 200
22 A Survival Guide by Nick Fox.................208
23 A Fair Exchange by Matt Williams.................216

PART EIGHT **GAINING AN EDGE**
24 The Essentials by Nick Pulford 220
25 Anoraks Are Back by Tom Segal.................234
26 A Winning Formula by Richard Birch.................238
27 Maximise Your Edge by Mel Cullinan 244
28 Systems Addicts by Peter May 252
INDEX 267

CONTRIBUTORS

NICK PULFORD is a freelance journalist, specialising in horseracing and football betting. Previously he was racing editor of the South China Morning Post in Hong Kong and has worked full-time for the Racing Post, Pacemaker, Thoroughbred Breeder and Raceform. He was also co-editor of *Flat Horses of 2003* and *Flat Horses of 2004*.

RICHARD BIRCH writes the Saturday betting column Get It Ready in the Racing Post, having joined the newspaper from the Press Association in 1995. He is also the Racing Post's Wimbledon greyhounds correspondent and has contributed to several racing publications, including the Racing Post's *Horses To Follow Flat* and *Jumpers To Follow* annuals.

MEL CULLINAN has worked for the Racing Post since 1990, pioneering the influential Mark Your Card column, and is also a leading tipster for the Racing Post Weekender. He is a regular contributor to the Racing Post's *Horses To Follow Flat* and *Jumpers To Follow* annuals.

PAUL CURTIS has been the Flat handicapper for the Racing Post since 1997, having joined the newspaper in 1993 from his previous job as a Ladbrokes betting shop manager. A member of the Racing Post Ratings team that won the National Press Challenge for tipsters in 1999 and 2002, he is also a regular contributor to the Racing Post Weekender and the Racing Post's *Horses To Follow Flat* annual.

GERALD DELAMERE has been a big-race analyst and tipster for the Racing Post since 1998, having filled the same role at the Sporting Life for the previous 12 years. A renowned paddock-watcher and going expert, he has contributed to the Racing Post Weekender and books such as *Counter Attack* and the Racing Post's *Jumpers To Follow* annual.

GRAHAM DENCH has reported for the Racing Post since joining from Timeform in 1986 and is now the paper's chief race analyst. He is also editor of the official form book and co-edited *Flat Horses of 2003* and *Flat Horses of 2004*. A regular contributor to the *Directory of the Turf* and Pacemaker, he also edited the early volumes of the Racing Post's popular Ten To Follow guides.

NICK FOX writes the daily Trading Bureau column in the Racing Post, having joined from the Sun in 1999, and is a regular contributor to other Racing Post publications. A dual winner of both the National Press Challenge and the Coral/Racing Post naps table for the jumps, he has written computer programs to help him bet successfully on horseracing and soccer with spread firms and exchanges.

STEVE MASON has been the jumps handicapper for the Racing Post Ratings team since 1993, having joined the newspaper in 1988. He won the National Press Challenge for tipsters in 1999 and 2002, as part of the RP Ratings team, and is a regular contributor to the Racing Post Weekender and the Racing Post's *Guide to the Jumps* and *Jumpers To Follow* annuals.

DR PETER MAY is the author of eight horseracing books, including *Forecasting Methods for Horseracing*, *Flat Racing For Profit* and *Jump Racing For Profit*, and has contributed to several racing publications, including Raceform Update, Raceform On Saturday and In The Know. He holds a BSc (Honours) in Mathematics and Computer Science, an MPhil in Expert Systems and a PhD in Artificial Intelligence.

NICK MORDIN is a speed ratings specialist, with a weekly column in the Racing Post Weekender. He has written four horseracing books, covering speed ratings, betting systems, handicapping and paddock watching.

RACHEL PAGONES is bloodstock editor with the Racing Post, having joined the newspaper in 2001. A bloodstock agent and pinhooker for the previous decade, she is a regular columnist on bloodstock matters for the Financial Times and American publication TBH MarketWatch.

TOM SEGAL writes the highly successful Pricewise column in the Racing Post, which he joined in 1997, having previously worked for Raceform. He also writes for the Racing Post Weekender and has contributed to several horseracing books, including the Racing Post's *Horses To Follow Flat* and *Jumpers To Follow* annuals and *Counter Attack*.

GRAHAM WHELDON is a leading expert on the effects of the draw, having written three books on the subject. Part of the Racing Post's Spotlight team during the Flat season and a contributor to the newspaper's Trading Post column, he also writes for the Racing & Football Outlook and Raceform Update. He has also worked for Weatherbys and as sports editor of Raceform On Saturday.

MATT WILLIAMS writes the Racing Post's Trading Post column, the ground-breaking daily guide to the betting exchanges. Before joining the Racing Post in 2000, he spent two years with Lambourn trainer John Hills.

JAMES WILLOUGHBY is special correspondent for the Racing Post, having joined the newspaper in 1999 after previous spells with Timeform and The Times. He is a familiar face on television, through his work on Attheraces and the Racing Channel, and has contributed to several racing publications including Pacemaker, *Flat Horses of 2003* and *Flat Horses of 2004*.

BETTING ON HORSES

INTRODUCTION

By NICK PULFORD

HORSERACE BETTING IN THE 21ST century is a complex, sometimes confusing, business. With more racing and more betting opportunities than ever before, the punter is faced with a bewildering array of choice. From the all-weather to the jumps, and from the betting ring to the exchanges, the battle to stay ahead of the game has never been more challenging.

This book offers a step-by-step guide through the minefield of modern racing and betting, offering practical advice on all aspects of the professional approach to picking winners and placing bets.

The book features contributions from the Racing Post's unrivalled team of experts, as well as other leading specialist writers and professional punters. Their views represent the most up-to-date thinking on racing and betting, and will be of interest to both experienced and novice punters.

The book is divided into two main sections. In the first section, Finding Your Winner, the experts examine how to assess ability and potential, as well as the effect of key factors on racing performance. Handicap ratings, speed ratings, race analysis, pedigree pointers and paddock clues all come under the microscope, along with important variables such as the draw, pace and going. The Racing Post's top tipsters look across the whole spectrum of racing, identifying the most profitable areas for betting and the winning approach to big races and major race meetings.

The second section, Choosing Your Bet, concentrates on the various sectors of the betting industry. There is a detailed examination of the pros and cons of the different bet types, off-course and on-course, along with an in-depth look at recent innovations such as betting exchanges and spread betting. The book concludes with Gaining An Edge, which draws together many of the book's strands and offers practical advice on how to make horse-race betting pay.

The book does not seek to promote a one-dimensional view on the approach to horserace betting. Instead, it reflects the diversity of opinion on the subject, drawing on the expertise and experience of leading specialists. Some experts favour win singles only, others espouse the virtues of each-way betting; some prefer the cut and thrust of the betting ring; others have switched successfully to new outlets such as the betting exchanges. It is all a question of choice.

All are agreed, however, that horserace betting can be profitable – and fun – if approached with a good understanding of the basic principles.

PART ONE

ASSESSING ABILITY

By NICK PULFORD

HORSERACING IN BRITAIN HAS TWO basic divisions: Flat racing, concentrated mainly in the summer months between April and October, and the winter season of jump racing, which starts in earnest in early November and continues until late April. There are more than 13,000 racehorses in training, competing for prize-money of almost £95 million spread across about 8,800 races per year. Those races are divided between 59 racecourses, which stage more than 1,200 race meetings per year (2003 figures compiled by the British Horseracing Board).

ADMINISTRATION The sport is governed by two organisations – the British Horseracing Board and the Jockey Club. The latter was founded in 1752 and was, until 1993, solely responsible for the governance and regulation of horseracing in Britain. In 1993, the Jockey Club decided to transfer certain functions to a new body, the BHB, which has four members: the Jockey Club; the Racecourse Association; the Racehorse Owners' Association; and the Industry Committee (representing trainers, jockeys, stable lads, breeders and others).

The BHB is now the principal administrative and planning body. Its main responsibilities include strategic planning of, and formulating policy for, British horseracing; representing the

11

interests of British horseracing to bookmakers; the collection and control of funds required for the administration of racing; central marketing and promotion of British racing; controlling the fixture list; race planning; and encouraging the breeding of bloodstock.

The Jockey Club has retained responsibility for licensing and 'integrity' issues. It is responsible for registering and licensing horses, racecourses, owners, trainers and jockeys. A requirement of licensing and registration is that racing participants abide by the Orders and Rules of the Jockey Club. The Jockey Club is also responsible for the conduct of racing, including: safeguarding the integrity of racing (essentially ensuring the public can trust the racing they are betting on); racecourse medical and veterinary arrangements for riders and horses; employment and direction of its race-course officials; and disciplinary matters. Through the Racecourse Holdings Trust, the Jockey Club also owns 13 British racecourses.

FLAT RACING Racing on the Flat accounts for about 60 per cent of all races run in Britain each year (approximately 5,200 in 2003). It is concentrated mainly in the summer months, with a seven-days-a-week programme that features some of the world's most famous races and race meetings.

The youngest runners are two-year-olds, who have a separate programme of races, though they are eligible for some all-aged races. It is rare for Flat horses to race much beyond the age of six, and certainly for them to be racing still when they reach double figures. It is generally reckoned that a Flat racehorse reaches its peak at four to five years of age.

Much of the attention is focused on the three-year-olds and especially the five Classic races which are restricted to them – the 1,000 Guineas and 2,000 Guineas at Newmarket in early May, the Derby and Oaks at Epsom in early June, and the St Leger at Doncaster in mid-September. These races form the centrepiece of

Kris Kin lands the 2003 Vodafone Derby, one of the five British Classics

three important weekend race meetings, but many of the other major festivals are held on weekdays. These include Chester's May meeting, Royal Ascot (mid-June), the Newmarket July meeting, Glorious Goodwood (late July/early August) and York's Ebor meeting in mid-August.

The turf Flat season starts in late March and runs until early November, but Flat racing is now held all year round following the advent of all-weather racing in 1989. There are three all-weather tracks – Lingfield, Southwell and Wolverhampton.

JUMP RACING National Hunt racing – more popularly known as jump racing – accounts for the other 40 per cent of British horseraces. It has three main categories: steeplechasing, over fences measuring around 5ft; hurdling, over smaller, less rigid obstacles; and National Hunt flat races (or bumpers). Most horses start racing at the age of three or four and usually graduate through the ranks, starting in bumpers, followed by a season of hurdling, after which they either continue to specialise in hurdling or move up to chasing. A hurdler's best years are often from the ages of five to seven, while chasers usually peak from the ages of seven to ten. The most durable often race until the age of 12.

Like the Flat, jump racing is now held virtually all year round, with a popular summer programme. The season officially runs from the start of May to the end of April, but the biggest races are held between November and April.

The season builds to a climax, principally at the three-day Cheltenham Festival in mid-March. This event is seen as jump racing's championship and features the Gold Cup, for the top steeplechasers, and the Champion Hurdle.

The most famous jumps race is the Grand National, which forms the centrepiece of a three-day festival at Aintree, usually held in early April. Most of the other important races are held at weekends during the winter months, with a final championship day staged at Sandown in late April.

STRUCTURE The championship races on the Flat and over jumps, and many other major races, are run at level weights – that is, all horses carry the same weight, meaning that the best horse should win. On the Flat, the weight carried by horses in these races (which include the five Classics) is 9st, while over jumps it is 12st (for races such as the Cheltenham Gold Cup and the Champion Hurdle).

The major level-weights races on the Flat make up what is known as the European Pattern, in which races are graded according to their importance. The top races are Group 1, followed by Group 2 and Group 3. The next highest category is Listed races, which, while not technically part of the Pattern, combine with Group races under the heading of black-type races (so called because winners and placed horses in such races are shown in black type in sales catalogues – a horse who has earned black type or has black type among its immediate family is therefore seen as more valuable).

uncommon knowledge

 Know your Flat races

Classics, claimers and gentlemen amateurs

The main race types in Britain (in approximate order of importance and prize-money value):

◇ **Group 1**
◇ **Group 2**
◇ **Group 3**
◇ **Listed races**
◇ **Conditions Stakes** Better-class race for horses below Class A. Weights are determined by age and/or sex, not by ratings
◇ **Rated Stakes** Valuable handicap with a limited weight range of 10-14lb, for horses at or just below Listed class
◇ **Classified Stakes** Race with a maximum rating, for horses who have run at least three times, or have run twice and won at least once
◇ **Handicap** Race where the weight each horse carries is determined by official ratings. Horses can only run in races where the maximum rating is higher than or equal to its rating
◇ **Nursery** Handicap for two-year-olds
◇ **Maiden** For horses who have never won
◇ **Novice** For two-year-olds or three-year-olds who have not won more than twice
◇ **Novice auction** For novices sold at public auction as yearlings or two-year-olds for a price not exceeding a specified figure
◇ **Maiden handicap** For maidens aged three or more who have run at least four times and have a maximum rating of 70

◇ **Auction maiden** For two-year-olds sold at public auction as yearlings or two-year-olds, for a price not exceeding a specified figure
◇ **Median Auction Maiden** For two-year-olds by stallions who had one or more yearling sold in the previous year with a median price not exceeding a specified figure
◇ **Claiming Stakes** Each horse's weight is determined by the price placed on them by connections. The lower the claiming price, the lower the weight. Horses can be 'claimed' (bought) by other owners and trainers for the specified price after the race
◇ **Rating Related Maiden** Maiden race for horses who have run at least three times and have a rating within a specified band
◇ **Seller** Low-class race where the winner is offered for public auction after the race
◇ **Apprentice Race** For apprentice jockeys only. In other races, apprentices are allowed to claim a weight allowance because of their inexperience. They can claim 7lb until they have won 20 races, 5lb until 50 races, 3lb until 95 races, after which they join the senior ranks. Weight allowances can be claimed in all race types except Group and Listed races
◇ **Amateurs** Race for amateur jockeys only
◇ **Ladies** Race for female amateur and apprentice jockeys only
◇ **Gentlemen** For male amateurs only

uncommon knowledge

 Know your jump races

Know your novices from your maidens and beginners

◇ **Grade 1**
◇ **Grade 2**
◇ **Grade 3**
◇ **Listed**
◇ **Open handicap** Better-class handicap for horses below Class A
◇ **Handicap** Race where the weight each horse carries is determined by official ratings. Horses can only run in races where the maximum rating is higher than or equal to its rating
◇ **Novice race** Chase or hurdle race open only to horses who have not won that type of race before the start of the current season
◇ **Open novice handicap** Better-class handicap for novices below Class A
◇ **Juvenile novices' hurdle** Hurdle race restricted to horses aged three at the start of the current season
◇ **Hunter chase** Weight-for-age chase confined to horses certified by a master of hounds to have been hunted during the current year, and ridden by amateur riders
◇ **National Hunt flat races** Also called bumpers, these are races without jumps designed to give young horses race experience.

Usually restricted to horses between the ages of four and six who have not run under any recognised rules of racing, apart from bumpers
◇ **Beginners Chase** Restricted to horses who have not won a chase
◇ **Maiden** For horses who have never won that type of race
◇ **Conditional jockeys** For conditional jockeys only (conditional is the NH term for apprentice). In other races, conditionals are allowed to claim a weight allowance because of their inexperience. Weight allowances can be claimed in all race types except level-weights Graded races
◇ **Amateurs** For amateur jockeys only
◇ **Claiming Stakes** Each horse's weight is determined by the price placed on them by connections. The lower the claiming price, the lower the weight. Horses can be 'claimed' (or bought) by other owners and trainers for the specified price after the race
◇ **Seller** Low-class race where the winner is offered for public auction after the race

The Pattern races form the pinnacle of each racing season, though they are relatively few in number. In Britain during 2003, there were 29 Group 1 races on the Flat, with 35 at Group 2, 59 at Group 3, and 151 Listed races. In all, then, there were 274 black-type races

Monty's Pass (19) on his way to winning the 2003 Grand National

(or just over five per cent of the total number of Flat races run in Britain).

It is a similar story over jumps, though the Pattern covers only races run in Britain and Ireland and races are classified as Grade 1, Grade 2 and Grade 3, again followed by Listed races. There were 27 Grade 1 races in Britain in 2003, 65 Grade 2 races, and 16 at Grade 3, with 31 Listed races (in all, about four per cent of the total number of jumps races held in Britain each year).

STRUCTURE If the purpose of horseracing were simply to find the best racehorse in each race, all races would be run at level weights and invariably the most talented horse would come out on top. Essentially, this was how racing started off and it was all pretty straightforward.

The problem was that it also became quite tedious. As horserace betting grew in popularity during the 19th century, so there was a need to provide more evenly balanced races, based on a system of weight penalties allotted to the better horses in each contest.

This practice eventually led to the creation of the modern handicapping system, which seeks to measure the merit of each horse's racing performances in terms of a rating. The official ratings are produced by the British Horseracing Board and used to allocate weights in handicap races, which make up the vast bulk of racing in Britain today.

The official handicappers assess the merit of each race and allocate a rating to each horse, expressed in pounds. These ratings are based mainly on the race distance, the winning time, the weight carried by the runners, their ages, and the margins separating the runners.

One important variable between different handicapping systems is the weight allowance for beaten distances, but a standard system on the Flat would use a sliding scale (as the race distance increases) of three pounds per length at five furlongs, two pounds per length over a mile and one pound per length at two miles. A particularly fast winning time might increase these allowances, say to three and a half pounds per length over five furlongs.

Over jumps, where races are longer and race times are slower, the allowances for beaten distances are much smaller than on the Flat. The standard system over jumps is to allow one pound per length, except at extreme distances.

Collateral lines of form between different horses and different races allow a complete set of ratings to be drawn up. This amounts to a universal handicap of all horses, ranging from the top performers, usually assessed in the high 130s on the Flat and the high 170s over jumps, down to the poorest runners, who might merit only a single-figure rating.

The ratings, expressed in pounds, indicate the respective levels of ability of each horse and, in theory, the amount of weight a lower-rated horse would need to receive from a higher-rated rival in order for both to be competitive in a given race.

For example, a horse rated 100 should

concede ten pounds to a 90-rated rival in a handicap in order for them to have an equal chance of victory. In a race run at level weights, the 100-rated runner would come out on top by a comfortable margin, according to the ratings.

A universal handicap also aims to allow comparison of horses from different eras. A top-class horse nowadays, rated 130 for example, should be the equivalent of a horse with the same rating from a decade ago.

The highest-rated horse in a handicap race is given the top weight and the other horses are then allocated weights according to the respective differences in their ratings. On the Flat the weights range from 9st 7lb to 7st 10lb, while over jumps the scale is from 12st to 10st.

There is a class structure to British racing. All black-type races are Class A, with the remaining events classified as Class B-G on the Flat and B-H over jumps. Prize-money usually decreases with each step down the class scale, with a horse's rating determining where it fits into the overall structure.

A Class B Flat race, for example, might be classified as 0-105, meaning it is open to horses with a rating between those figures (horses who have won or placed at Listed level or above usually exceed a rating of 105, which rules them out). In practice, the ratings differential of horses entered in such races might be 80-105 – if this were the case, a horse with a rating of 105 would be allocated top weight (9st 7lb), with the rest allocated weight according to their rating compared with the top-rated horse. Thus a horse with a rating of 98 (seven less than the top-rated 105) would be on 9st (7lb below the top-rated's weight of 9st 7lb). A horse rated 80 would be given the minimum of 7st 10lb (25lb below the top-rated's 9st 7lb).

PRIVATE RATINGS As in many other sports, pure 'class' in horseracing is difficult to define and quantify. The official ratings may form the basis for handicap races, but that does not mean they are entirely accurate. If they were, every handicap would finish in a dead-heat because the weights allocated would cancel out the differences in ability between the horses.

Races are run under varying conditions and there is no definitive, unarguable guide to one racehorse's ability over another. The picture is complicated in Britain by the number and variation of racecourses, which increases the difficulty of making accurate form comparisons between different races.

Such comparisons are, however, the basis of virtually all betting selections and there are a vast number of 'private' handicapping services which seek to find an edge over the official figures. These ratings fall into two broad categories – form ratings and speed ratings. Form ratings use benchmark horses in races to determine the ratings of the other runners, while speed ratings are based on the time taken to run a race, after making allowances for the ground conditions and the standard time for the course and distance of the race.

The pros and cons of each approach are discussed later in this section by Paul Curtis, part of the three-man team that compiles the highly regarded Racing Post Ratings, and Nick Mordin, one of the world's leading authorities on speed ratings.

FORM RATINGS The basic handicapping principles are widely accepted and often there appears to be little variation between BHB ratings and non-official figures such as Racing Post Ratings. However, even a difference of one or two pounds in the respective ratings can be vital in assessing a tight handicap, which is why many serious punters rely on at least one set of non-official ratings when making betting selections.

The official ratings adhere more rigidly to the black-and-white of the form book (one reason being that the handicappers have to be as fair as possible to the horses' connections when making their assessments), whereas non-official

Geos (near side) collars Rooster Booster on the line in the 2004 Tote Gold Trophy at Newbury, one of the Jumps season's big handicap hurdles

handicappers have more scope for deviating from the strict figures. While an improving horse might go up eight pounds in the official ratings after a win, a private handicapper could factor in the horse's potential for improvement and raise the horse by ten or 12 pounds. On the horse's next run, therefore, the horse could be as much as four pounds 'well in' when comparing the non-official rating with the official figure.

Even when the official and non-official ratings are the same, the non-official handicapper can use a plus sign next to the rating to indicate that the horse is probably capable of achieving a better rating – another useful guide for the punter.

Handicapping is not merely about mathematics – it is about accurate interpretation and application of the basic principles. The real art of handicapping in a betting sense is knowing when to follow those principles, and when not to, and how to adjust the figures according to other factors such as course and going. This is one reason why the Racing Post Ratings service has proved so successful in tipping competitions in recent years, as it takes a first-class set of ratings and applies them to each individual race. Later in the book (in chapter 13, page 110, and chapter 14, page 126) the Racing Post Ratings team take a detailed look at how their ratings work across the different race types and offer an insight into where the best betting opportunities lie.

SPEED RATINGS

Speed ratings are a relatively new phenomenon in racing compared to form ratings and are chiefly a product of the American racing scene, where speed as a method of analysis was first mentioned in the early 1900s. It did not gain wide acceptance, however, until the US speed guru Andy Beyer wrote Picking Winners in 1979 – a mould-breaking book which revolutionised the analysis of horseracing in the States and, to a lesser extent, in Britain.

It may seem obvious that the fastest horse in a race should win, but horseracing is not that straightforward. Unlike athletics, where pure times are a good guide to results because all times are recorded under similar conditions (400m tracks with little surface variation), the analysis of finishing times in horseracing presents a host of logistical problems.

The most obvious is the wide difference in racing conditions on the various racecourses, making direct comparison of race times impossible. The picture is complicated by the unreliability of the advertised going and, in some cases, the race distances, and by the fact that horses do not pace themselves (as athletes do) but are directed by their jockeys, bringing issues of pace and tactics into the equation.

Speed experts attempt to factor in all these variables to produce a set of ratings which, like form ratings, allow comparison of horses which have been running in different races and under different conditions.

Speed ratings make adjustments to pure times by assessing the merit of each race against

Runners on the all-weather at Lingfield. Speed ratings, according to expert Nick Mordin, are particularly useful on the all-weather tracks

the clock – chiefly by comparing individual race times against racecourse standard times.

Assessment of a set of race times at a particular meeting enables the calculation of a going allowance (which seeks to quantify the effect of the ground conditions), which is then used to adjust the time of each race (according to the distance) and each horse (according to the distances by which they won or were beaten). This set of calculations produces a raw speed rating.

Published speed ratings, of course, are much more complex than this simple formula. They have developed significantly over the past three decades to include a host of other factors, though experts argue over the merits of taking into account such variables as the weight carried by a horse or the direction and strength of the wind at a race meeting.

One significant complication for British students of speed ratings is the absence of sectional timing at most racecourses, which reduces scope for assessing the pace of a race – a vital factor in compiling accurate speed ratings.

making ratings work for you

OFF THE MARK

RACING POST RATINGS (FORMERLY known as Postmark) have been a feature of the Racing Post since its inception, providing an independent opinion on the value of the form of all races run in Britain and Ireland, plus the top races from overseas.

By PAUL CURTIS

The purpose of form ratings such as RP Ratings is to provide a measure of performance for every horse to have run in the several thousand races analysed each year, from the lowest of sellers to the championship Group 1 events. But while it may please the purist to know how this year's Derby winner compares with recent winners, that's not going to pay the bills and a potentially more profitable way of using ratings is as a tool to forecast future results.

The Racing Post employs three handicappers, two for the Flat and one for jumps, who not only compile the RP Ratings but use them to arrive at the selections found daily in the Post.

The computerised system we use at the Racing Post will automatically calculate ratings for all runners in a particular race once a marker rating has been decided upon and a pounds-per-length figure has been set. This rating shows how much better or worse a particular horse's performance was against other runners in the race. Because we produce figures and selections on a daily basis we already have 'pre-race' ratings, or the figure we thought a horse capable of running to in a particular race,

uncommon knowledge

Racing's currency is pounds and lengths

How ratings are compiled

Races are usually rated up the morning after the race, for inclusion in Raceform, and the thought processes used to compile the figures can be very similar to those employed as a punter.

First, one would look for a solid 'marker' in a race, a horse that has finished reasonably close-up and might have been expected to have run its race under the prevailing conditions. That horse, or rather the rating it is thought capable of running to, is then used as the initial benchmark for the race, with the other horses rated according to the distance they were in front of or behind the 'marker'. This is done using a pounds-per-length scale, which for good ground on the Flat would look something like this:

5f: 3.5lb
6f: 3lb
8f: 2lb
10f: 1.7lb
12f: 1.5lb
14f: 1.3lb
16f: 1lb

This scale would vary slightly depending on ground conditions and race times, while 1lb per length is generally used for all but extreme distances over jumps.

and the result rating program allows us an at-a-glance assessment of how each horse has performed above or below pre-race expectations.

The thought processes in arriving at handicap ratings can be similar to those employed as a punter, with all the variables such as track, trip, ground etc being thrown into the mix. For example, if one knows that a horse requires give underfoot or a distance of ground to be seen to best effect, it is unlikely to have run to its best over a fast six furlongs. One would expect a horse's form to follow its established pattern and this knowledge of preferred conditions can help weed out dodgy results or performances.

The tipping part of the job can prove very beneficial when it comes to compiling ratings, as it gives an insight into the race, the way you expect it to be run, where the pace is, draw biases, those horses you anticipate improvement from, etc. Although in theory it is possible to handicap a race 'cold', in practice it is very difficult. One might produce satisfactory figures without knowing anything about the race, but one is then only reacting to past events. The insight gained from analysing a race beforehand helps us to look ahead and, at least in part, gives the ratings a more predictive nature.

Race times can have a big influence on form ratings, particularly when dealing with unexposed horses, such as when rating two-year-olds. Once the race times have been noted it is possible to arrive at the 'definitive' RP Ratings for each race at a meeting.

Definitive is in inverted commas because in practice there is no such thing. The theoretical part of the job is to place each horse in an overall handicap, so that horses that have never met can be assessed against each other. Such ratings are never set in stone, however, and there is always a degree of fluidity. Potential for movement can vary greatly, from early season two-year-old events where little is known about the runners and the value of form can shift dramatically, to solid top handicaps such as the Royal Hunt Cup or John Smith's Cup where initial assessments are unlikely to be more than a pound or two awry.

That's not to say that initial ratings for early season two-year-old events like the Brocklesby are mere guesses, as there is plenty of historical evidence that can be used to assign ratings to races where there is little form to go on. Course, trainer, time of year and race times can all be factored in, plus we have a fair idea from previous seasons of what standard is required to win certain races. We now publish the average required standard expected of the winner for many non-handicap races in the Racing Post, and this can be a useful guide to see whether those to have run have shown form approaching the usual winning standard.

THE RATINGS EDGE
The theoretical handicap can be seen as a huge jigsaw, where each race, however minor, has an effect on

the overall picture. As each new result is assessed there is a knock-on effect, and ratings for past results will be raised or lowered as a result. Thus a horse can find its mark improving or declining without even setting foot on the racecourse.

Most ratings services, RP Ratings included, operate on the same scale as the BHB official handicappers, ie, 0-140 on the Flat and 0-175 over jumps, where each point on the scale represents 1lb of weight. The Flat, then, works on a theoretical handicap with a top weight of 10st, and the jumps 12st 7lb.

The major difference in the Racing Post's approach, though, is that RP Ratings does not operate a current handicap, or master ratings as they are commonly known. Every horse eligible for handicaps in Britain and Ireland has an official handicap mark, a figure that the official handicappers consider that horse capable of running to currently. This approach is necessary for the framing of weights for the thousands of handicaps run in Britain each year. RP Ratings does not run a live handicap, however, instead using historical records of a horse's performances to decide what it might be capable of under the prevailing conditions and giving them a more predictive nature.

If a horse has produced a figure of, say, 100, four runs ago, but has run poorly in three subsequent starts, what rating is that horse currently capable of running to? Their official mark might well have slipped a few pounds to, say, 97, to reflect those below-par efforts, but nowhere on their record is there a performance rating in the high 90s. That figure is an attempt by the official handicappers to gauge the animal's current ability, with a view to trying to compile a fair and open handicap.

By not having to bother with a current handicap in the Racing Post, RP Ratings avoid this necessary slippage and can treat each horse on its individual merits. As the ratings are a tipping-based service, the ability of each horse to show its form under forecast conditions is decided at the overnight stage – hence in the above example we would look for reasons why the 100-rated horse might not have run to its mark since. Track, trip, ground or draw might have been against it, and if conditions are in the horse's favour it would invariably be given the benefit of the doubt. If not, it would be downgraded for the racecard, but would still retain its top figure. As long as that form is solid and has not been devalued by others, the 100 rating will stick despite a slipping official mark, and its ability to reproduce it will be assessed on an ongoing basis.

This is an area where RP Ratings do particularly well as the tipping methodology comes into play. Because our figures are not so heavily weighted towards recent form, there are many instances where we can identify apparently out-of-form horses who have slipped in the weights, yet are ideally suited to forecast conditions. It may be the return of soft ground or to a favourite track, or perhaps the stable has just struck form. Whatever the reason, if one delves beneath the surface there are often well-handicapped horses lurking.

THE PROBLEM AREAS Where ratings tend to fall down is when dealing with unexposed horses, or races where such horses feature prominently. We usually have an idea of what is required to win a particular race, but while such information is useful for compiling ratings after the event, it's not much use beforehand.

There is no magic sliding scale for ascertaining when old form becomes irrelevant, and with racecard ratings decided at the overnight stage such decisions are made almost every day. A current handicap system would eliminate such worries, but it would also mean missing out on some good-priced winners.

As ever, it's a judgement call and conditions will play a big part in the decision-making process, as would the likely prices on offer. In the above example, with such small margins the recent form would probably get the edge,

The three-year-old problem

The three-year-old division has long been the Achilles heel of the tipping side of our service, which is understandable given the nature of the beast.

Trying to weigh up the previous year's nursery form against unexposed maiden form can be very difficult, while the level of ability a horse retains is far more volatile between the ages of two and three than at any other time.

It takes time for the three-year-old form to settle down and the relevance of nursery form, usually the most solid two-year-old form but getting past its sell-by date by early summer of the following year, illustrates a difficulty with the RP Ratings approach to tipping, that being the difficulty of weighing up recent form with older performances.

Using the example of the 100-rated horse again, what should one do from the ratings perspective if it comes up against a horse that ran to 99 last time and meets off level weights? The BHB figures would favour the recent form, yet RP Ratings would initially give the older form the edge.

but not if it is likely to offer poor value. The ability to oppose likely overbet horses and not be a slave to the figures is a distinct advantage of the RP Ratings approach.

THE CLASS FACTOR Class is another area where ratings can struggle, as although there are reasonably well-established guides to what ratings on the 0-140 scale equate to in terms of ability, it can be difficult to move between bands.

0-45	regional racing
45-60	sellers/modest handicappers
60-70	fair handicappers
70-80	decent handicappers
80-95	useful handicappers
95+	top handicappers
105+	Listed class
110+	Group 3
115+	Group 2
120+	Group 1
130+	top-class

That scale gives an indication as to what the
ratings mean in terms of class, but there is plenty
of flexibility between bands, particularly at the
top end of the scale where top handicappers
merge with lesser Pattern-class performers.
Every race is judged on its merits, and, although
one might expect a 120+ rating from a Group 1
race, if the form isn't up to it, it will fall short of
the anticipated standard. Similarly, because
a race carries only Listed status does not mean
that it cannot produce a rating superior to that
usually associated with the grade if the race
attracts sufficient quality performers.

A horse's current handicap mark is valid
no matter what the grade, so a horse rated
50 in a 0-50 handicap can be expected to carry
top weight, but faced with a 0-70 affair could
find itself somewhere near the foot of the weights.

Handicap ratings assume that, all things being
equal, the horse would have as good a chance
in either race, but the reality tends to be
quite different. On good ground this hypothetical
50-rated horse would find it far easier to concede
weight to lesser rivals than to win in receipt
of weight from classier individuals.

A far higher proportion of handicaps are won
by horses near the top of the weights compared
to those at the bottom, the exception being when
conditions get testing, particularly over a distance
of ground. This is the class effect and it is
something that can make a mockery of even
the very best handicap ratings.

A classic example would be the winner of a
solid mid-grade handicap who scrapes into a
classier affair under a penalty. There is nothing
wrong with its winning form and it might
look well treated under a penalty, but up against
superior opposition it can't keep up. Despite
receiving weight, it is not enough to compensate
for the fact that it just can't run fast enough.

This sort of scenario is often seen on the
all-weather, where weight generally has less of
an effect than on turf and running in the correct
class is as important as a handicap mark. An
even greater proportion of handicaps on sand

uncommon knowledge

**Digging deeper
into a race**

Behind the figures

The ratings published in the Racing Post cover three areas, offering a figure for a horse's latest, best (in the past 12 months) and master figure, the latter being the rating that goes on the card and our assessment of what each horse is capable of under the conditions.

While RP Ratings have a good record as a tipping service, however, there is no substitute for a personal understanding of the figures. The Racing Post usually publishes three lines of form, and while recent form is the most relevant it doesn't always show how the ratings work. Full records for every horse, including their RP Rating for each race, can be found on the Racing Post website.

One of the major benefits RP Ratings have over the official figures is that we aren't really answerable to anyone with regard to what figures we assign a horse. It's far easier for us to take a chance, and hopefully find an edge, when we're not going to get our ear bent by the animal's trainer

because it's hiked 17lb for a cheeky two-length win.

We also have more scope to take the run of the race into account. For instance, if a big-field handicap splits into two groups the official assessor cannot do anything about the 'winner' of the disadvantaged group. Should we wish to, we can treat such races as two separate events for RP Ratings purposes.

Conversely, a wide-margin winner can expect a hefty rise in the weights, whereas RP Ratings might be able to reflect the fact that the horse was flattered by the run of the race. The official handicappers have to be seen to be fair to all, a position that can prove profitable for those who don't feel the pressure to justify their actions.

Compiling handicap ratings might not be everyone's cup of tea – to cover the thousands of races run in Britain each year would require a level of dedication beyond the means of most people – but they are the most important foundation of successful punting.

are won by those towards the head of the weights, the weight received by less talented runners simply not being enough to compensate for their lack of speed.

However you deal with it, the class factor is a problem when compiling handicap ratings and using them for making selections, and the best policy is probably just to be aware of it. If a horse fails in better grade then don't necessarily hold it against it, while a horse dropped in class is often well worth another look.　■

figuring out who runs fastest

SPEED'S ALL YOU NEED

THE BEST PERFORMER IN MOST sports is the one who can run the fastest, jump the highest, throw the furthest or lift the most. There is no question about the relative merits of competitors. Their precise level of ability can be measured to the ounce, millimetre or hundredth of a second.

By NICK MORDIN

In horseracing, things are very different. All the rankings of horses published in the entire world are a matter of guesswork. Nobody seems to have figured out an objective way to quantify the exact merit of a racehorse.

It need not be that way. Surf to the website www.emiratesracing.com, the website of the Emirates Racing Association, and you can see how the racing game will almost certainly be played in the distant future.

The ERA appears to have stumbled upon something that enables us to compare one racehorse very accurately with another. The something in question is the remarkably fast and consistent racing surface of their flagship track, Nad Al Sheba.

At other racetracks the relative speed of the surface varies from day to day, but at Nad Al Sheba the surface is almost always exactly the same speed. As a result, you can bet that a horse who runs a mile and a quarter in two minutes, two seconds is actually a second faster than one who runs the same distance in two minutes, three.

Super fast, consistent Nad Al Sheba: one day all tracks will be this way

The surface at Nad Al Sheba is so fast that even if it slows up considerably it allows a horse to race at maximum speed. I wish all racecourses could be this way, and I'd bet good money that one day they will be. The ability to directly compare a time recorded at one course with that recorded at any other would offer the game huge promotional advantages. It would put horseracing on the same footing as other sports. Anybody, even the most inexperienced fan, would be able to tell which runner was fastest simply by glancing at the times they had run.

Until that happy day is reached we are going to have to make do with speed ratings.

Speed ratings provide a numerical estimate of how fast a horse ran on a particular day. They are based on the apparent speed of the racetrack and of the horses who ran on it.

Very few people outside America bother to compile their own speed ratings. As a result they offer punters in Britain a significant edge. Speed ratings will often put you on to horses that other methods would never select. For this reason alone, they are worth producing.

I am convinced that speed ratings offer the

most accurate way of estimating the merit of
a racehorse. If you would like to produce
your own, it is not that hard. You can crank out
usable ratings in as little as an hour a week.

Here's how. First, you will need something
that shows the results of races along with
how much faster or slower they were than
the standard times produced by the Racing Post.
I recommend the Racing Post Weekender's
pullout form supplement. The daily results in
the Racing Post will do just as well.

Now, turn to the result of the first race at the
first meeting listed. At the bottom of the
result you will see the time of the race, along
with how much slower or faster than standard
this time was. For example, you might find that
a two-mile race was run 16.4 seconds slower
than standard.

The next step is to divide the number of
seconds a race was run slower or faster than
standard by the number of miles the race
was run over. In the example above, you'd divide
16.4 by two, since the race was run over two
miles. This would tell you that the race was run
8.2 seconds per mile slower than standard. If
the race were three miles you'd divide by three.
If it were six furlongs (0.75 of a mile) you'd
divide by 0.75, and so on. Do this for every race
on the card and write down the result next to
the time of the race. When you've finished, you
will be able to see which was the fastest race at
the meeting and which was slowest.

Now, go to the fastest race and divide the
Racing Post Rating awarded to the winner
by 3.8. This is the speed rating for the fastest
race of the day. For example, if the RPR for the
winner of the fastest race was 120, the speed
rating should be 31.57 (since 120 divided by
3.8 equals 31.57).

To work out the speed ratings for other races
simply deduct one point for every fifth of a
second per mile the winner ran slower than the
fastest race, as judged by the standard times.
For example, if the race was 8.2 seconds per
mile slower than standard and the fastest

uncommon knowledge

 Speed ratings

Foreign forays can help you stay ahead of the crowd

Probably the biggest edge you can obtain from speed figures nowadays is the insight they can give you into foreign races.

On a typical day's racing in Britain, there will be about a dozen horses engaged who have significant recent foreign form. Most will come from France or Germany. It is not that hard to work out ballpark speed figures for them. All you have to do is look up the races they ran in overseas and base your ratings on their official handicap marks.

To look up French form, surf to www.france-galop.com and click on the 'base de données' (database) button. I'm not going to go into the details of exactly how to use the France-Galop database. With a little trial and error you'll soon find out for yourself. You'll be able to call up a horse's form, look at the results and times from a given day and access the official ratings (by hitting the 'valeur' button). To look up German form, find the German race in which a horse ran using the Racing Post website, then, to access its full form, use the database at https://www.horse.de/galopp/deutsch/impressum/index.html to look up the race it ran in and click on the horse's name (this will show you its last ten starts). Then go to www.direktorium.de and use the 'renntermine' button to access the database of German results complete with race times and official German GAG ratings (you can obtain these by clicking on a horse in a race result and calling up their individual file).

There are eight or more races run on a typical French or German card. On most days there are several races run over the same distance. To work out rough figures you will need to do three things: find the time it took the horse to run the race (ie, the official time, plus a fifth of a second for every length it was beaten); second, look up the times of all the other races run at that distance on the same card; third, look up the official ratings of the winners at all these races and convert them to an equivalent Racing Post Rating.

It's easy to convert official French 'valeur' ratings to RPR – multiply them by 2.2. Converting official German GAG ratings to RPRs is more difficult: 102 GAG equals 124 RPR and one GAG point equals two RPR points. So a GAG of 70 is equal to an RPR of 60 (since 70 is 32 less than 102, 32x2 is 64 and 124 less 64 is 60).

Now you can work out rough figures for the foreign races in a similar way to British ones – basing ratings on the RPR equivalent for the fastest race run that day at the trip over which the horse you're looking up ran over. For example, if the winner of the fastest race had the RPR equivalent of 110 then you award it a speed rating of 28.95 by dividing it by 3.8 as I explained above. Then you deduct however many fifths of a second per mile slower than this your horse ran.

race was 5.0 seconds slower than standard the winner's rating should be 16 points lower (since the difference between the two races is 3.2 seconds and there are 16 fifths of a second in 3.2 seconds).

To work out speed ratings for beaten horses, deduct the number of lengths per mile they were beaten from the winner's speed rating. For example, if a horse is beaten ten lengths in a two-mile race it gets a rating five points lower than the winner.

What is set out above is a grossly simplified method for producing speed ratings. It is based on research which shows that 3.8 RPR points equals a fifth of a second per mile, as well as the assumption that Racing Post Ratings and Racing Post standard times are completely accurate.

Ideally you should produce your own set of standard times and file the ratings earned by every horse in alphabetical order in a word processing document for easy reference. You should also base the speed rating for the fastest race of the day on speed figures you have previously awarded the winner and those they beat, as well as the past ratings of runners in other races run on the day.

I know it sounds pretty complicated when I set all the mathematics down in a compressed manner as I have done here. But you will soon learn it all if you simply practise. With experience, you will begin to think in terms of speed ratings and develop a strong sense of how good a horse is from the ratings you've awarded it.

Whether you use the methods set out here or the advanced ones in my book Mordin On Time (available from www.bestbetbooks.com), I have a few suggestions about how to use the speed ratings you produce.

Firstly, at a bare minimum, whenever you award an unusually big speed rating to a horse, make a note of it and make sure you follow it in its upcoming starts. By unusually big I mean bigger than you would expect. It is interesting to know that a horse ran a fast time when winning a Group 1 or a Grade 1 race, but that doesn't help you much from a betting perspective.

You expect big speed ratings from such races. The fast times worth knowing about are the unexpected ones run by lightly-raced or seemingly low-class horses in minor contests.

If you keep a notebook of horses who run unusually fast times you will be amazed at how often they win at real value prices. The key is not to give up on them too soon. If a horse to whom you gave a big speed figure loses next time out, don't assume you have made a mistake. It was probably running in unfavourable circumstances.

Keep following it until it rises to the kind of class level your ratings say it belongs in. I know from experience how painful it can be to oppose a horse I've given a big speed figure to only to see it come up and beat my selection at big odds.

If you want to get into compiling speed figures, I'd advise you start out making the simplistic ratings I have outlined in this article. Then read my book, or Picking Winners by Andy Beyer (available from www.drf.com), and learn the intricacies of accurate speed ratings. After that, try compiling ratings for the all-weather tracks and honing your skills there before you attempt to crunch out numbers for every race.

If you know how to write software or understand Microsoft Excel or similar programs, you can take a good deal of the grunt work out of speed figures – especially if you learn how to import the comma-delimited results you can produce using Raceform Interactive software.

There is no end to the refinements you can employ when making speed ratings. The great thing about them is that you can start off very simply and obtain really good results. I hope I have inspired a few of you to try compiling them for yourself. Not too many, though – speed ratings offer terrific betting value for the very reason that so few punters use them.

Get your hands on your equipment

TOOLS OF THE TRADE

IF KNOWLEDGE IS POWER, BRITISH punters have never been in a stronger position than they are in the new millennium. While the amount of racing has grown enormously in recent years, the coverage of the sport – especially in specialist publications – has more than kept pace with the fixtures explosion and given punters a wealth of information at their fingertips.

By NICK PULFORD

First stop for most punters, big and small, is the Racing Post – Britain's only daily newspaper dedicated to horseracing and sports betting. The Post lists all the runners, riders and form at every race meeting in Britain and Ireland, plus the major races in Europe and the rest of the world, along with a vast range of important statistics.

Want to know the trainers and jockeys who are in (or out of) form, which trainers and jockeys do best (or worst) at a particular course, which trainer/jockey combinations are most successful, or which trainers have sent their horses the furthest to a race meeting? All those stats, and more, are in the Racing Post.

So, too, is a wealth of information on the horses – those with previous course and/or distance wins, those having their first run for a trainer, those wearing first-time blinkers/visor/tongue tie, those gelded since their last outing, those reappearing quickly, those set to go up in the handicap . . . the list is almost endless.

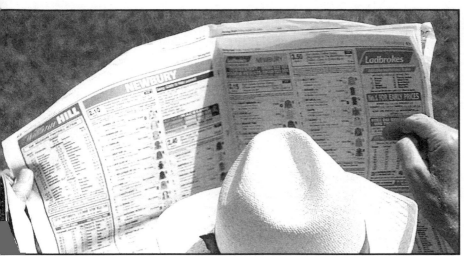

Paper prophets: the Racing Post contains a wealth of information

The Racing Post's scope is limited only by its size – there is only so much information that can be packed into a newspaper. Even more statistics are available on the Racing Post website, including full career form for every British- and Irish-trained horse, plus major runners from other countries. There is also the Smartbet service – a direct link from the site to major bookmakers, allowing users to select a horse and then place a bet.

There is also a group of weekly newspapers – the Racing Post Weekender, Raceform Update and Racing & Football Outlook – which are published on Wednesdays and provide in-depth previews of the following week's racing, with entries, ratings and statistics. The Weekender and Update also offer a collectable results pullout, which provides a handy form reference as the season progresses.

Raceform is known chiefly for the Form Book – which contains the British Horseracing Board's official race results plus analysis from Raceform's team of expert racereaders.

The Form Book is sent out to subscribers on a weekly basis and builds up into a complete record. It is also available as a bound volume at the end of each racing season.

The Form Book services are also available with Raceform Interactive, which provides a vast horseracing database for the PC, allowing the user to analyse past form and future declarations. Several menu options are built in to the software, allowing the data to be retrieved and analysed in many different ways.

Timeform, established in 1948, is another highly respected name in the world of racing, chiefly for its invaluable ratings. The company provides a range of detailed publications for the serious racing enthusiast, the most famous being the Timeform Black Book – a weekly A-to-Z of British racehorses, including commentary and rating for every horse that has run during the season.

Another popular service is Timeform Perspective, which presents the information race by race rather than horse by horse. It is similar to the Form Book in providing results and analysis of all British races on an ongoing basis.

Computer Timeform incorporates all the information found in Timeform Perspective and has a database covering two complete seasons racing, allowing users to process the information according to different variables.

Of the many other publications on racing,

 Useful contacts

Racing Post
1 Canada Square,
London E14 5AP
Tel: 020 7293 2001
Fax: 020 7293 2630
www.racingpost.co.uk
(The **Racing Post Weekender**, **Raceform Update** and **Racing & Football Outlook** can

all be contacted via the above address)

Raceform
High Street, Compton,
Newbury, Berkshire
RG20 6NL
Tel: 01635 578080
Fax: 01635 578101
www.raceform.co.uk

Timeform
25 Timeform House,
Northgate, Halifax,

West Yorkshire HX1 1XF
Tel: 01422 330330
Fax: 01422 398017
www.timeform.com

Superform
Furlong Press, High
Street, Shoreham By
Sea, West Sussex BN43
5ZZ
Tel: 01273 452441
Fax: 01273 464817
www.superform.com

perhaps the most widely used among the professional tipsters and backers is Superform. Founded in 1974, the service is available via post or on the internet and – like Raceform and Timeform – offers comprehensive form, ratings and analysis on British horseracing.

TELEVISION British punters have always been well served by television coverage of racing, with the BBC and Channel 4 (and, previously, ITV) devoting considerable time to the sport, but the service became even better with the advent of Attheraces in 1999.

Attheraces – a joint venture between Channel 4, BSkyB and Arena Leisure – was made available to cable and satellite subscribers, transforming the picture for the ordinary punter. It acquired the rights to broadcast live pictures from 49 British racecourses, including all the major venues, and provided the first wide-scale opportunity for the general punter to watch almost every race, putting them on an equal footing with the professionals.

Its future was shrouded in doubt in early 2004 due to poorer returns than expected from betting revenue, but at least a blueprint has been established for how TV racing should be broadcast.

Tom Segal, who writes the influential Pricewise column in the Racing Post, says punters should take every opportunity to judge races for themselves on television rather than relying solely on the opinions of others in print.

"The methods that have served me best over the years are, firstly, to watch as many races as you can – especially those you haven't had a bet in, because you are able to watch that race with no bias – and, secondly, to keep thinking," Segal says.

"I watch as many races as I can, although preferably with the sound turned down. I have learned that if you stick to what you believe you know, or have seen, there is no-one to blame but yourself."

PART TWO

ASSESSING POTENTIAL

By NICK PULFORD

RACEHORSES REVEAL THEIR ABILITY at different rates and in different spheres. So-called 'early' two-year-olds on the Flat might possess such precocious speed that they can dominate their peers at the start of their careers, but are unable to sustain that dominance once their later-maturing contemporaries begin to overtake them in physical development.

There are many factors which influence a racehorse's development, including its physical build, training regime, breeding, the type of races in which it competes, and the distance and going over which it runs. For punters, it is just as important to be able to weigh up these factors as it is to assess the ability a horse has already shown in its races.

This section looks at key factors which determine a horse's potential, with contributions from three of the Racing Post's leading experts.

Graham Dench, editor of the Form Book and one of the sport's most respected race-readers, provides a professional's guide to race analysis.

Bloodstock expert Rachel Pagones looks at the influence of breeding on performance, including a guide to the Derby – a fascinating race to solve from a pedigree viewpoint.

Finally, Gerald Delamere, one of the most renowned paddock judges in Britain and Ireland, examines the lessons that can be learned from close examination of horses before and during races.

43

let's get critical

RACE
ANALYSIS

IT WAS WAY BACK IN 1996 THAT

By GRAHAM DENCH

the Racing Post added the analysis section to its results service, and it has been evolving ever since. Fashions have come and gone, yet the same basic principles stand. Analysis aims to interpret the result, rather than describe the action – to read between the lines and put the form in context in terms of good or bad, reliable or unreliable and so on. Above all, it seeks to steer the reader towards horses to back, and horses to avoid.

It sounds simple, doesn't it? But in coming to his conclusions the analyst may draw on literally hundreds of different strands of information, many of them subconsciously, and the importance he attaches to each fragment of the jigsaw will always be subjective.

WEIGHING UP A RACE

In its simplest terms, the overall quality of a race can usually be gleaned from the qualifications under which it is run and the classification it has been assigned, which since the introduction of 'regional racing' on the all-weather tracks now extends from Class A (Group races and Listed races) down to Class H (found exclusively at 'regional' meetings and catering generally for the lowest of the low).

Broadly speaking, the higher the classification, the better the horses involved, and the more reliable the form will be. But it's not as simple

Reliable form: big handicaps such as the Royal Hunt Cup at Ascot attract better-class horses and throw up more next-time-out winners

as that. Even a Group race can represent unreliable form if, for example, it is run at a crawl and develops into a sprint, while a low-class affair can still represent rock-solid form provided it is run at a true pace and contested by horses who have run well under similar circumstances in the recent past.

It is an over-simplification, but the most reliable form tends to be found in valuable races that attract the better-class horses and are run on the fairer courses. They may be the hardest in which to find the winner, but they are second to none as a source of future moneyspinners. As you would expect, the big handicaps at Royal Ascot and York, for example, throw up a much higher proportion of next-time-out winners than bread-and-butter races at Chepstow or Hamilton contested by less predictable types, some of whom will struggle ever to win and others who may be being prepared for another day.

Races at almost any level in which there is good support for a wide variety of horses tend to provide stronger form than those in which perhaps one horse is backed to the exclusion of all others, or in which nothing at all seems to be much fancied. Races, especially maiden and novice races, that are dominated by well-bred horses from leading stables tend to be stronger than those fought out by undistinguished types from two-winners-a-year yards.

Form can prove unreliable for a huge variety of reasons. Races that are run at a muddling or inconsistent pace (in the absence of sectional times, which are still in woefully short supply in Britain, this usually has to be judged principally by eye) seldom work out reliably, and nor for that matter do races in which the leaders go off too fast, since they tend to flatter the more patiently ridden runners who often overhaul them as the pacesetters' exertions take their toll. In both cases it can pay to forgive horses unsuited by the way the race developed, and to treat with a degree of caution those who have done well, unless there are good grounds for anticipating similar circumstances to prevail.

Similarly races run on tracks where there is an obvious draw bias – one side of the track rides faster than the other, either because of uneven watering or harrowing, compaction by safety vehicles and so on – are also likely to produce unreliable results, as are races run under conditions so extreme that only a small minority can cope.

Alarm bells should also ring in conditions races in which complete no-hopers finish uncomfortably close, or in handicaps in which horses well out of the proper weights finish close up, unless there are grounds for accepting the improvement. The results of races which are especially tactical in nature, where one or two jockeys outfox their rivals and steal a march, also need to be taken with a pinch of salt.

SPOTTING AN IMPROVER
Spotting horses who are better than their bare form is one of the key ways to make betting pay, but what do you look for? In these days when even the most mundane of sellers is replayed time and again and scrutinised from every angle, few horses

that are unlucky in running escape the eagle eyes of the professional race readers, so when they run next time the bad luck factor is nearly always built into their odds.

Better to look for horses who acquitted themselves well, less conspicuously, in spite of the factors that were against them – the poor draw, the slow pace, the inept ride, the impossible task, the unsuitable distance or going. Or for winners who can be rated better value than their winning margin – not those that win pulling up, with their riders showboating, but the ones that perhaps idle in front and only scramble home after getting there too soon, or else get up to win despite a shocking blunder out in the country.

Horses who seem to be running over the wrong distance are always worth keeping in mind for the future. It is no secret that certain trainers qualify their horses for handicaps by running them over inadequate trips, and only allow them to race over an appropriate distance once they have been assessed. But the official handicappers are wiser to this now than they used to be, so they take few chances, and in any case the odds usually reflect the potential improvement.

Better to look for horses who run as if needing further, taking time to find top gear and doing their best work when the race is all over, or alternatively those that show such speed that they fail to last home, so can be expected to improve when dropped back in distance.

Non-triers are a fact of life, like it or not, and more than ever since the advent of betting exchanges. There are many ways of stopping a horse, and nowadays they tend to be rather more subtle than used to be the case. Occasionally you spot a horse who has clearly been prevented from doing its best by being restrained throughout, or at least until after the race has begun to develop in earnest, but more often it is a case of deliberately losing ground at the start, losing ground throughout by racing wide, forcing the pace on a horse that prefers to come from behind, and so on. If you spot one,

uncommon knowledge

 Between the lines

Spotting horses that are being prepared for the big handicaps requires a fair amount of reading between the lines, but an understanding of the modus operandi of some of the specialist stables is a big help, since some trainers follow the same routes year in, year out. Familiarity with the handicapping system and the race conditions – when the weights are published, the penalty clauses, and so on – is invaluable.

uncommon knowledge

Learn to spot the warning signs

Horses to avoid

It is part of the Racing Post analyst's brief to highlight horses to avoid, but this is an area fraught with danger. To paraphrase, hell hath no fury like an owner scorned, and the modern fixture list caters so much better for bad horses than good ones that nearly every dog has his day. What's more, in the right circumstances and at the right odds even the worst rogues can be tempting if they are not entirely devoid of ability.

Nevertheless, it is only proper that punters should be alerted to horses of whom they should at least be wary.

Horses who run up long strings of placings, failing to put their heads in front even when presented with a golden opportunity, need to be treated with caution as far as win bets are concerned at least, even if they do not display the usual signs associated with one that simply won't go by.

Equally, horses that are so highly strung that they race too freely and rarely have any energy left at the business end also must be treated with caution, as do those who compromise their chance by habitually starting slowly.

Horses with a history of unsoundness are best steered clear of when they are risked on really firm ground and, despite all of the modern advances in training techniques, it is asking a lot of a long-absent horse to win in really testing conditions.

Horses from stables that are out of form are also best avoided, pending signs of a revival. For a variety of reasons, some unfathomable, form in the majority of stables is cyclical.

and the often dramatic fluctuations on the betting exchanges obviously help in this respect, good luck to you, but remember that if connections are unscrupulous enough to stop a horse one day, then there is no guarantee it will be doing its best next time.

Horses who appear to run well when out of their class can be particularly interesting, provided there are good grounds for trusting the form. Supporting them when back down in grade will always be speculative, and it is a matter of assessing the reliability of the form and weighing it against the odds available.

Equally it is possible to unearth a star at one

of the gaff tracks, more often over jumps than on the Flat, but not exclusively so. Impressive winners at the gaffs are often underestimated when they step up in class, especially if they are from unfashionable stables, but if their subsequent Racing Post Ratings back up the good visual impression then back them to follow up. After all, Cheltenham winners, and even Royal Ascot winners, from time to time initially reveal their potential at tracks like Folkestone.

Paddock inspection is not as rewarding as it once was, since radical changes in training techniques and the proliferation of all-weather gallops over the last 20 years or so have raised fitness standards. However, that is not to say that there is nothing to be gained from it – the paddock is still the best place to judge young horses with little or no form, and valuable clues to a horse's well-being can also be gleaned from its appearance and general demeanour.

MAKING ANALYSIS PAY The only way to make a long-term profit from any form of gambling is to bet only when the odds available exceed the probability of winning. Unfortunately in horseracing there are no hard and fast rules – it will always be subjective, and a matter of personal opinion.

But money can be made by being selective, avoiding habitual losers and hype horses, and concentrating on backing potential improvers about whom there is more than meets the eye. Follow them under the conditions alluded to in the Racing Post analysis, or better still find them independently by following some of the basic guiding principles.

Inevitably there will be setbacks – the 'improver' will turn out to be nothing of the sort, and a horse nobody would touch with a barge pole will get up to beat the one that went into the notebook months previously – but stick at it. The more you put into it – studying replays, sifting through form and statistics – the luckier you get.

how important is sire power?

BREEDING MATTERS

PEDIGREE IS UNDOUBTEDLY A By RACHEL PAGONES
useful instrument in the punter's toolkit. At the
most basic level, the name of a horse's sire alone
gives you a good idea of what sort of trip he can
handle. Of course the dam is, theoretically,
equally important. But most mares produce
fewer than 15 foals in a lifetime, whereas many
stallions generate close to 100 – sometimes more
– foals per year. Consequently, statistics
relating to pedigree have a heavy male bias.

A more sophisticated way to assess a horse's
stamina is through the Dosage system, which
for some reason tends to inspire great passion
in people. They either love it or disdain it. I find
it quite useful as a way to highlight the dominant
influences of speed and class in a pedigree. It's
especially pertinent to unexposed three-year-
olds facing top-class middle-distance competition
– exactly the Derby scenario. More on this later.

Another helpful theory – and one that is
virtually free from controversy – is that of nicks.
A nick is a cross between a particular sire
and broodmare sire. An example of a successful
nick is that between Sadler's Wells and mares
sired by Darshaan. As proof of the strength
of this cross, consider: Darshaan mares produced
ten European stakes winners in 2003; only three
were by Sadler's Wells, and those three were
High Chaparral, Islington and Yesterday. They
were the only runners out of Darshaan mares
to win European Group 1 races in 2003.

Son of his father: a Sadler's Wells colt is led around the sales ring

There are several other things pedigrees can suggest about a horse's potential. Precocity, temperament, preference for type of going, even the likelihood of a debut win can be predicted by a horse's pedigree – sometimes. Like everything else in racing, trying to pick a winner on the basis of its pedigree is an inexact science.

Probably the most important proviso to bear in mind when using pedigree as a tool is this: the better the quality of the race, the more pedigree matters; the lower the quality of the race, the less relevant pedigree becomes. This is because, in low-calibre races, it's fairly easy for an individual to outclass its untalented rivals; but in a high-class event filled with talented athletes who are tested to the limits, it really does matter whether a horse is bred to handle the race conditions.

RANDOM OR PREDICTABLE? Before getting into details, let's briefly review what is known about heritability of racing potential in the thoroughbred. The sorry answer is: not much. Despite around 300 years of going by the breeders' maxim "breed the best to the best and hope for the best", nobody can tell us, in any given mating, which traits will be inherited from the sire, which from the dam, or even whether they will be inherited at all.

Is there a gene for speed? No, say the geneticists – who, by the way, are in the process of creating a gene linkage map of the thorough-bred. When they do, they will be able to look at a horse's genetic profile and say definitively that this gene has been passed down by the dam, and that one by the sire. Right now, it's mostly guesswork. Despite the common wisdom that sire and dam contribute equal parts to the whole of their offspring, this is not so, according to Professor Twink Allen, director of the Equine Fertility Centre in Newmarket and a world-renowned authority in equine reproduction.

Allen told me that the relationship between paternal and maternal inheritance can basically be described as random. He said any given horse could inherit 70 per cent of the male line and 30 per cent of the female, or vice versa. That's something to bear in mind when looking at an animal whose sire was best over ten furlongs and whose dam won over six. Does this mix mean you'll end up with a miler? As breeders who have tried the concept have found – not at all. But thankfully, in spite of our dim knowl-edge of the reasons for it, racing talent is heritable. The problem is, we don't know what has been inherited from whom until we see the horse in action.

What's a punter to do? Use the knowledge you have to come up with the most likely result – then test your hypothesis. That's all anyone can do with any betting system, because none of them are anywhere near infallible. Pedigree knowledge can tilt the odds in your favour; in betting, that's about as good as it gets.

STAMINA There is a very easy, if some-what rudimentary, way of assessing stamina potential. It is called the average winning distance. The Racing Post publishes the average winning distance of the progeny of sires – which it calls the stamina index – of two- and three-year-old maidens and big-race entries in its form section. The Racing Post Weekender is even more helpful, publishing this information for all Flat entries. (Of course, we've already established that we don't know whether the horse will inherit its stamina from the sire or dam. Just remember this is the average winning distance for all horses by this sire, and assume the horse is more or less average).

The Weekender also includes the stamina index of broodmare sires. This can be helpful to an extent; say the horse in question has a sire with a stamina index of 6.4 furlongs, and his broodmare sire's comparable figure is 12.2 furlongs. There's a good chance your horse will have more stamina than one bred to a mare sired by a sprinter. It is worth remembering, though, that this is the average winning distance for all horses produced by the sire of the mare, not the average for all horses produced by daughters of that sire.

THE DOSAGE SYSTEM A more sophisticated way of assessing stamina is the Dosage system. As I mentioned earlier, Dosage has its detractors. One well-known bloodstock analyst said of the system's proponents: "Those people should be put in pedigree jail!"

I think the big advantage of Dosage is that it narrows down the possible influences in a pedigree from all sires to a relatively few, select sires. These sires are called chefs-de-race, and they are categorised according to the type of runners they produce. Chefs-de-race fall into the following categories: Brilliant, Intermediate, Classic, Solid, Professional. From left to right, these cover the gradient from speed to stamina; essentially, from five-furlong sprinter to two-mile stayer.

The modern Dosage developers, Steven Roman and Steve Miller, have done a massive amount of research into which stallions have been influential over time, and what type of influence they exert. For that reason alone I find the system helpful.

There are three Dosage calculations: the Dosage profile, Dosage index and centre of distribution. To me, the most helpful is the profile. It's obtained by going back through the first four generations of a horse's pedigree and assigning a numerical value to each chef-de-race in it. First-generation chefs get 16 points, those in the second generation eight, in the third, four and in the fourth, two.

High Chaparral's profile looks like this: 6-1-22-9-2. The '6' represents points in the Brilliant (sprinting) category, the '1' points in the Intermediate (miler) category, and so on. Clearly the heaviest concentration is in the Classic (middle-distance) area with a good dose of influence in the Solid (staying) category. But there is also speed – six points worth – and High Chaparral's record as a top-class middle-distance colt who also won a Group 1 at two seems in accordance with his Dosage profile.

In contrast, the sprinter Song has the following profile: 11-0-3-0-0. Clearly a lot of speed and not much else. As to the index (DI) and centre of distribution (CD), suffice to say that the higher the number, the more speed in the pedigree, and the lower, the more stamina. By way of example, High Chaparral's DI is 0.82 and his CD is 0.00; Song's DI is 8.33 and his CD is 1.57. You can access Dosage information for most horses on the website Pedigree Online (www.pedigreequery.com). More information on Dosage and a list of chef-de-race sires can be found on Roman's site (www.chef-de-race.com).

NICKS These change over time as stallions come and go, so it is worth updating your statistics now and then. Recently, the best-publicised cross has been Sadler's Wells on Darshaan mares. Other examples are Sadler's Wells (and his sons Barathea, El Prado and In The Wings) with Rainbow Quest mares, and Sadler's Wells and other Northern Dancer-line sires (for example Green Desert, Hernando,

uncommon knowledge

 Firm, soft and no preference

Going concerns

Individual sires' statistics change over time, and you need to do a little work to keep up. It is generally known that horses by Sadler's Wells like some cut in the ground, and after Zafeen flopped in the 2003 Irish 2,000 Guineas, while Indian Haven won, it became common wisdom that Zafonic's runners prefer firm ground, while Indian Ridge's thrive on soft. As always, there are exceptions, and the stakes-winning Zafonic colt Zarfoot could only handle soft ground – perhaps a legacy from his dam Harefoot, a daughter of Rainbow Quest.

Nureyev's runners have a good firm-ground record, as do his sons Fasliyev (from limited statistics) and Spinning World. So do Gone West (and, as noted, his son Zafonic). Horses by Woodman and his son Hector Protector tend to handle soft ground well. So, as a rule, do French- and German-bred horses. There are many sires, though, whose runners show no preference.

Peintre Celebre, Polish Precedent and Unfuwain) with mares by Shirley Heights, who is Darshaan's sire.

Another tried-and-true cross is that between sons of Northern Dancer and Mr Prospector mares; recently Storm Cat has done particularly well when crossed with mares by the great Mr P. This cross produced Group 1 two-year-old winners Denebola and One Cool Cat in 2003. Mares by Mr Prospector's son Miswaki also do very well when crossed with sons of Northern Dancer; the unfortunate Landseer, for instance, was a result of this nick.

It works in reverse, too. Mares from Northern Dancer-line sires cross well with Mr Prospector stallions. An example is multiple Group 1 winner Russian Rhythm, a product of Mr Prospector stallion Kingmambo and Nijinsky mare Balistroika.

PRECOCITY Heidegger's uncertainty principle comes into play here. That is, the mere act of observing the phenomenon can change it.

Here's how it works: a trainer acquires a horse by a stallion with a reputation for precocity. He puts the youngster into training early and runs it early. Thus it has a greater chance of exhibiting precocity – ie winning a race early in its two-year-old season – than a horse that doesn't see a racecourse until it turns three. Conversely, when trainers buy horses by sires they believe produce late-bloomers, they tend to train those horses like late-bloomers – whether they are naturally backward or not. The main thing to remember is that speed favours precocity, because the early races for juveniles are mostly sprints.

There is another type of precocity, which involves debut wins. Work I did in conjunction with the Racing Post database showed that horses by Nureyev, Gone West and Gone West's son Zafonic have exceptional strike-rates with their debutants.

NORTHERN DANCER-LINE SIRES There are so many of them, and they are so influential, that they deserve a separate category. The main lines in Europe are Sadler's Wells, Danzig, Nijinsky and Nureyev, while Storm Cat is gaining ground in America.

On the racecourse, Sadler's Wells is an influence in the miler-to-middle-distance category. As stallions, though, his sons tip the balance towards stamina – hence the large number covering jumps mares. An exception is Barathea, a top miler whose average progeny also fall into that category. Another difference: Sadler's Wells is a lousy all-weather sire, while Barathea's strike-rate is better than most.

Sadler's Wells' best son at stud is In The Wings, who passes on most of the qualities of his sire. In The Wings' best son, on the race-course and at stud, is Singspiel. Interestingly, Singspiel's finest to date, Moon Ballad, was better on dirt than turf.

The late Nureyev has excelled mostly as a miling influence. But he has produced runners as diverse as Prix du Jockey-Club winner Peintre Celebre (now sire of top-class middle-distance

uncommon
knowledge

 The Danzig influence

Danzig is considered the most influential active stallion in the world. Among his male-line descendents are Anabaa, Green Desert, Key Of Luck and the late Chief's Crown and Danehill. Danzig's influence is for precocious speed, and his descendents also do well on the all-weather. Some of his best all-weather descendents are Sheikh Albadou, Polish Patriot, Strolling Along, Danzig Connection, Roi Danzig and Grand Lodge. While Danzig's runners tend towards speed, Anabaa, Chief's Crown (and his son Grand Lodge), Danehill and Key Of Luck have all produced Group/Grade 1 middle-distance winners.

competitors Dai Jin and Super Celebre) and Fasliyev, an unbeaten two-year-old and Europe's leading first-season sire in 2003. He has one of the highest strike-rates of any sire on the all-weather, and his sons Great Commotion, Theatrical, Wolfhound and Polar Falcon, as well as grandson Ashkalani, all fare well on artificial surfaces. Triple Crown winner Nijinsky has been a middle-distance influence above all else. So are his sons Hernando and Kahyasi, who incidentally also have strong all-weather records.

THE DERBY There is nothing like it and, from a pedigree analyst's standpoint, it is special too. That's because the Derby field is made up of well-bred horses facing Group 1 competition over a mile and a half for the first time. It is the perfect scenario for picking a winner based on pedigree. If you go the Dosage route, here are some trends culled from the last ten years: seven of the ten winners had ten or more points in the Classic (middle-distance) category, and four had more than 20. Only two (Erhaab and Benny The Dip) had no points at all in the Solid and Professional (staying) categories. The highest Dosage index (Erhaab's) was 3.86, the lowest was 0.80 (Shaamit) and the average was 1.66. The highest centre of distribution was 0.79 (Erhaab), the lowest was -0.10 (High-Rise) and the average was 0.32.

Sire power? Sadler's Wells is the clear winner – although it was not until 2001 that he had his first winner of the race, Galileo. He promptly produced another, High Chaparral, and he was sire or broodmare sire of seven out of ten runner-ups. Another runner-up, Silver Patriarch, is by his son Saddlers' Hall. The other sires of winners were Chief's Crown, Mtoto, Silver Hawk, High Estate, Fairy King (a full brother to Sadler's Wells), Grand Lodge and Kris S.

A final word on Derby pedigrees. Stamina alone is not enough. Tactical speed is crucial. Six of the past ten winners had at least ten points in the Brilliant/Intermediate categories, and only two had fewer than eight.

watching and walking

READING THE SIGNS

I HAVE BEEN WATCHING HORSES in the paddock for over 40 years, but there is no way I would consider myself an expert. The real experts are those who know how to judge a yearling or an older animal at a horses-in-training sale, but the requirements at the sales are totally different to those which are needed for betting purposes. If you judged a horse in the paddock as you would in the sales ring, you wouldn't bet too often.

WHAT TO LOOK FOR The make and shape of the thoroughbred would demand a book of its own. On the Flat you have juveniles, three-year-olds and older horses, sprinters, milers, middle-distance horses and stayers, and within all these categories there are different makes and shapes.

Over jumps, horses range from the Flat-bred, speedy sorts to the weak, rangy, chasing types who often start off in bumpers and novice hurdles but only mature when they reach seven or eight years of age.

The old proverb 'beauty is in the eye of the beholder' applies neatly to paddock watching. The same horse may evoke very different opinions around the paddock and, equally, any horse can be the pick of the paddock one day and look outclassed on another.

I like a well-made animal with a frame to grow into, rather than the small, narrow type that

By GERALD DELAMERE

Get your eye in: studying horses before a race can be profitable

will struggle when asked to carry weight. A case in point in the 2003/04 jumps season was Iris Royal, whom I backed for big handicaps at Ascot and Cheltenham when he was set to carry less than 11st, but not on his next run when he had 11st 12lb to carry. He won the first two, but was pulled up in the latter.

A depth of girth is essential, as this provides plenty of heart room. But too much length leads to weakness and unsoundness. A horse's neck needs to be in proportion to its body and swan necks are unattractive, as is straightness in front.

An honest head is highly desirable and often defines a horse's character. A scowling look with the white of the eye – as often depicted in oil paintings – is not a good sign, and nor is a small head stuck in the air during the pre-race preliminaries.

Ears are one of the most important parts of an animal and you can learn plenty from a horse's ears, both in the paddock and when racing. Half-cast ears (neither pricked nor flattened) are a particularly worrying sign.

I like alertness and a horse full of wellbeing.

When a horse is bouncing around the paddock ("mad for the road", as they say in Ireland), that is a positive pointer. On the other hand, horses who become edgy and fractious, and start sweating, suggest that they are not on good terms with the job in hand.

A good walker is another positive. A horse who puts his feet in the right place and has a good rhythm when walking is more likely to do it when galloping, rather than knocking into himself.

THE COAT Horses show how well they are through their coats, just as humans do through their skin, and this is a most important area for paddock watchers. A gleaming coat is always a good sign and I put them into five categories – outstanding, well, fine, okay and poor.

Hormonal changes make differences in both sexes. You can sometimes spot a filly in season in the paddock by her demeanour or by traces of a discharge around her anus. A filly or mare turning in her coat is very difficult to read in the autumn and I have never met anyone who could get this right all the time. One thing that is consistent is that when the coat goes properly and their hormones settle down, fillies can be most genuine.

On the jumping front, for the past four or five seasons Martin Pipe hasn't been clipping out his jumpers, which means they don't mark as easily. A regular paddock comment for his horses nowadays is "fit and hairy".

Another point to note during the jumps season is that a gelding will never look as well as a colt in mid-winter.

SWEATING The cause of sweating is difficult to pinpoint, as is when to take heed of this factor and when to ignore it.

Where the sweat is located on a horse's body is one of the key questions. I don't worry about a bit of sweat down the neck, but dripping from under the saddle and behind is a bigger concern.

uncommon knowledge

 Watching juveniles

Close scrutiny of youngsters can give you an edge

Punters can gain a significant edge by looking at two-year-olds, especially early in their racing careers. With little or no form to go on, the paddock is one of the best sources of information about a two-year-old's wellbeing and potential.

Fitness is a huge factor in two-year-old races, especially early in the season and on softer ground. You can learn a lot from the muscle definition down a horse's hind-quarters and on its neck, and from whether the horse looks fat around its belly. The round-barrelled horse has caught us all out, but it should not do so more than once.

The best clue to fitness is a clear outline of a horse's ribs, though it isn't always a straightforward matter to spot one because, side-on, horses often look to be carrying a bit of condition.

It is better to watch the horses coming round a bend in the paddock, as the hint of a rib or two will be obvious from this viewpoint.

The line (or crease, as it is sometimes called) down a horse's hind-quarters is an important indicator of how much work a horse has done.

Leggy juveniles can often be weak and the same trait is demonstrated by those that are still 'up behind' (which means that a horse's hind-quarters are much higher than they are at the withers).

Noisy young horses and those who become coltish will often show inexperience once racing, whereas those who appear calm and focused usually perform much better.

Whereas many defects can be ignored in older horses, you would not be haring off to the ring to back a debutant with bad hocks or a swan neck, or one who is back at the knee.

Sweating between the hind legs is not a huge problem if the rest of the coat is cool. This secretion doesn't put me off as much as a free-sweating horse does.

The absence of sweat can also be significant, if the horse in question normally sweats up. As with all aspects of paddock watching, uncharacteristic behaviour is often the most worrying behaviour.

GROUND CONDITIONS

The going is one of the most crucial guides to a racehorse's prospects, if not the most crucial. I started walking courses decades ago, having come from a farming and hunting background, including a period as Master of the Hounds, when I had a decision in whether to hunt or not. Add to that an uncompleted BSc in agriculture and you can see I am better qualified for giving a judgement on the state of the ground than on most of the jobs I do!

AN UNEVEN PLAYING FIELD

The most infuriating thing about coming in from walking the course is when you bump into someone and, having given them the details of your findings, they then proceed to tell you what it's like in the car park or in their back garden!

Rule number one is, forget the car park – it isn't cultivated or watered. The majority of Flat courses are regularly watered, most by the pop-up system which throws out water in a circular or arc motion. This means that certain areas get less water, a problem that can be exacerbated by wind conditions.

Over decades this results in a tremendous unevenness on racecourses. This can be of huge importance in straight-course sprint races, where one rail can have a major advantage over the other.

After watering and then rain you regularly find the ground on a racecourse will vary from firm to soft. There are areas on most courses that are always fast or always soft due to different soil types and drainage. The newer watering systems such as the Upton Irrigator give a more even distribution, but they can't change 15 years of unevenness overnight.

The 'little and often' approach is best for watering. If the clerk of the course waits until the going becomes firm and piles it on, water will always find somewhere more receptive to go and this leads to patchy going.

York's 2003 August meeting saw good to firm

Big bias: the inside rail at Chester is one of the best-known advantages

for three to four horse-widths on the round-course rail, but outside that it was good to soft. With maximum fields a near-certainty for 'Royal Ascot at York' in 2005, the uncompetitive nature of races with a massive draw bias is a huge worry.

A QUESTION OF BIAS Compaction plays a huge role on racecourses where the ground has been pounded in, for more than 100 years in some cases.

Parts of some courses are well known for biases caused by this factor – the stands rail in Epsom sprints, the inside rails at Chester, Beverley and Windsor, and the far rails on the Newmarket July course and on Sandown's sprint track.

But add a large quantity of rain and areas where horses normally race are shunned – the stands side at Brighton, Haydock, Sandown, Kempton and Salisbury come into their own in such circumstances. This is because the top of the ground cuts up easier once the rain gets in, as it is less settled and matted in from frequent use.

PART THREE

THE KEY VARIABLES

FINDING WINNERS IS ABOUT MUCH more than identifying the horse with the greatest ability or potential. A host of modifying factors play a part in assessing a race and each horse's chance within it, especially in the modern era of specialisation within racing.

By NICK PULFORD

The great horses of the past ran up sequences of victories over widely varying distances and under different conditions, but such domination is rare nowadays.

There is a saying that the best racehorses will handle any going, for instance, but few form judges would subscribe to that view. Racing has become so competitive that most horses have preferences for going, distance, course and so on, which all play a part in determining its chance in a given race. Trainers look for the key to each of their horses – the combination of factors which bring out its best form – and punters need to unlock the same information to make a success of betting.

THE GOING If there is one factor above all others which has to be taken into consideration before placing a bet, it is the going. Ground conditions are the single biggest variable in a horse's race record and it follows that they will be one of the greatest influences on the outcome of a race, especially at the extreme ends of the going spectrum.

The rule when assessing going preference

Man with a stick: punters can suffer from inconsistent going reports

is to look at a horse's overall form and find its best runs. If they came on a certain type of ground, that is a good guide to its preferred going.

Even if that same horse has won on a different type of going, the form might be suspect if the performance does not figure among its better efforts. A horse might win a couple of uncompetitive, soft-ground races and appear to have a preference for that type of going. However, its best run might have been a third place on good-to-firm ground, suggesting that it is likely to prove best on that type of surface.

David-Lee Priest, in his book Against The Odds (Raceform, 2003), found that Flat horses he termed 'soft' performers (ie, horses who had shown a distinct preference for ground softer than good) had a good strike-rate and profit-to-stakes success when meeting such conditions again.

The evidence was less conclusive for 'firm' performers (horses who had shown a distinct preference for good-to-firm or harder ground) in their favoured conditions, while a similar test for jumps horses revealed no significant bias, leading the author to conclude that "it is far more important to consider the going preferences of runners on the Flat when the going is softer than good".

Narrowing down a horse's going preferences is not always straightforward. What about a horse making its debut, or having its first run on a particular type of going? Some clues can be found in a horse's action – a round action, where the horse brings its knee high in almost a cycling motion, usually denotes a suitability for softer ground, while a closer-to-the-ground action is indicative of a preference for faster going.

Another source of information is the horse's breeding – did its sire and dam have any going preferences? Have its siblings shown similar traits? Pedigree pointers are an under-researched area in punting methods, but it is obvious that they can pay dividends.

The major stumbling block for punters, however, is the lack of accuracy and consistency in going reports. Most British racecourses assess the going using the age-old method of a man poking the ground with a stick, though some have adopted more accurate measuring devices, such as the recently developed GoingStick.

In any case, racing has been plagued over the years by going reports which prove wrong and, despite more advanced watering systems, ground conditions which vary on different parts of the track. Such problems can have a major effect on a horse's chance and punters are wise to have a degree of scepticism both about the predicted going and the official going listed in a horse's form record, which might give a misleading impression of its ability to handle certain ground conditions.

DISTANCE Just as horses have going preferences, so they also have specific distance requirements. Genes may play a more significant role in this respect, with stamina and speed arguably inherited, though modern training methods can develop both aspects of a horse's make-up.

Pedigree analysis is not a foolproof method of assessing a horse's best distance, but it is a good starting point. Stallions produce a mass of evidence on the racetrack to enable punters to gauge both the ability and versatility of their stock.

This is especially true in the modern era of large-scale breeding, with as many as 150 foals sired each year by some stallions, enabling racing patterns to develop quickly among their offspring. These, in turn, are usually built on by breeders, who will see, for instance, that a sire is good at producing precocious two-year-olds or sprinters and send mares which conform to the stereotype, thereby reinforcing the established pattern.

This is all to the assistance of the punter, who can use the evidence to assess a horse's distance requirements. One reference source is the average winning distance of a sire's progeny – the average winning distance of a sprint sire like Pivotal will be around 6.5 furlongs, while for classic middle-distance sires such as Sadler's Wells or Rainbow Quest it is over ten furlongs-plus. This, of course, was no bar to Sadler's Wells siring the 2,000 Guineas winners Entrepreneur, King Of Kings and Refuse To Bend, so the dam's side of the pedigree also has to be considered.

King Of Kings, for instance, was out of a mare by the speed influence Habitat and proved to be a miler pure and simple – as did Sadler's Wells' Breeders' Cup Mile winner Barathea, from a similar female line. Refuse To Bend's dam never won beyond six furlongs, which might have been a clue to his apparent failure to stay when favourite for the Derby. Refuse To Bend was a good example of the complexities of pedigree analysis, however, as his half-brother Media Puzzle (by Theatrical) won the Melbourne Cup over two miles, which suggested that the 2,000 Guineas winner might stay at least a mile and a half.

uncommon knowledge

 A mile is not simply a mile

It pays to read between the lines of a horse's bare form when assessing distance requirements. A hurdler that stays two miles on a stiff track or on rain-softened ground might be capable of a step up in distance, but equally it might be tapped for speed over two miles on a fast track and/or ground. This is one of the reasons why form from the Cheltenham Festival is often overturned the following month around the quicker course at the Aintree Grand National meeting.

uncommon knowledge

**When stamina
runs out**

Only so low you can go before none of them stays

One interesting theory on the stamina question is provided by Nick Mordin, the renowned speed ratings expert. He argues that lower-class horses do not really stay beyond sprint distances, as evidenced by the widening gap between the best times achieved by higher-class and lower-class horses as race distance increases.

In his book Mordin On Time (Aesculus), he writes: "In a top-class race, it is worthwhile to try to sort out which horses are better stayers. But in really low-class events, there's no point doing this. Basically, none of the horses stays."

Mordin says that a good horse can win in a lower class at any distance simply by having a class or fitness edge over its rivals, and argues that this is not based on stamina. He argues that a horse with a good speed rating in a lower-class race should not be ignored simply because it is running over an apparently 'wrong' distance.

The Derby presents one of the most fascinating pedigree puzzles, with at least half of the runners usually untested at the 12-furlong distance before the race. The stamina debate over the top colts often starts after the preceding year's top juvenile events, but a few golden rules can help to narrow the field for ante-post punters (see chapter 7, page 50).

Another area where distance capabilities are a vital factor is three-year-old middle-distance handicaps, which often feature horses stepping up beyond a mile for the first time. Every season there are numerous examples of horses who show much-improved form once they enter this sphere, especially from top trainers whose stables tend to attract well-bred, stamina-laden animals.

On the Flat, too, knowledge of a course's characteristics is vital in assessing stamina. A pure five-furlong horse is needed on Epsom's ultra-fast downhill straight course, whereas

Sandown's sprint track is mainly uphill and winners there are often capable of staying six furlongs or more, while the real speedsters are usually found wanting at the finish.

DISTANCE Horses for courses is one of racing's well-worn phrases, but it has more than a ring of truth to it. One of British racing's greatest attractions is the variety of its 59 courses and that variation leads to different form patterns, probably more marked than in any other major racing nation.

Whereas the United States, for instance, has fairly uniform track layouts – oval, left-handed and usually just over a mile round – British racecourses come in all shapes and sizes. Three of the most famous Flat tracks illustrate the differences – Goodwood's right-handed loop traverses the South Downs before returning right-handed into the finishing straight, Epsom's famous mile-and-a-half switchback is horseshoe-shaped, while Chester's circular city track is barely a mile round and has very tight turns.

The individuality of British courses stems from the piecemeal development of racing over the past four centuries. When King Charles II (or 'Old Rowley', hence the Rowley Mile) founded the Newmarket meetings following his restoration to the throne in 1660, spectator viewing was not top of the agenda and hence the town's two racecourses start out of sight of the grandstands and basically consist of two long straight stretches with a turn about a mile from the finish.

Following this less than perfect model, Britain's racecourses continued to develop according to the contours of the land, each assuming its own character. History also dictated which of the racecourses became most important – Epsom's status stems from the fact that it was the chosen venue in 1780 for the famous race named after the 12th Earl of Derby. While its unique gradients have played a vital role in the Derby's history, Epsom's inherent 'unfairness' means that it would be highly unlikely to be chosen now as the home of the most important Classic in the British racing calendar.

Understanding the characteristics of each racecourse is a vital weapon in the punter's armoury. The most basic difference is whether a course is left- or right-handed – roughly two-thirds of Britain's tracks are left-handed (22 of the 37 Flat courses, and 26 of the 42 jumps venues). It can become obvious that certain horses prefer to go left-handed rather than right-handed, or vice versa, while some sprinters show their best form on a straight track rather than a turning course.

There are, of course, further variations on course layout. Even a horse best at going left-handed is unlikely to be suited equally by a tight track like Chester and a galloping course such as York. Part of the reason is that races develop in different ways on different tracks – a course with a long straight, such as York, allows the long-striding horse time to wind up gradually to the finish, whereas Ascot's relatively short straight favours the horse with an instant burst of acceleration. The influence of track layout on the pace of the race also means that some courses, such as Goodwood, favour front-runners, while others are more suited to hold-up horses.

The influences on a horse's suitability for a particular course can also be man-made – namely the fences on a chase course. The degree of difficulty of the obstacles can vary widely from course to course and it pays to be wary of suspect jumpers over stiff fences such as those found at Wetherby or Sandown. The pace of the race plays an important part here, too, because a horse who has achieved three bloodless wins over easier fences in the run-up to the Cheltenham Festival might be caught out by the faster pace and stiffer fences at the most competitive meeting of the season. And it is a similar story over the Railway fences down the back straight at Sandown, where jumping rhythm is put to the test by the quick succession

uncommon knowledge

Horses for courses

It's not just people – horses can be left-handed too

Aidan O'Brien advanced the opinion that High Chaparral was better going left-handed after the horse had finished third in the 2003 Prix de l'Arc de Triomphe. Although High Chaparral had won going right-handed, including the Irish Derby, O'Brien argued that his most impressive wins had been over left-handed courses – a view backed up by Racing Post Ratings, which made his best left-handed form six pounds superior to his top right-handed performance.

Punters who picked up on those ratings differences might have given themselves an advantage even before O'Brien ascribed High Chaparral's lesser form going right-handed to a shoulder problem. In the betting-exchange era, the edge gained by astute punters can be put to good use by laying a popular horse like High Chaparral on a course which doesn't suit him.

The great steeplechaser Desert Orchid was best on a right-handed track – 25 of his 27 career victories came right-handed, with 23 of them achieved at just four tracks (Sandown, Kempton, Wincanton and Ascot). This made him vulnerable on a left-handed track and he lost on four of his six visits to the big meetings at Cheltenham and Aintree. If betting exchanges had been available in the days of Desert Orchid, layers could have profited from his weakness going left-handed – though, famously, he eventually triumphed in the 1989 Cheltenham Gold Cup.

of obstacles. Which brings us back to horses for courses. The number and variation of British racecourses inevitably means that some horses will show a particular aptitude for a certain track – perhaps even a higher level of form at that track than elsewhere. Basically, the more idiosyncratic tracks are more likely to produce course specialists – so multiple course winners are often found at Brighton, Bath and Chester.

Again, however, it is wise to dig deeper into possible reasons for an apparent course preference and a good example is the sprint handicapper Zuhair, widely regarded as a Goodwood specialist after gaining six wins there from 1999 to 2003. However, five of those successes came at the Glorious meeting, while he was beaten in eight out of nine visits to the track at other times of the year – suggesting that there might have been other factors at work to explain his effectiveness in late July/early August.

The all-weather also produces specialists but the difference between the racing surfaces at Southwell and Wolverhampton (Fibresand) and Lingfield (Equitrack) means that the form between the three all-weather tracks is not transferable in many cases.

THE DRAW The effect of the draw is one of the most contentious issues in Flat racing and a season seldom passes without a controversy over the draw's effect in a big race, usually one of the major sprint handicaps. This is one reason why some races, such as the Lincoln Handicap over the Doncaster straight mile and the six-furlong Stewards' Cup at Goodwood, now draw connections by lot and allow them to choose the stall number for their horse, rather than allotting the draw by the usual random process.

Results show that the draw can be a major influence, particularly over distances of a mile or less, though its effect can vary according to the track conditions.

Even modern watering systems have failed to create a level playing field at some tracks, which show a clear draw bias year after year, and in chapter 10, page 82, expert Graham Wheldon provides an in-depth study of the effect of the draw at British racecourses.

Professional backer Alan Potts says he can use the draw to eliminate at least half the runners in a race before he even turns to the form book. But he says that many pundits and punters think too vaguely about the draw.

"You often hear people say 'a high draw is favoured', but that begs two questions – what is a high draw? And what do they mean by favoured?" Potts says. "You've got to put specific numbers to any perceived draw bias.

"For instance, in the big handicaps down the

Luck of the draw: runners burst from the stalls. A horse's stall position can make the difference between winning and losing a race

straight course at Royal Ascot, I will split the field into groups and allocate a price to each group based on the chance of the winner coming from that group according to the draw. It might be even-money the winner coming from stalls 25-30, 2-1 on stalls 1-6 and 5-1 all the rest.

"Then I price up each runner's chance of winning their group – say 2-1 for the horse with the best chance from stalls 25-30.

"Combining the two prices in a double gives you a price about each horse winning the race – evens about stalls 25-30 and 2-1 about the favourite in that group doubles up to 5-1, which represents the odds of that horse winning the race. So you're looking for odds of 5-1 or better about that horse."

FITNESS In any athletic sport, form and fitness are two of the key factors in determining success or failure, and horseracing is no different. In-form, fit horses are what every punter should be looking for, as Tom Segal, who writes the Racing Post's highly successful Pricewise column, explains: "The main factor in any race is current form. Horses drop down the handicap because they can't run fast any more, yet so often we hear all that garbage about how this or that runner is 5lb lower than their last winning mark.

"Surely you want exactly the opposite – a horse getting better who is 5lb above its previous winning rating. I always try to concentrate on horses who are getting better, not those who only have a chance if they come back to form. Linford Christie used to run fast but he can't now, and no-one would think of backing him if he ran in a top sprint, but often we get sucked into backing horses on former glories."

Form ratings – not the bare form figures – are the best guide to current form as they are designed to grade a horse's performances on a comparable scale and therefore allow a comparison to be made between horses who have been running in different events. Clearly they are not infallible, but Racing Post Ratings show the benefits to be gained from using a good ratings service (as outlined in a detailed analysis in chapter 13, page 110, and chapter 14, page 126).

Form tends to be most consistent at the height of the Flat or jumps season, for the obvious reason that most horses have had several runs by then and their wellbeing can be assessed more accurately. Early in the season, fitness from the gallops plays a bigger role but is not always easy to assess for the punter, who is denied access to the information of its home-work. In other major racing countries, such as the United States and Australia, work is done in public on the racetrack and sectional times are available to enable punters to gauge the fitness and ability of every horse.

In the absence of that information, British punters must rely on other guides to fitness, such as paddock inspection and a horse's form record, which might suggest that a horse is easy to get fit as it runs well first time out or after a mid-season break.

A consideration here is the record of the trainer in getting horses to a peak for their first run –

uncommon knowledge

Watch out for the favourites

The races trainers like to win – again and again

Trainers become associated with success in particular races, often those with some special place in the racing calendar. Richard Hannon is the man to follow in the Weatherbys Super Sprint at Newbury with five wins in the first 13 runnings – the race carries a particularly attractive prize for two-year-olds, an area in which Hannon specialises.

Luca Cumani was renowned in the 1990s for his success in the Galtres Stakes at the York Ebor meeting, winning the race eight times in that decade – as one of the few black-type races restricted to fillies and mares, it was not surprising that Cumani targeted the race year after year with his best female runners.

In Ireland, Aidan O'Brien has dominated the top two-year-old races in Ireland such as the National Stakes (six wins in eight years, 1996-2003) – a consequence of the fact that the strength of his stable means he will always try out his best juveniles in those contests.

former trainer Jack Berry was renowned for his ability to strike with early two-year-olds, while Sir Mark Prescott rarely has a tilt at a big race, even with a horse who has been off the track for a long time, unless it has a genuine chance (he won the 2003 Cambridgeshire with Chivalry, who had not run for 343 days, and the 1996 King's Stand Stakes with seasonal debutant Pivotal).

Other trainers are adept at getting horses to run consistently well once they hit top form and some horses, particularly sprinters, can notch several wins in quick succession – David Nicholls, Mark Johnston and Mark Brisbourne are three with a notable record in recent years of winning with the same horse within the space of two or three days. One reason for a winning horse reappearing quickly can be to take advantage of a lower handicap mark before its official rating is revised upwards – while this is no guarantee of success, such 'momentum' horses are always worthy of note.

A horse's form is inextricably linked to the form of its stable as a whole, and this is another key area for punters to consider.

Form can tail off quickly at the end of a long season, especially as the ground changes (getting softer on the Flat as winter approaches and faster over jumps during the spring and early summer).

Just as form and fitness can be difficult to weigh up at the start of a horse's campaign, so the end of the season can be an unprofitable time for the unwary punter.

Steve Mason, who compiles Racing Post Ratings for the jumps, says: "The importance of continuity in the form is highlighted when the performance of our selections is broken down on a month-by-month basis. April and November are what I would describe as transitional months. January through to March is the heart of the jumps season proper – there is continuity in the form and, as I would expect, this is a period when our selections do particularly well."

COMMITMENT Horses, and indeed stables, rarely maintain the same level of form for an entire season. Factors such as illness and injury play a big part in form fluctuations, but equally it is evident that trainers target certain races, race meetings and periods in the season for their horses to hit peak form. The clues provided by a stable's pattern of winners and losers can be invaluable in looking beyond the form to decide whether a horse is likely to run to its optimum level.

One of the most important factors is a trainer's record at a particular course or meeting. Some trainers have become well known for their successful traits over the years – Barry Hills and Geoff Wragg are the ones to follow at Chester's May meeting, Mark Johnston is particularly successful at Royal Ascot and

uncommon knowledge

 Big fish, small ponds

It's worth looking at the statistics for smaller courses to see which bigger trainers do well there – certain Newmarket trainers do well at northern tracks from a handful of runners, often their developing two-year-olds.

In a similar vein, it is always worth looking out for horses who have been sent a long distance to compete or who are the only runner for their trainer at a particular meeting. This may indicate that a horse has been primed for the race, though it is arguable that the significance of such factors has decreased given the recent growth in racing opportunities and improved travel for horses.

Glorious Goodwood, David Nicholls' horses also excel at Glorious Goodwood, while Hills again does well at Doncaster's St Leger meeting. Over the jumps, Nicky Henderson has built up an enviable record at the Cheltenham Festival.

Equally, some of the same trainers have periods when their stable goes through a comparatively poor patch. Johnston and Hills have enjoyed comparatively little success at York's Ebor meeting over the years, while Nicholls' horses struggle at the big meetings at York and Doncaster.

Clearly these trends are often a reflection of a trainer's preferences – Barry Hills likes Chester's May meeting so much that he starts planning his strategy the previous autumn. Or they can be a consequence of a trainer's campaigning style – John Gosden's stable comes alive in the autumn, hence his good record at the Doncaster St Leger and Prix de l'Arc de Triomphe meetings.

The stats are often compelling, but it pays to keep an open mind and watch for changes. John Dunlop would have been a trainer to avoid at Chester's May meeting until the late 1990s but has a good recent record there; champion jumps trainers Martin Pipe and David Nicholson both struggled for years to notch the big winners at the Cheltenham Festival but eventually their records at the season's most prestigious fixture matched their achievements elsewhere.

As most of the main trends are well known, it is also worth watching out for emerging trainers who may be quietly building up some impressive statistics at a particular course or meeting. Gerard Butler, for instance, has been particularly successful at Chester since he started training and has a record to rival course specialists Hills and Wragg – indeed, Butler has acknowledged that he follows the Hills/Wragg method of galloping horses around the track on the morning of the race to let them get a feel for the tight turns.

Impressive course statistics are not limited to the big trainers. Many successful smaller trainers have enviable records on their local tracks, such as Len Lungo over the jumps at Ayr.

Another clue to a horse's commitment for a particular race can be the jockey booking. A senior jockey replacing an apprentice is often viewed as a signal of intent, but equally an apprentice taking a few pounds off the horse's weight can be a positive sign, especially if the horse has performed well for an apprentice in the past. In races restricted to amateurs, ladies and apprentices, where riding ability can vary widely, the bookings of the top jockeys in that sphere always catch the eye.

Another major element to consider is a horse's position in the handicap. A horse's handicap mark is a crucial factor in its success – every horse eventually finds its level and, especially later in its career, it is unusual for a horse to find enough improvement to enable it to win off a higher mark than before. A horse with a top winning mark of 70, for example, will struggle if it ends up in the 70s after several good runs and is likely to need a return to a mark in the 60s to rediscover winning form.

Trainers, of course, are aware of this factor and it is common sense to assume that trainers will maximise their efforts with a horse – for instance, by paying more attention to a jockey booking – when it is running off a handicap mark that befits its ability.

GENUINENESS Horses are often blamed for a punter's mistakes, being labelled as 'dogs' if they fail to deliver the expected win. While it is true that some horses dislike racing, more often than not there is a physical reason for any apparent lack of fighting spirit – a bleeding attack or an unresolved injury, for example.

Tony Morris, the esteemed pedigree expert, has pointed out the folly of attributing human characteristics to horses, such as a will to win.

"A horse doesn't think like a human being, has no idea why that stick with the red circle on top is planted in the ground, possesses no natural inclination to get anywhere any quicker than its fellows, and only a rider's encouragement can make it conquer the pain barrier, which is a concept that it can't begin to understand," he wrote in the Racing Post.

"Racing, actually competing against others with a little human being aboard, is a totally artificial pursuit, foreign to the horse's nature. It just isn't something that a horse would choose to do."

Whatever the reasons, however, the Form Book is packed with examples of horses who run consistently without winning, or travel well on the bridle without finding anything in the finish, or whose form tails off badly. Trainers can take corrective measures with such horses – notably by applying equipment such as blinkers, a visor or a tongue tie. Racing is littered with examples of horses who have improved significantly after a change to their tack – Persian War, a three-time Champion Hurdle winner (1968-70) and one of the best of all time, was transformed by a tongue tie, while Ezzoud, a dual Juddmonte International winner in the 1990s, was much better in blinkers or a visor, finishing out of the places only twice in 14 top-level races after being tried with the equipment.

Equipment changes are judged to be so important that many racing nations enforce public notification by connections – an area in which the Jockey Club has recently begun to catch up by introducing compulsory notification of tongue ties and cheekpieces, as well as blinkers and visors.

Moving to a different trainer can appear to bring a change of attitude from a horse, with any improvement in form often ascribed to 'a change of scenery'. Whether the improvement is mental or physical, a new training regime often brings out the best in a horse and some trainers, such as David Nicholls, are renowned for their ability to improve horses from other stables.

Equally, some trainers are adept at getting the best from every horse and their cast-offs rarely improve – Henry Cecil in his prime was a good example, and the animals who went to the horses-in-training sales out of his stable did not usually step up on their form with a different trainer.

It is worth checking Trainer Trace in the Racing Post's Signposts section for horses who have changed stables, but the importance of the information always hinges on the relative abilities of the trainers involved.

OTHER FACTORS A host of other factors can affect a horse's performance, though many are hard to quantify and their influence is disputed. This category includes non-notifiable equipment such as sheepskin nosebands, which are fitted to horses by trainers – some as a matter of routine – as an aid to concentration.

Physiological changes, notably a filly or mare coming into season, are widely held to have an impact on performance. A female horse generally comes into season every three weeks for a few days, which is the time when she prepares to accept a stallion, and the Jockey Club's chief veterinary officer Peter Webbon told the Racing Post: "It's more a behavioural change rather than a physical one, so it could affect a horse mentally. For instance, she might not be prepared to go for gaps like she would otherwise."

It is not easy to detect when a filly is in season, even for a trainer, but females can often be forgiven one poor run because the factor might be at work. Russian Rhythm's only defeat against her own sex was blamed on her being in season for the 2002 Cheveley Park Stakes, while the winner of that race, Airwave, was beaten in the 2003 King's Stand Stakes when reportedly in season.

Other fillies and mares, however, have won despite being in season and trainer James Given, a qualified vet, told the Racing Post: "It's not black and white. Some fillies have been known

uncommon knowledge

**Different
gear**

Cheekpieces, blinkers and visors – what they do

Blinkers consist of a hood with eye cups that are fitted over a horse's head. They limit a horse's vision and reduce distractions, with the aim of concentrating its mind on racing. They are used on curious or nervous horses who may want to look around, horses who do not run properly and tend to lean against horses by their side, or those who need to increase early speed, particularly in sprints. A visor is similar to blinkers, but has a slit in each eye cup to allow some lateral vision. A tongue tie is a strip of material tied around a horse's tongue and jaw to keep it from retracting or extending its tongue, which can clog its air passage.

Cheekpieces – also known as 'French blinkers' – are strips of sheepskin which are attached to the cheekpieces of a horse's bridle. As they partially obscure a horse's rear vision, they act in a similar way to blinkers and are capable of having a similar effect. Storming Home, the 2002 Champion Stakes victor, is one example of a big winner who wore cheekpieces.

to run better in season, although the opposite is more common."

Surgery can also lead to a major shift in form and it is worth watching for horses who have been gelded as the operation often transforms a previously unco-operative animal. Other operations such as hobdaying and tubing, which are used to correct respiratory problems, are commonly cited by trainers as the reason behind a win and there have been calls for this information to be available to the racing public before a race.

Another contentious issue is the body weight of horses, which is public knowledge in countries such as the United States and Australia but remains an unknown factor for British punters. Some pundits believe a horse's body weight offers an invaluable insight into its fitness, though its importance is disputed. ◼

be quick on the draw

BEAUTY IN THE BIAS

THE DRAW IS THE SINGLE MOST important factor in the outcome of almost every Flat race at distances short of a mile, and quite frequently over longer trips too. That was the case when I wrote my first book on the effects of the draw in 1997 and is still true today, with the draw having affected more sprints during 2003 than in any other Flat season in living memory.

Biases do, however, change over time at most courses – hence the need to keep tabs on things on an ongoing basis – due to such factors as drainage work, course alterations or a switch to different watering methods. They can even swing within the space of a couple of months, which is why I never struggle to fill a page each week in the Racing & Football Outlook throughout the turf season.

As an example, over the past two seasons I've done my money in Kempton sprints more than once, mostly because of constructive watering, but also because of fields not splitting at the expected point.

As with several other courses, there are many variables to take into account at Kempton (this is why I feel statistics are rarely of much assistance in pinpointing biases). Firstly, there is the going, as the bias here is completely different on soft ground than on fast. Then there is the field size and whether and where the field will split (Kempton can accommodate 24

By GRAHAM WHELDON

Unlikely candidate: the Cesarewitch at Newmarket might be a marathon, but the draw bias can apply even at extreme distances

runners in sprints and the stalls can be positioned far side (high), stands' side (low) or down the centre).

This is why each race has to be considered on its merits and why I price up every non-maiden sprint staged throughout the year, factoring in the anticipated effect of the draw. Sometimes the Racing Post tissue/bookmakers' prices fail to do likewise, and this is where the draw player continues to gain his edge.

For example, in the race won by Prime Recreation at Kempton in March 2003 (one race at the track I got spot on) I had made the winner, drawn 16 of 16, 5-1 co-favourite, along with Our Chelsea Blue, berthed next door, and Woodland Blaze (11). This was because the stalls were on the far rail (high) and because the field was unlikely to split (the runner drawn in 1 was still eight stall-widths from the stands' rail). Conversely, the Racing Post prices had not accounted for a potential draw bias, and the winner went off overpriced at 9-1.

An example of bookmakers offering prices that factor in an incorrect draw bias came at Royal Ascot during the summer of 2003. The opening day's results had suggested a major bias in favour of the stands' side (low), and that was duly borne out by the result of the Royal Hunt Cup the following afternoon.

However, things changed somewhat on the Thursday, with New Seeker able to overcome racing in a far smaller group to win the Britannia from stall 27. By that stage (that race was the last on the card and not over until 5.35pm) the bookmakers had already sent their prices for the following day's seven-furlong handicap, factoring in a big low bias.

This fact was not missed by Pricewise, who put up Attache from stall 30 at 33-1 (as did yours truly on the Racing & Football HotLine). The far side duly came out on top, with Attache scoring at 10-1, which was probably the sort of price he would have been in the first place had the layers been able to wait until after the Britannia.

It isn't just straight-course races that are affected by the draw, though, as some big-field, round-course handicaps can also be played as bias races.

The most obvious example of this is the John Smith's Cup at York, a 1m2f handicap in which low numbers have done particularly well over recent years. Two other less-exposed races to bear in mind are the 2m4f Ascot Stakes at Royal Ascot and the 2m2f Cesarewitch at Newmarket, both of which show a bias in favour of high numbers.

There are several jockeys whose reading of the draw and course bias makes them worth following. These 'draw jockeys' used to be headed by the now-retired Ray Cochrane and Michael Roberts, both of whom were different class.

The best three on the northern circuit nowadays are Robert Winston, Dean McKeown and Dale Gibson, but there are no outstanding candidates in the south, apart from the obvious top jockeys like Kieren Fallon and Richard Quinn.

The draw biases I have outlined in this chapter

apply to straight-course races unless otherwise stipulated. Punters should also note that most races (outside Festival meetings) are now restricted to 20 runners under a recent BHB rule, which means it is now particularly worth looking at the position of the stalls, as many courses can accommodate more than that number.

ASCOT (RIGHT-HANDED) 2003 saw some
major biases appear (most notably at the Festival of Racing meeting, when runners were switching right over to the far side), but things were never consistent, with a lot down to watering. Low numbers had looked to hold the advantage during the first couple of days of the Royal meeting, but only once in the past ten years has the stands' rail ridden genuinely faster at this fixture; otherwise those drawn very high in big fields have at least held their own. That again proved the case later in the week, with Ratio (22 of 29) dead-heating in the Wokingham to follow up wins for Attache (30 of 27) and New Seeker (27 of 29). Over longer trips, runners tend to head wide down the side of the course on soft ground.
Stalls Almost always go on the stands' side (low).
Biases The far side (high) always rides quicker on soft/heavy ground. High numbers have an excellent record in the 2m4f Ascot Stakes.
Splits Runners usually converge towards the stands' side, apart from in fields of 22+ or under exceptional circumstances (very soft ground or when the far side is clearly riding quicker).

AYR (LEFT-HANDED) The draw usually
only becomes a major issue in sprints at the Western meeting, with fields rarely big enough during the rest of the season for groups to form (high is almost always best in fields of 25 or fewer, whatever the ground). There was a turnaround in the Silver and Gold Cups last season, with the far side (low) coming out on top in both races. High numbers had dominated for many years previously, not least during the

mid-1990s. The change was almost certainly down to a fresh (hardly watered) strip of ground being unveiled down that side and it will be interesting to see whether the management takes the same approach this season. The general view is that low numbers are best in big fields over 7f 50y and 1m, but this rarely pans out, with fields often in single figures.

Stalls Usually go up the stands' side (high) in sprints, but occasionally go on the other side (normally in the run-up to the Western meeting to preserve the ground).

Biases High numbers are usually best in sprints whatever the ground, apart from the odd occasion when the stalls are placed up the far side (low). A watching brief is advised on the Silver and Gold Cups to see whether the 2003 results are maintained.

Splits Fields only usually split in the Silver and Gold Cups.

BATH (L-H) The draw is of far less importance than the pace at which races are run. In big fields, runners drawn low are often inclined to go off too fast to hold a rail position (the course turns left most of the way, including one major kink) and this can see hold-up horses drawn wide coming through late. Conversely, in smaller fields containing little pace, up front and on the inside is often the place to be.

Stalls Always go on the inside (low).

Splits Fields always stick together, but soft ground (very rare) can see a split, with the outside rail (high) favoured.

BEVERLEY (R-H) A high draw is essential on good to soft or faster ground over 5f and also on the round course, particularly in races of 7f 100y and 1m 100y. In sprints, runners have to negotiate a right-handed jink not long after the start and it seems harder here than at probably any course for runners drawn low to get over to the favoured rail (there is also a camber). When conditions are genuinely testing, however, there is a strip of ground by the stands' rail that rides significantly quicker than the rest of the course, and under such conditions those drawn very low hold a decisive advantage. The course management experimented with moving stalls to the stands' side over 5f in 2002 (unsuccessfully, as it led to a huge low bias) and had planned to do so again in 2003, but were forced to abort after being unable to provide a level playing field (apparently the rail strip has become compressed thanks to the ambulance). They will try it again in 2004, but only in small fields, since otherwise the high-drawn runners will still be near enough to the far rail. Major work is going to be carried out in a bid to level the course out once and for all.

Stalls Go on the inside (high) at all distances, but will be tried stands' side again over 5f at some point in 2004.

Biases High numbers are massively favoured at 5f on good to soft or faster ground, but very low draws take over on soft/heavy (hold-up horses are usually best avoided whatever the going). High numbers are also best on the round course.

Splits Very rare and only likely over 5f on soft ground.

BRIGHTON (L-H) Much depends on the going and time of year; on good to soft or slower ground runners often head for the outside rail (high), while in late season it is often just a case of whichever jockey finds the least cut-up strip of ground. Otherwise, low-drawn, prominent racers tend to hold sway in fast-ground sprints, with double figures always facing an uphill task over 5f 59y.

Stalls Always go on the inside (low) in sprints.

Splits These occur frequently in the second half of the season, as jockeys look for a fresh strip on ground that seems to churn up easily. George Duffield often takes an exploratory route.

CARLISLE (R-H) In recent seasons, runners racing with the pace and hardest against the inside rail (high) have done well in big fields early in the campaign. This is entirely down to the fact that the Flat course and jumps course are one and the same, and that those racing nearest the fence are running where the hurdle wings were positioned, while those wider out are on the raced-on surface. Things have tended to level out as the year has progressed, however. On soft ground, the bias swings completely, with runners racing widest (low) and grabbing the stands' rail in the straight favoured at all distances.

Stalls Normally go on the inside (high) but can go down the middle in sprints (usually on slow ground).

Biases High numbers are best in early-season sprints as long as the ground is no slower than good. Look to back low numbers on soft/heavy ground, although such going is seldom seen here, because there is no racing after early September.

Splits Rarely will two groups form in the straight, but on easy ground runners often spread out.

CATTERICK (L-H) When the ground is testing, the stands' rail is definitely the place to be, which suits high numbers in 5f races, and high-drawn prominent racers at all other distances. However, when the ground is good to firm or faster, horses drawn on the inside (low) often hold the edge, and there were several meetings in the 2003 season when those runners racing prominently hardest against the inside rail dominated (over all distances, presumably as a result of watering).

Stalls On the inside (low) at all distances these days (they often used to go on the outer over 5f 212y).

Biases Low numbers are best in sprints on fast ground (particularly watered firm going), but the stands' rail (high) rides faster under slower conditions.

Splits Fields have usually stuck together in fast-ground 5f races in the past, but splits could become more common on genuine good ground.

CHEPSTOW (L-H) High numbers enjoyed a massive advantage in straight-course races in 2000 and the course management took steps to eradicate the faster strip, using the 'earthquake' machine employed at Goodwood in the late 1990s. This led to little in the way of a draw bias for the next two years, but it was back with a vengeance in 2003 (presumably caused by compaction) when the winners of the 18 14+-runner, straight-course races were drawn: 12 of 15, 17 of 19, 10 of 16, 12 of 20, 9 of 19, 16 of 17, 17 of 20, 16 of 20, 13 of 15, 8 of 15, 17 of 18, 16 of 16, 5 of 20 (far side), 13 of 18, 5 of 19 (far side), 16 of 16, 17 of 19 and 15 of 15. Interestingly, the two winners who managed to score up the far side both contested 7f races (interesting, because some believe the bias increases the longer the trip). There were also numerous smaller-field winners who won thanks to grabbing the stands' rail in front, Material Witness and Benbaun being two notable examples.

Stalls Always go on the stands' side (high) on the straight course.

Biases High numbers are massively favoured on the straight course (up to 1m14y) whatever the ground, and the good news for draw players is that the bias only increased as the 2003 season progressed.

Splits Jockeys on low-drawn runners sussed out in 2003 that they had more chance going to the far side than staying off the fence near side, so splits are again likely to be common in big-field straight-course races.

CHESTER (L-H) It is well known that low numbers are favoured at all distances here, even in the 2m2f Chester Cup, and the bias is factored into the prices these days. However, sprints (in particular handicaps) are still playable. Six of the eight events last year with 10+ runners were won by stall 1, 2, 3 or 4.

Stalls On the inside (low) at all distances bar 1m 2f 75y and 2m 2f 117y (same starting point) when they are positioned on the outside. Certain starters ask for the stalls to come slightly off the inside rail in sprints.

Biases Low numbers are favoured at all distances. Soft ground seems to accentuate the bias until a few races have been run, when a higher draw becomes less of a disadvantage as the ground on the inside becomes chewed up.

DONCASTER (L-H) Draw biases here are

usually as reliable as they come (despite something very odd happening midway through the St Leger meeting in 2003, expect things to settle down again). High numbers dominate in sprints, low numbers take over on the straight mile (as long as there are enough runners for a split) and either rail can have the advantage at 7f. Going into September 2003, the results from the previous two and a half seasons were spectacular, with 17 of the 25 16+-runner sprints won by a horse in the top six stalls, and stall 1 landing six of the 12 races over the straight mile.

Stalls Always on the stands' side (high) on the straight course.

Biases High numbers are best in sprints, very high and very low numbers are favoured over 7f, while very low draws are best over the straight mile (as long as they are taken to the far side). The softer the ground becomes, the greater the biases.

Splits Fields tend to stick together in sprints, apart from in fields of 20+, but it is not uncommon for a few to go far side at 7f and 1m.

EPSOM (L-H) When the going is on the

soft side, jockeys tack over to the stands' side for the better ground (this strip rides quicker in such conditions, as the course cambers away from the stands' rail towards the far side). In 5f races, the stalls are invariably placed on the stands' side, so when the going is soft the majority of the runners are on the best ground from the outset. Prominent racers drawn low in round-course races are able to take the shortest route around Tattenham Corner, and on faster ground have a decisive edge over 6f, 7f and 1m 114y. Over 5f, high numbers used to hold quite an advantage, but the bias is not so great these days.

Stalls Always go on the outside (high) over 5f and 6f (races over the latter trip start on a chute) and inside (low) at other distances, bar 1m 4f 10y (centre).

Biases Low-drawn prominent racers are favoured at between 6f and 1m 114y.

Splits Good to soft ground often leads to a few trying the stands' side route.

FOLKESTONE (R-H) Before 1998, Folkestone was never thought to have much bias, but now the draw is often crucial on the straight course (up to 7f). Whatever the ground, the far rail (high) rides faster than the stands' rail, which in turn rides quicker than the middle of the track. Last season, runners invariably went across to the far side over 6f and 7f (jockeyship often played a part, with several races going to whoever had secured the front up the rail, including Richard Hughes more than once). However, over 5f, when the stalls were up the stands' rail, fields often split, with low numbers just about holding sway (it seems that the ground lost by switching across over the minimum trip cannot be regained from racing on the faster ground). Slow ground swings things even more in favour of high numbers.

Stalls Usually go up the stands' side (low) on the straight track, but occasionally down the centre (they can't go up the far side as the ambulance needs access).

Biases High numbers are favoured over 6f and 7f, and also over the minimum trip when 14 or more line up. However, very low numbers have a good record in smaller fields over 5f. Front-runners are worth considering at all distances.

Splits Fields tend to divide only over 5f.

GOODWOOD (R-H and L-H) The course management took steps to end the major high bias that affected the Stewards' Cup throughout the late 1990s by breaking up the ground by machine in 1998. However, the inside strip has since become compressed again and the bias has returned with a vengeance in the last couple of seasons (the first one home up the stands' side in 2003, the progressive Frizzante, was beaten around four lengths). All other sprints also tend to develop away from the stands' rail now, apart from on soft/heavy going (when low numbers continue to enjoy the edge) and it usually pays to concentrate on the top half of the draw in fields of 12+. High numbers are favoured on the round course, particularly at between 7f and 1m1f, except on good to soft or slower ground, when jockeys tend to tack over centre to stands' side in the straight.

Stalls Invariably on the stands' side (low).

Biases High numbers are best at between 7f and 1m1f, and the faster the ground the more pronounced the bias (keep an eye out for the rail on the home turn being moved during Glorious week). High numbers are best in sprints of 12+ runners, apart from on soft ground, when low take over.

Splits Although fields tend not to break into groups in most sprints, runners often spread out to about two-thirds of the way across in fields of around 20.

HAMILTON (R-H) Extensive drainage work was carried out in the winter of 2002 in a bid to level up the two sides of the track but, after encouraging early results, the natural bias in favour of high numbers (far side) kicked in again, particularly after the first soft-ground fixture. It seems the course is stuck with this bias, which can only be altered by watering on faster going (be careful after a dry spell, as things can often swing in favour of low numbers). High numbers are also best over 1m 65y, thanks to runners encountering a tight right-handed loop soon after the start.

Stalls It is not uncommon for the ground to become too soft for the use of stalls, but they usually go on the stands' side (low).

Biases High draws are best in soft/heavy-ground sprints, but the bias becomes middle to high otherwise (often switching to low on watered fast ground). Despite the stiffness of the course, front-runners do particularly well at all distances.

Splits Look for high numbers to peel off in fields of 8+ when the stalls are stands' side, unless the ground is very fast.

HAYDOCK (L-H) High numbers used to enjoy a major advantage in soft-ground sprints, but that seems to have been turned full circle by drainage work carried out in the late 1990s, with the far side (low) now best on very bad ground. Otherwise, runners usually head for the centre these days, the draw rarely making much of a difference (although very high numbers can be worst off in big fields on faster going).

Stalls Usually positioned down the centre in the straight.

KEMPTON (R-H) This has become one of the most complicated bias courses in the country during recent seasons, with ground, watering, field size and stall positioning four factors to consider in every sprint. In mid-summer, when fast ground and small fields usually prevail, the stalls are generally put down the centre, and jockeys tend to stay there in one group. However, when 10-16 line up, runners often split if the stalls are down the middle (no guaranteed bias), while they usually stick to either rail if the stalls are stands' side (low) or far side (high). Under the latter circumstances, very low numbers or very high numbers respectively enjoy the advantage. In big fields (17-20 – the course can take 24 but no more than 20 are allowed to run under the new BHB rule) it is not uncommon for fields to split wherever the stalls are positioned, and much then comes down to watering. The judgement call continues to be low (definitely on soft ground) but the far side (high) has been known to dominate, particularly in early season. High-drawn, prominent racers had an excellent record over 7f and 1m (Jubilee and Round courses) in 2003.

Stalls Can go anywhere, and often down the centre in mid-summer.

Splits Splits are common in double-figure-field sprints.

LEICESTER (R-H) Between 1998 and 2001 the centre-to-far-side strip (middle to high) enjoyed a decisive advantage over the stands' rail and jockeys eventually chose to avoid the near side. That changed in 2003, with very low numbers more than holding their own. Expect more of the same, and for the stands' rail to ride considerably quicker on slower ground.

Stalls Invariably go up the stands' side (low).

Splits Given the switch in bias, fields are more likely to stick together in one group, although it is always worth looking for a 'draw jockey' positioned very high in big fields.

LINGFIELD TURF (L-H) The draw advantage is nothing like as defined as in years past, and 2003 saw things turn full circle. In the first half of the year, the middle of the track (low) at least held its own with the stands' rail, and then completely took over around July, when high numbers might as well have not turned up. From the middle of August, though, that changed, with the stands' rail becoming dominant. The one factor that can have a massive effect on the draw is heavy rainfall on firm ground. Presumably because of the undulating nature of the track and the fact that the far rail on the straight course is towards the bottom of a slope where it joins the round course, rainfall seems to make the middle and far side ride a deal slower. In these conditions, the top three or four stalls have a massive edge.

Stalls Go up the stands' side (high) at between 5f and 7f, and down the middle over 7f 140y.

Biases High numbers are massively favoured on fast ground after recent rain, but otherwise the most recent meeting is usually the best guide.

Splits It is unusual to see two distinct groups, but runners often fan out centre to stands' side in big fields.

LINGFIELD ALL-WEATHER (L-H) There is little in the draw at longer distances, but there is over 5f, with stalls 1-5 enjoying a major advantage over boxes 6-10. It is also best to be low to middle in 6f races, and over 1m2f, where those drawn wider than 7 tend to struggle. That said, being drawn next to the inside rail can also be a disadvantage, with stalls 1 and 2 not performing well (boxes 3-7 are favoured).

MUSSELBURGH (R-H) The bias in favour of low numbers at 5f looked greater than ever in 2003, even on fast ground. That said, nobody tried going right to the far side from a very high draw, a tactic that had proved successful the previous summer, with most edging towards the main pack centre to stands' side. The bias in favour of high numbers at 7f and 1m is not as strong as many believe.

Stalls Usually go up the stands' side (low) over 5f nowadays, but they can be rotated.

Splits Look out for runners drawn very high in big-fields over 5f on fast ground – they occasionally go right to the far rail.

NEWBURY (L-H) It is hard to remember a race before 2003 in which the far side (low) had come out on top in a straight-course race where the field had split, but that changed in the Weatherbys Super Sprint, in which If Paradise ended the high-number dominance by scoring from the 1 box. Ultimately, there is probably little between the two flanks these days, apart from on soft ground, in which case the stands' rail (high) is the place to be. When the ground is testing, it is not uncommon to see runners race wide down the back straight and down the side at between 1m 3f 56y and 2m (particularly over 1m 5f 61y). In such circumstances, a high draw becomes a huge advantage.

Stalls Can go anywhere for straight-course races.

Splits It is not often that fields are big enough for a split to occur.

NEWCASTLE (L-H)

On the straight course, it used to be a case of high numbers best on good or firmer and low numbers having an advantage when the ground rode good to soft or softer. That changed in 2001, when the far side proved best whatever the going, and again in 2003, when ultimately there was rarely much between the two sides on fast going (on four occasions less than half a length separated the flanks, in races won by Karminskey Park (May 22), Strensall (July 26), Caribbean Coral (October 1) and If By Chance (October 22)). The far side (low) still rides considerably quicker on slow ground, however. Over the straight mile, the stands' rail (high) is the place to be apart from on bad ground.

Stalls Invariably on the stands' side (high), only being switched to the inside under exceptional circumstances.

Biases Low numbers are best at up to 7f on good to soft or slower ground, but there is rarely much between the two sides on faster going. Very high numbers are best over the straight mile, apart from on very testing ground.

Splits Two groups are usually formed when 14+ go to post, and often when 8-13 line up. The majority tend to go far side in sprints, but most stick stands' side over the straight mile.

NEWMARKET JULY COURSE (R-H)

The major draw biases seen under the former clerk of the course have become a thing of the past since Michael Prosser took over, and now only the occasional meeting will be affected. The course is permanently divided into two halves by a rail (the Racing Post now carries information regarding which side is to be used) and, as a rule, the two outside rails (stands' rail when they are on the stands'-side half, far rail when they are on the far-side half) ride faster than the dividing rail.

Stalls Can go either side on either half of the track.

Stands'-side half: On fast ground (particularly watered) very high numbers are often favoured at up to 1m, when there is a narrow strip hard against the fence that rides quicker. However, on good to soft or slower ground, runners racing down the centre are favoured.

Far-side half: There is rarely much in the draw, apart from on slow ground, when the far side (low) rides much faster.

Splits Runners just about tend to form two groups in capacity fields, but are more likely to run to their draw here than at tracks such as Newcastle.

NEWMARKET ROWLEY MILE (R-H)

Similarly to the July Course, the draw seems to have been evened out since the clerk of the course change. Occasionally a bias will appear, but they are hard to predict these days.

Stalls Can go anywhere and are rotated.

Biases High numbers have dominated the 2m2f Cesarewitch in recent years, the 2002 and 2003 winners having come from 36 of 36. The logic here is that those on the inside can be switched off early, while low numbers have to work to get into position before the sole right-handed turn.

Splits It is not unusual for jockeys to come stands' side on slow ground in round-course races.

NOTTINGHAM (L-H) On the straight course,

it used to be a case of low numbers being favoured when the stalls were on the far rail and high numbers when they were stands' side, with low being best when the stalls spanned the entire course. These days, though, it is less clear-cut and the feeling at the end of the 2003 season was that there is ultimately little between the two sides. As in the previous year, the occasional meeting showed an advantage in favour of one side or the other, but even after the inside rail had been pulled in to unveil fresh ground in the autumn, there still was little between the flanks. The bias in favour of low numbers at 1m54y is only slight.

Stalls Tend to go on the stands' side (high) unless the ground is very soft.

Splits Fields usually split in sprints when 14+ line up.

PONTEFRACT (L-H) Low numbers have always been considered best here for the same reason as at Chester – the course has several distinct left-hand turns with a short home straight. However, this is definitely not correct – if anything, high numbers have the edge in sprints, whatever the ground, and massively so on soft/heavy. Drainage work in the late 1990s was intended to eradicate the outside-rail bias on slow ground, and worked immediately afterwards, but in 2003 there were signs that it is now riding much faster (doubters need only look back at Frankie Dettori's riding of Rules For Jokers from stall 18 at the meeting on October 6). Of the nine 16+-runner sprint handicaps staged, six went to a runner drawn 15 or higher, including four from the 18 box – statistics too overwhelming to be labelled a fluke.

Stalls Inside (low) unless the ground is very soft, when they are switched to the outside rail.

Biases Very high numbers did particularly well in big-field sprints during the 2003 season, and there is definite evidence that the outside rail now offers the advantage on any ground bar fast (runners sticking to the inner on soft/heavy may be worse off by as much as 20 lengths).

Splits Although it is uncommon to see distinct groups, high numbers usually race wide these days on good to soft or slower ground. It is possible some will try going right to the outside rail in future.

REDCAR (L-H) It is not unusual to see big fields throughout the season here, but the draw rarely plays a part, with runners inclined to converge towards the centre. That said, there were a couple of breakaways in 2003 which nearly came off, not least Local Poet, who finished second in the big sales race from stall 1 (raced with one other far side).

Stalls Go towards the stands' side (high).

Splits Unusual and of little consequence when they are seen.

RIPON (R-H) The draw is often the sole deciding factor in big-field sprints, but the picture became rather more clouded in 2003, presumably because of watering. In the nine handicap sprints in which fields split, the far side came out on top only once, when Hidden Dragon won the Great St Wilfrid from 23 of 23 (all other winners coming from single figures). However, there was a definite spell of far-rail (high) domination in mid-summer. Similarly, there was a period earlier in the season when the stands' rail enjoyed a massive advantage, highlighted by The Wizard Mul's race in late May, a race in which the near side was responsible for the first five home (first one far side, Isengard, won next time). The best guide here these days, by some distance, is the most recent meeting.

Stalls On the stands' side (low) apart from under exceptional circumstances.

Biases Low numbers are best in sprints of 12 runners or fewer, but things can change in big fields. Front-runners (particularly from high draws over 1m) enjoyed a tremendous time of things on the round course in 2003, and any horse trying to make ground from behind and out wide is always facing a tough task.

Splits Fields tend to stay together in races of 12 or fewer, but a split is near guaranteed when 15 or more line up. Look for 'draw jockeys' who might chance going far side in fields of 13-14.

SALISBURY (R-H) It is difficult to win from a single-figure draw in big-field fast-ground sprints, and also over 7f, but proven stamina and race suitability become the most important factors over the testing straight 1m. This far-side bias is at its greatest in early and late season, before and after the erection of a temporary rail (which usually goes up in July). The draw swings full circle on slower ground, as jockeys then invariably head towards the stands' rail (good to soft seems to be the cut-off point).

Stalls Far side (high) unless ground is soft, when they are often moved to the near side.

Biases High numbers are best on the straight course on fast ground, there is not much in it on good to soft, while low take over on soft/heavy.

Splits Fields only tend to divide on good to soft ground; otherwise they all converge towards either rail, dependent upon going.

SANDOWN (R-H)

On the 5f chute, when the going is on the soft side and the stalls are on the far side (high), high numbers enjoy a decisive advantage. On the rare occasions that the stalls are placed on the stands' side, low numbers enjoy a slight advantage when all the runners stay towards the stands' rail. However, when a few break off and go to the far side high numbers comfortably hold the upper hand again. High numbers enjoy a decent advantage in double-figure fields over 7f and 1m on good going or faster, but jockeys invariably head for the stands' side on slow ground.

Stalls Usually go far side (high) over 5f, as the course is more level that side.

Splits It is unusual for runners to split over 5f, with capacity fields rare and jockeys all inclined to head for the far rail.

SOUTHWELL ALL-WEATHER (L-H)

During 2003 the 5f bias seemed to swing back towards the stands' side (high) following two years of far-side domination. It is best to be drawn low over 6f due to the proximity of the start to the first bend, but over 7f and beyond it is preferable to be middle to high, especially over distances with a long run to the first bend.

THIRSK (L-H)

Used to be the biggest draw course in the days of the old watering system (which was badly affected by wind) but, while biases still often show up, they are not as predictable. Field sizes, watering and going always have to be taken into account in fields of 12 or more (11 or fewer runners and it is rare to see anything bar one group up the stands' rail, with high numbers best). Otherwise, low numbers are almost always favoured on good or softer ground. Either rail can enjoy the edge on watered fast ground (the one place not to be is down the middle). Front-runners enjoyed a tremendous time on fast ground on the round course in 2003, and low-drawn prominent racers are worth considering whatever the distance.

Stalls Always go up the stands' side (high).

Biases High numbers are best in sprints when 11 or fewer line up, but it's hard to know which side is likely to do best in bigger fields on fast ground. The far (inside) rail is always best on good or slower going (the slower the ground, the greater the advantage).

Splits Runners invariably stay towards the stands' side in sprints of 12 or fewer runners (unless the ground is soft) and frequently when 13-14 line up. Any more and it becomes long odds-on two groups.

WARWICK (L-H) Low numbers are favoured in fast-ground sprints, but not by as much as many believe, and the prices often over-compensate. However, when the ground is genuinely soft, high numbers can enjoy a major advantage, as the outside rail then rides much faster.

Stalls Always on the inside (low).

WINDSOR (FIGURE OF EIGHT) It is typical to see large fields all season, and the draw almost always plays a part. In sprints, things are set in stone, with high numbers best on good or faster going (particularly watered fast ground), with not much between the two sides on good to soft, and with the far side (low) taking over on soft or heavy ground. In longer races, high-drawn prominent racers enjoyed a whale of a time on fast ground in 2003, and again it looked difficult for runners who were switched off the stands' rail to make up the leeway (because the course turns sharply left soon after the finish, those pulled wide must think they are being asked to quicken up into a dead-end). On slower ground, jockeys head centre to far side, and right over to the far rail on genuine soft/heavy (again, it is difficult to make ground from behind under such conditions).

Stalls Can be positioned anywhere for sprints.

Biases High-drawn prominent racers are favoured in fast-ground sprints, and also over 1m67y. On good to soft going, there is rarely much between the two sides, but it is a case of nearer to the far rail (low) the better on bad ground.

Splits Tend to occur only on good to soft ground, and even then it's rare to see two defined groups.

WOLVERHAMPTON ALL-WEATHER

(L-H) At most meetings the ground against the inside rail rides much deeper than the rest of the track, except after very wet or very cold weather when the track is usually deep harrowed. Statistics generally reflect this bias, with stall 1 having a poor record over most trips up to 1m 1f 79y (best to be middle to high). The bias is at its strongest over 5f, with stalls 1 and 2 having a poor record, although over 7f 100y and 1m 100y it's also a disadvantage to be drawn on the extreme outside, as both starts are very close to the first bend.

YARMOUTH (L-H) High numbers enjoyed

a major advantage for much of the 1990s, but this was put to an end by the switch from pop-up sprinklers (which were affected by the offshore breeze) to a Briggs Boom in 1999. These days a bias will appear occasionally (the far side (low) rode much faster in the summer of 2002) but it is hard to predict, and runners often head for the centre whatever the going.

Stalls Go one side or the other.

Splits It is common to see groups form, often

Sprinting at York: the draw is not as unpredictable as many believe

including one down the centre, in big fields.

YORK (L-H) The draw is nothing like as unpredictable in sprints as many believe, although things are never quite as clear-cut in September and October as earlier in the season. Essentially, on good or faster ground, the faster strip is to be found centre to far side, which means in capacity fields, the place to be is stall 6-12, while in fields of 12-14 runners drawn low are favoured (the course can accommodate only 20 runners). On soft/heavy ground, the stands' side (high) becomes the place and high numbers often get the rail to themselves, as this is not a bias well known by jockeys. Low numbers are best on fast ground on the round course, although watering can reduce the bias.
Stalls Can go anywhere.
Biases Prominent racers drawn centre are favoured in fast-ground sprints, but high numbers take over on soft/heavy ground. Low numbers are best in big fields on the round course, apart from on slower going, when runners leave the inside in the home straight.
Splits Defined groups are rare.

how was the race run?

STAY WITH THE PACE

PACE: THE FINAL FRONTIER. AS THE analysis of racing has confronted brave new ideas, one area has become increasingly shrouded in mystery and riddled with misunderstanding.

The truth is that the precise influence of pace on the outcome of a horserace – and how to incorporate it in analysis – will never begin to be understood until British racecourses are equipped with sectional timing. Fortunately, with the testing of state-of-the-art systems well in advance, that day is finally arriving.

In the meantime, while we do not have the data to make a fully objective analysis, it is important to be clear-headed about the limitations of pace analysis.

Several quasi-applications of pace have sprung up in the last few years. The concept that a slow early gallop favours horses prominently positioned, while a fast pace suits those restrained, has been widely accepted as a fundamental principle. Fair enough, but the application of these relationships in real-life situations is not straightforward and leads to races being misinterpreted.

For instance, I have lost count of horses who are supposed to have 'stolen' slowly run races from the front and who go on to win again under supposedly adverse circumstances. Similarly, there are any number of examples of horses who are wrongly given extra credit for

By JAMES
WILLOUGHBY

104

uncommon knowledge

Horses for courses

Punters must contextualise

All examples of pace analysis must be contextualised with the influence of racetrack configuration and ground conditions. A front-runner who is allowed a soft time has a much better chance of success at Kempton than Newmarket, for instance. In this regard, it is less important to understand why a particular course favours a running style than to be aware of the fact that it does. A statistical guide to the success rate of front-runners at various courses is available from several sources.

Ground conditions also both promote and compromise particular running styles. Here we are descending into the realms of the truly subjective, because empirical evidence is just about all there is to go on. Summer storms on watered ground at Goodwood, for instance, seem to promote front-running winners to the same extent that Polytrack racing at Lingfield favours those coming from off the pace. One day, with the advent of sectional timing, we will perhaps know why.

'doing best of the front-runners' in fast-run races in the belief that they would have fared better had the early pace been slower.

THE THREE-PART RULE One of the root causes of errant analysis is the widespread preoccupation with dividing races into just two parts. According to prescribed theory, a slow early pace corresponds with a sprint finish; a fast early pace with a slow finish. This is an over-simplification and inevitably leads to misunderstanding.

It is far better to think of races having a beginning, middle and end. For horses to benefit from a pace scenario, they must have two of the three sections run to suit. Even if the early pace is slow, it does not suit a front-runner to kick for home too soon. Horses can only maintain top speed for less than a quarter of a mile and decelerate sharply once they can no longer sustain all-out effort.

A great example of this was the 2003 Dewhurst

Stakes at Newmarket. Most observers correctly identified that the early gallop was moderate and therefore expressed surprise that the winner, Milk It Mick, was able to come from last place to success. Either he is a superstar, they concluded, or the form is just not very good.

Extend the pace analysis of the Dewhurst to three sections, rather than two, however, and it is far more understandable what went on. The middle part of the race was strongly run and the pace peaked too early to suit the front-runners, so the winner was able to pick up horses who had been softened up.

The run of the race was such a vital factor in the Dewhurst that correct interpretation of the form depends on proper analysis of the pace. This is so often the case that starting to think of races in three dimensions is crucial.

WHY THE MIDDLE MATTERS

Here are the four basic shapes of the tempo of races: fast-fast-slow; fast-slow-fast; slow-slow-fast; slow-fast-slow. The pace in the middle section of a race is inversely proportional to what happens at the end.

Therefore, it arguably has more influence on the result than the early pace. Next time a horse jumps out of the stalls and dictates a slow pace, the most pertinent question to ask yourself is at what point was it forced to accelerate? If taken on in the middle section, its victory could be deeply meritorious, even though the early gallop was steady. Conversely, do not be fooled into thinking that a horse who makes all at a fast early pace deserves extra credit if it was allowed to slow the tempo.

BEFORE THE RACE

If the objective analysis of the influence of pace is difficult after the event, it is doubly problematic beforehand. If pre-race discussions about pace were made in a vacuum and had no influence on the thinking of jockeys and trainers, it would be easier for punters to turn knowledge into profit. However, the prominence of pace prognostications in the media tends to increase the chaos factor.

If a horse is tipped up because it is likely to have an uncontested lead, for instance, it is common for the connections of at least one of its rivals to react by making sure it is taken on up front. This can turn the likely scenario on its head, the resultant fast and contentious pace ending up to the detriment of the horse supposed to be favoured.

Similarly, when pundits comment that the presence of several front-runners in the line-up makes a fast pace likely, one or more of the pace-setters may elect to take back in order that their chance is not ruined. As a result, a front-runner who was thought to be at a disadvantage can benefit from being able to dominate.

SPEED MAPS While these scenarios serve as a caveat to the usefulness of pace analysis, there is no need to throw the concept out of the window. It is well worth assimilating the likely running styles of horses in a race as a matter of course. For a shortcut, try Lawrence Taylor's excellent speed maps available every day free on attheraces.co.uk.

Pace maps which detail the runners with early pace have an important application in predicting draw advantage on straight tracks. Again, however, this is a factor which can be skewed by human influence.

Jockeys who believe they are badly drawn tend to go off hard in order to compensate, while their colleagues on the opposite side of the course take things easily in the misapprehension that they have an edge. The advantage of being well drawn therefore turns out to be ethereal.

The subject of pace and its many ramifications and applications for analysis still remains a complicated subject. As the nascence of sectional timing in Britain is just around the corner, the opportunity to gain increased knowledge finally presents itself. Unless punters tread carefully with pace, however, the education could easily prove costly.

PART FOUR

RACE
TYPES

By NICK PULFORD

A MANTRA OFTEN REPEATED BY betting experts is: specialise, specialise, specialise. With almost 9,000 races per year in Britain, spawning an infinite variety of betting opportunities, no punter can hope to stay on top of the form across the racing spectrum and it can pay to concentrate on a type of race – two-year-old events, for example, or the all-weather.

This section identifies the race types that might be more profitable than others, using the unrivalled expertise of two of the Racing Post Ratings team – Steve Mason (jumps) and Paul Curtis (Flat). Along with Simon Turner – the third member of the team – they have proved consistently the best tipping service in the National Press Challenge, which measures the performance of tips for all races. They won in 1999 and 2002 and finished runner-up in 2003, the year in which they also won the prestigious Coral/Racing Post naps competition.

Having proved highly successful at tipping in every race in the calendar, they use their expertise to identify the most profitable race types and, just as importantly, the times of the year when their ratings perform best.

There is further insight on the biggest races and meetings from Tom Segal, who writes the Pricewise column in the Racing Post. He outlines the betting approach for the Cheltenham Festival, the Grand National, the five Classics on the Flat and Royal Ascot.

ratings approach to the flat

A USEFUL PERFORMER

WITH TIPS FOR EVERY FLAT RACE IN

BY PAUL CURTIS

Britain, the National Press Challenge does not lend itself to selectivity. There are many races among the 4,000-plus Flat races run every year where, if given the choice, you wouldn't tip, let alone have a bet.

The sheer number of selections demands a different strategy to that employed by the selective punter, and Racing Post Ratings tips could be said to follow a 'scattergun' approach. That is to say, while there are many solid form selections to be made every year, there are equally many races, particularly at the lower end of the class scale, where one is making a best guess and hoping that one or two will stick, often at rewarding prices. With this in mind an overall level-stakes loss of 6.5%, with a strike rate of 26%, for the period in question is no mean feat.

I consider ratings the single most important factor in the selection process and, while many other variables come into the tipping equation, a reliable set of ratings is the best starting point. With the help of programmer Kevin Smith, I have been able to compile a detailed analysis of RP Ratings performance over the four years from 1999 to 2002, and looking at the data from the National Press Challenge (table 1) I would suspect that, similarly to the jumps, at least the top five performers over the past few years all use ratings of some description as their base.

1 NATIONAL PRESS CHALLENGE					
newspaper	wins	runs	profit/loss	strike-rate	profit/loss %
SPOTLIGHT	4434	17227	-£2,237.67	25.7	-13.0
The Star	4319	17140	-£1,643.43	25.2	-9.6
The Sun	4261	17202	-£843.88	24.8	-4.9
RP RATINGS	4257	16500	-£1,082.62	25.8	-6.5
Daily Mirror	4197	17170	-£2,036.98	24.4	-11.9
Telegraph	4187	17172	-£2,014.12	24.4	-11.7
The Guardian	4144	16401	-£1,375.51	25.3	-8.4
The Express	4050	16713	-£1,329.68	24.2	-7.9
The Times	4032	16418	-£662.92	24.6	-4.0
POSTDATA	4009	17177	-£1,659.51	23.3	-9.7
Daily Mail	3999	17191	-£2,013.92	23.3	-11.7
Independent	3765	16779	-£2,220.05	22.4	-13.2

A CONSISTENT APPROACH The reasoning behind Racing Post Ratings is to find the horse with the best form chance at the weights in any given race, and while this can be straightforward in maidens or level-weights races, it is a lot more complicated when dealing with exposed handicappers.

Opinion can differ, as can the interpretation of what makes a well-handicapped horse. How far do you go back when trying to identify the horse with the best chance at the weights? In many handicaps, there are horses who have plummeted in the ratings for one reason or another and are dangerously well handicapped if coming back to form. Trip, ground or draw might have been against them – or perhaps a change of stable or the application of headgear might spark a revival in their fortunes.

Invariably, any argument to find the best-handicapped horse in a race is a subjective one, but what RP Ratings tries to do is to be consistent in its approach to this conundrum.

There is often little mileage in opposing in-form, well-handicapped horses at the top of their game, especially if they are on the

2 RACING POST RATINGS TIPS

year	wins	runs	profit/loss	strike-rate	profit/loss %
Flat					
1999	813	3175	-£219.00	25.6	-6.9
2000	752	3045	-£349.55	24.7	-11.5
2001	802	3124	-£214.82	25.7	-6.9
2002	817	3128	-£131.49	26.1	-4.2
Total	3184	12472	-£914.86	25.5	-7.3
All-weather					
1999	287	922	£88.96	31.1	9.6
2000	275	986	-£51.06	27.9	-5.2
2001	261	1004	-£38.66	26.0	-3.9
2002	250	1116	-£166.99	22.4	-15.0
Total	1073	4028	-£167.75	26.6	-4.2
Combined					
1999	1100	4097	-£130.04	26.8	-3.2
2000	1027	4031	-£400.61	25.5	-9.9
2001	1063	4128	-£253.48	25.7	-6.1
2002	1067	4244	-£298.48	25.1	-7.0
Total	4257	16500	-£1,082.61	25.8	-6.5

upgrade. But when such horses are in short supply, a little more imagination is required and with only two people – Simon Turner and myself – responsible for selections, it is a lot easier to maintain a consistent approach to these more challenging races.

As with the jumps, although without quite such startling success, 1999 remains the best year on record for RP Ratings selections (table 2). The loss of £130.04, at a rate of 3.20%, was enhanced by a decent profit on the all-weather, an area that, with the exception of 2002, has outperformed the turf selections.

The all-weather might not be to everybody's liking, but an overall loss of just 4.20% suggests that with some selectivity it can prove a profitable area.

3 RACING POST RATINGS TIPS BY MONTH

year	wins	runs	profit/loss	strike-rate	profit/loss %
Flat					
March	42	171	£22.66	24.60	13.30
April	214	806	£50.89	26.60	6.30
May	420	1763	-£165.39	23.80	-9.40
June	588	2276	-£202.61	25.80	-8.90
July	647	2436	-£185.95	26.60	-7.60
August	617	2297	-£145.03	26.90	-6.30
September	397	1517	-£69.85	26.20	-4.60
October	220	1032	-£185.04	21.30	-17.90
November	39	174	-£34.55	22.40	-19.80
All-weather					
January	220	774	-£30.53	28.40	-3.90
February	195	690	-£61.74	28.30	-8.90
March	113	423	£0.51	26.70	0.10
April	45	172	-£22.64	26.20	-13.10
May	45	173	-£21.63	26.00	-12.50
June	60	187	£38.29	32.10	20.50
July	51	175	-£12.63	29.10	-7.20
August	19	64	£8.06	29.70	12.60
September	28	121	£23.20	23.10	19.20
October	53	207	-£20.01	25.60	-9.70
November	107	498	-£58.91	21.50	-11.80
December	137	544	-£9.74	25.20	-1.80

MONTH BY MONTH As one might expect, the best period for tipping on the sand is December/January, the heart of the all-weather season (table 3 shows performance on a monthly basis). A limited pool of horses coupled with generally consistent ground makes for favourable tipping conditions, with each month showing a profit in two of the four years under review despite three-year-olds-only events showing a loss.

RP Ratings also started 2003 in good form with another decent profit in January, again with little help from the new three-year-olds, and, with selectivity, the all-weather could prove an even more profitable area over the winter.

Against this, the figures suggest that the all-weather should be avoided in November. This is a transitional month, with jaded turf horses trying their luck against established all-weather performers getting ready for the season proper. With little continuity, it is very difficult to bet successfully in November.

Conversely, performance at the height of the turf season over the four-year period is relatively poor. Perhaps surprisingly, the best time to follow RP Ratings in the four years under review has been the beginning and end of the season – March/April and September.

Unlike other form services, RP Ratings does not concentrate wholly on recent form and we use many of the other factors that go into the selection process to arrive at a tip. This is never more important than at the start of a new season, when first-time-out records or a change of stable can be as important an indicator to a horse's chance as form, and while the service tips its fair share of favourites, an eye is kept on the value angle. An overall profit of a shade over 3% on all selections in March/April is decent enough, but the figures are even better if one concentrates solely on the turf, with a 7.5% profit to level stakes.

Another factor behind the good early/late season performance is that the volume of racing is relatively low. I'm quite sure that the poor performance during the summer months is largely down to the vast number of races once evening racing gets under way, with time necessarily being stretched a lot more thinly than at other times of the year.

This is illustrated by the performance in the four-year-old-plus division, which makes up the lion's share of all selections. Significant losses in 1999, 2000 and 2001 were turned around in 2002, with a 10.7% profit on all all-aged events. Figures for 2003 show a minor loss, but that still represents a major improvement on

Ages	wins	runs	profit/loss	strike-rate	profit/loss %
4 RACING POST RATINGS TIPS BY AGE RESTRICTION					
1999					
2yo	269	821	-£28.02	32.8	-3.4
3yo only	220	835	-£108.61	26.3	-13.0
3yo+	611	2441	£6.59	25.0	0.3
2000					
2yo	246	780	-£38.84	31.5	-5.0
3yo only	225	831	-£96.55	27.1	11.6
3yo+	556	2420	-£265.23	23.0	-11.1
2001					
2yo	269	829	-£22.69	32.4	-2.8
3yo only	226	867	-£82.14	26.1	-9.5
3yo+	568	2432	-£148.66	23.4	-6.1
2002					
2yo	294	855	-£40.06	34.4	-4.7
3yo only	249	939	-£72.96	26.5	-7.8
3yo+	524	2450	-£185.45	21.4	-7.6
Four-year total					
2yo	1078	3285	-£129.61	32.8	-3.9
3yo only	920	3472	-£360.26	26.5	-10.4
3yo+	2259	9743	-£592.75	23.2	-6.1

1999, 2000 and 2001 and it is no coincidence that this reversal has come about in the two years since Simon Turner started to share responsibility for RP Ratings selections. This has eased the summer workload considerably and allowed for more time to study each race. It will be interesting to see if this improved mid-summer performance is maintained.

AVOID 3-YEAR-OLDS-ONLY EVENTS

Although the all-aged events contribute most to total losses over the four-year period, as a percentage three-year-old events fare worst with a loss of 10.4% to level stakes (table 4).

May and June have proved the worst months,

5 RP RATINGS TIPS BY HANDICAP/NON HANDICAP

Race type, age	wins	runs	profit/loss	strike-rate	profit/loss %
Handicap 2yo	109	560	-£59.70	19.5	-10.7
Handicap 3yo only	381	1826	-£167.14	20.9	-9.1
Handicap 3yo+	1103	6138	-£369.56	18.0	-6.0
Non-handicap 2yo	969	2725	-£69.91	35.6	-2.5
Non-handicap 3yo only	539	1646	-£193.12	32.7	-11.7
Non-handicap 3yo+	1156	3605	-£223.20	32.0	-6.2

and this can be put down to the number of unexposed horses coming into handicaps. Early season three-year-olds are notoriously hard to pin down in terms of form, while there is also a clash of formlines: two-year-olds who have earned their marks in nurseries are pitched against lightly raced types, at whose ability and potential we can make only an educated guess.

It is rare for three-year-olds to get into their first handicaps off obviously lenient marks as the official handicappers are understandably cautious and many unexposed three-year-olds are untippable: they have yet to show form good enough to win from their allotted mark. Furthermore, once an unexposed horse starts to show its true colours, it can tend to be overbet, which probably explains the significant losses despite a decent 21% strike-rate (table D).

Nevertheless, performance in three-year-old handicaps outstrips that of non-handicap events, the latter showing an 11.7% loss to level stakes (table C). This area covers a wide range of events from the poorest seller to the Derby, but as conditions events one would expect better results and a healthy strike-rate of nearly 33% suggests there is little value in following form horses in three-year-olds-only events.

TWO-YEAR-OLDS SHOW IMPROVED PERFORMANCE Overall performance on two-year-olds of a shade under 4% outstrips that on all selections despite a poor return from

C RP RATINGS TIPS BY MONTH (3yo+ handicaps)

Month	wins	runs	profit/loss	strike-rate	profit/loss %
January	78	358	-9.52	21.80	-2.70
February	68	340	-57.53	20.00	-16.90
March	62	275	37.96	22.50	13.80
April	54	320	-3.70	16.90	-1.10
May	105	652	-32.71	16.10	-5.00
June	166	886	-6.45	18.70	-0.70
July	177	981	-92.09	18.00	-9.40
August	138	831	-123.49	16.60	-14.90
September	98	560	12.01	17.50	2.10
October	60	381	-51.34	15.70	-13.50
November	45	288	-34.63	15.60	-12.00
December	52	266	-8.05	19.60	-3.00
Total	1103	6138	-369.54	18.00	-6.00

D RP RATINGS TIPS BY MONTH (3yo only handicaps)

Month	wins	runs	profit/loss	strike-rate	profit/loss %
January	25	88	-12.18	28.40	-13.80
February	25	75	7.66	33.30	10.20
March	18	65	25.61	27.70	39.40
April	32	137	3.51	23.30	2.60
May	45	279	-43.06	16.10	-15.40
June	71	363	-64.42	19.50	-17.70
July	76	341	-8.63	22.30	-2.50
August	62	266	20.47	23.30	7.70
September	12	110	-54.35	10.90	-49.40
October	15	94	-33.75	17.20	-26.70
November	0	8	-8.00	0.00	-100.00
Total	381	1826	-167.14	20.90	-9.10

nurseries, suggesting that this is an area where profits can be made. The vast majority of juvenile events are not handicaps and a loss of 2.5% on these events (table 5) could certainly

6a RACING POST RATINGS TIPS BY ODDS (2yo)

Race type	odds group	wins	runs	profit/loss	strike-rate	p/l %
Handicap	1 to 2.25	37	102	-£2.06	36.3	-2.0
Handicap	10+	5	97	-£28.00	5.2	-28.9
Handicap	2.5 to 4.5	33	169	-£25.34	19.5	-15.0
Handicap	5 to 9	25	181	-£8.00	13.8	-4.4
Handicap	less than 1	9	11	£3.70	81.8	33.6
Non-handicap	1 to 2.25	377	969	£3.77	38.9	0.4
Non-handicap	10+	2	52	-£26.00	3.8	-50.0
Non-handicap	2.5 to 4.5	185	799	-£23.23	23.2	-2.9
Non-handicap	5 to 9	43	316	-£4.75	13.6	-1.5
Non-handicap	less than 1	362	589	-£19.70	61.5	-3.3

6b RACING POST RATINGS TIPS BY ODDS (3yo+)

Race type	odds group	wins	runs	profit/loss	strike-rate	p/l %
Handicap	1 to 2.25	272	841	-£100.34	32.3	-11.9
Handicap	10+	61	1172	-£269.40	5.2	-23.0
Handicap	2.5 to 4.5	422	1879	-£13.83	22.5	-0.7
Handicap	5 to 9	300	2143	£34.55	14.0	1.6
Handicap	less than 1	48	103	-£20.54	46.6	-20.0
Non-handicap	1 to 2.25	462	1245	-£48.23	37.1	-3.9
Non-handicap	10+	6	88	-£9.80	6.8	-11.1
Non-handicap	2.5 to 4.5	242	1157	-£128.28	20.9	-11.1
Non-handicap	5 to 9	72	494	-£0.65	14.6	-0.1
Non-handicap	less than 1	374	621	-£36.25	60.2	-5.8

be improved upon with a little selectivity.

Returns are further enhanced when you concentrate on short-priced non-handicap selections (table 6a), particularly those from evens to 9-4, which show a small profit on the best part of 1,000 selections. A near 40% strike-rate shows that winners are not in short supply and it appears that backing form-choice favourites in two-year-old conditions events is not the road to the poorhouse that the blind backing of market leaders would often prove.

The strike-rate for odds-on chances in these events rises to over 60 per cent, but the returns are not so encouraging, although once again a 3.3% loss on the best part of 600 selections could be improved upon with a little sifting.

Only the relatively few non-handicap selections at 10-1 or over show a loss greater than that on all selections across the age range, and ruling out these big-priced selections from the two-year-old conditions events restricts the losses to 1.6%. Figures for 2003 show further improvement, with the evens to 9-4 range progressing to a positive 1.1% return to level stakes.

It is a similar story with nurseries, the short-priced selections again faring best, with odds-on shots in nurseries showing a profit. Unfortunately, there are only a handful of such horses each year, but an 82% strike-rate shows that they are worth noting. Those between evens and 9-4 are slightly more plentiful and show a small loss on around 100 selections. That loss was turned around in 2003 and, with selectivity, betting on short-priced two-year-olds with strong form claims can prove profitable.

FOLLOW OLDER HORSES IN HANDICAPS
In contrast to the juveniles, short-priced selections in handicaps for three-year-olds and upwards fare poorly, those starting at 9-4 or shorter returning a loss of 12.8% (table 6b).

Things get much better when operating at more rewarding odds, however, with selections priced between 5-2 and 9-2 showing a minor loss of 0.7% and those between 5-1 and 9-1 turning in a decent 1.6% profit.

Perhaps surprisingly, and in common with the three-year-olds-only events, RP Ratings performs better from the profit-and-loss angle in handicaps than conditions events. All things being equal, one would expect better performance from a form service in non-handicap events, but while strike-rates in the low 30s are respectable, the profits in

7 RACING POST RATINGS TIPS BY CLASS

Race type, class	wins	runs	profit/loss	strike-rate
Handicap A	11	41	£9.71	26.8
Handicap B	68	532	-£154.27	12.8
Handicap C	240	1324	-£83.54	18.1
Handicap D	412	2117	-£174.27	19.5
Handicap E	524	2730	-£200.72	19.2
Handicap F	290	1489	£53.37	19.5
Handicap G	48	291	-£46.67	16.5
Non-handicap A	247	892	-£105.41	27.7
Non-handicap B	65	225	-£39.35	28.9
Non-handicap C	214	585	£15.94	36.6
Non-handicap D	1108	2868	-£134.78	38.6
Non-handicap E	376	1219	-£62.37	30.8
Non-handicap F	461	1508	-£119.62	30.6
Non-handicap G	193	679	-£40.63	28.4

conditions events are not.

The approach adopted for non-handicaps is no different to that for handicaps, so perhaps the form horses are overbet. The big difference between the two divisions is that there is greater scope for a form service to find a value bet in a handicap than in a conditions event. Often, RP Ratings will be forced to select the form choice in non-handicaps despite the selection being unsuited to race conditions, when there might be a better-value fancy to expose any perceived weakness in the form choice.

An obvious example of this scenario would be the 2003 Champion Stakes, where Alamshar went to post the clear form choice on his King George win, but with a big question mark over his ability to reproduce that performance in a race ripe for an upset.

In common with short-priced selections, those starting at double-figure prices also performed poorly, and it is clearly in the mid-range of prices that one finds the best blend between strike-rate and SP, an area RP Ratings successfully exploited when winning the Coral/Racing Post naps competition for the 2003 Flat season.

CLASS NO GUIDE TO SUCCESS I anticipated that data sorting by race class would show some preference for higher-grade events, but table 7 clearly shows this not to be the case. A profit in Class A handicaps is attained from a small sample size and might not be an accurate guide, and in any case is completely wiped out by a heavy loss in Class A non-handicaps.

Similarly, a profit in Class F handicaps is sandwiched between losses at Class E and G level, while Class F is among the worst performers in non-handicaps. The figures in this table have something of a random feel to them, and for RP Ratings success or failure is clearly spread right across the class range.

DISTANCES A CONFUSING PICTURE Having run data breaking down RP Ratings performance by race distance some years ago I anticipated a strong showing in 7f-10f events, with poor performance over sprint trips, when the data was re-run for this four-year period (table 8).

Perhaps too much emphasis was placed on the earlier results as performance in sprints, particularly handicaps (table 8a), is much improved. However, it is difficult to establish a pattern from this analysis of tips by distance, with significant disparity between returns for five and six furlongs. This could be explained by course biases tending to be stronger over five furlongs than six, with handicaps at the likes of Beverley and Chester quickly whittled down to a handful, while the minimum trip can lend itself to more specialist performers.

It is more difficult to reason the vast difference in performance over seven and nine furlongs against that over a mile, however. The intermediate distances might lend themselves to trip specialists, but that does not explain why performance at a mile is so poor. Similarly, performance at a mile and a quarter falls some

8 RP RATINGS TIPS BY DISTANCE (3yo+)

Race distance (furlongs)	wins	runs	profit/loss	strike-rate	profit/loss %
5	249	1160	-£25.21	21.5	-2.2
6	298	1324	-£135.11	22.5	-10.2
7	326	1340	£84.33	24.3	6.3
8	326	1524	-£195.02	21.4	-12.8
9	163	676	£22.07	24.1	3.3
10	236	1008	-£145.62	23.4	-14.4
11	145	541	-£0.66	26.8	-0.1
12	273	995	£28.59	27.4	2.9
13	35	197	-£84.47	17.8	-42.9
14	79	382	-£76.86	20.7	-20.1
15	14	54	£1.87	25.9	3.5
16	100	436	-£22.75	22.9	-5.2
17	9	55	-£26.65	16.4	-48.4
18	3	30	-£8.13	10.0	-27.1
19	0	1	-£1.00	0.0	-100.0
20	1	10	-£7.63	10.0	-76.3
21	1	6	£0.50	16.7	8.3
22	1	4	-£1.00	25.0	-25.0

way short of that over 11 and 12 furlongs with no apparent good reason.

On the plus side, those races not restricted to two- or three-year-olds return a respectable profit of just under 3% over a mile and a half, while that percentage profit improves to over seven when concentrating on open handicaps. While there are pockets of profit when breaking down RP Ratings selections by distance, overall it is hard to identify any discernible pattern.

CONCLUSION One of the more interesting findings to emerge from this study is that there seems to be a pattern to how RP Ratings selections perform throughout the year. A decent start to the year is followed by a lull in May/June as early-season form is overhauled by the better

8a RP RATINGS TIPS BY DISTANCE (3yo+ handicap)					
Race distance (furlongs)	wins	runs	profit/loss	strike-rate	profit/loss %
5	150	799	£28.63	18.8	3.6
6	133	783	-£85.21	17.0	-10.9
7	147	777	£82.86	18.9	10.7
8	142	938	-£172.60	15.1	-18.4
9	85	425	£33.29	20.0	7.8
10	90	572	-£93.61	15.7	-16.4
11	51	287	-£20.50	17.8	-7.1
12	133	610	£44.45	21.8	7.3
13	20	147	-£68.71	13.6	-46.7
14	45	278	-£57.87	16.2	-20.8
15	11	46	£1.06	23.9	2.3
16	83	385	-£27.08	21.6	-7.0
17	9	52	-£23.65	17.3	-45.5
18	3	26	-£4.13	11.5	-15.9
19	0	1	-£1.00	0.0	-100.0
20	0	6	-£6.00	0.0	-100.0
21	1	6	£0.50	16.7	8.3

class of horse that starts appearing. The first three years of data show poor performance in July and August also, but a large part of that is down to the vast number of races run in mid-summer and, with the workload eased considerably, performance in these two months has improved enormously.

September has traditionally proved a good month, but by October things are starting to tail off with inconsistent going a major problem at the backend of the turf season. November is a real transitional month, particularly on the all-weather, and would be a good time to take a break, before things start to settle down again on the sand in December.

It would be difficult to build these findings into any sort of system, but it would seem to pinpoint the best periods to be concentrating on form-based selections.

6 RACING POST RATINGS TIPS BY ODDS

Race type	odds group	wins	runs	profit/loss	strike -rate	profit/loss %
Handicap	1 to 2.25	441	1322	-£126.33	33.4	-9.5
Handicap	10+	81	1552	-£371.00	5.2	-23.9
Handicap	2.5 to 4.5	591	2613	-£13.93	22.6	-0.5
Handicap	5 to 9	384	2848	-£58.70	13.5	-2.1
Handicap	below 1	96	189	-£26.43	50.8	-14.0
Non-handicap	1 to 2.25	1070	2847	-£90.56	37.6	-3.2
Non-handicap	10+	9	170	-£39.80	5.3	-23.4
Non-handicap	2.5 to 4.5	518	2435	-£237.75	21.3	-9.8
Non-handicap	5 to 9	136	985	-£41.85	13.8	-4.2
Non-handicap	below 1	931	1539	-£76.28	60.5	-5.0

Two-year-olds are worth considering for those who like to see a regular supply of winners, short-priced form horses faring particularly well. With a bit of weeding out of those badly drawn or possibly unsuited to conditions, a decent profit could be achieved.

If three-year-olds are your thing, then early season would again be the best time to catch them, with profits in the three-year-old handicaps showing in February, March and April, while July and August also fare well when one considers the poor overall performance for three of the four years. Figures for 2003 show that three-year-olds-only handicaps again broke even during the mid-summer period.

Perhaps the best angle to take from this study, though, is the performance of selections in three-year-old-plus handicaps, which outperforms the overall performance in the Press Challenge despite offering some of the most challenging races from a winner-finding point of view. A profit on 3yo+ handicap tips in the 5-2 to 9-1 price range on over 4,000 selections suggests this area is worth concentrating on and focusing on these selections in the more productive months could further enhance returns.

While I am not convinced that there is a

A RP RATINGS TIPS BY MONTH (3yo+)

Month	wins	runs	profit/loss	strike-rate	profit/loss %
January	165	598	-17.78	27.60	-3.00
February	145	548	-60.76	26.50	-11.10
March	110	452	5.32	24.30	1.20
April	130	554	31.94	23.50	5.80
May	233	1081	-92.07	21.50	-8.50
June	317	1375	-72.17	23.10	-5.20
July	360	1495	-106.47	24.10	-7.10
August	312	1317	-121.06	23.70	-9.20
September	199	892	19.23	22.30	2.10
October	114	585	-71.87	19.50	-12.30
November	85	440	-68.74	19.30	-15.60
December	88	405	-40.57	21.70	-10.00
Total	2258	9742	-595.00	23.20	-6.10

B RP RATINGS TIPS BY MONTH (3yo only)

Month	wins	runs	profit/loss	strike-rate	profit/loss %
January	55	176	-12.75	31.30	-7.20
February	50	142	-0.97	35.20	-0.70
March	44	141	15.60	31.20	11.10
April	99	352	-19.35	28.10	-5.50
May	159	638	-90.84	24.90	-14.20
June	183	679	-82.04	26.90	-12.10
July	145	548	-54.58	26.50	-9.90
August	104	409	-11.33	25.40	-2.80
September	43	191	-43.19	22.50	-22.60
October	33	166	-46.42	19.90	-28.00
November	5	25	-9.38	20.00	-37.50
December	0	5	-5.00	0.00	-100.00
Total	920	3472	-360.25	26.50	-10.40

system lurking in this, and would not suggest the backing of RP Ratings selections blind, there is some success to be had from concentrating on the highlighted areas with selectivity. ■

ratings approach to the jumps

ONE JUMP AHEAD

THE INTRODUCTION OF THE NATIONAL
Press Challenge by the Racing Post in 1990
ensured that the tipsters 'lucky' enough to be
included in the table were monitored like never
before. Like a punter who does not keep a
betting record, a tipster who is not monitored
lives in a selective world where successes are
trumpeted and failures ignored.

By STEVE MASON

The world of the National Press Challenge is
much less forgiving. Selection boxes at all meetings, with the exception of the minor cards
on particularly busy Bank Holidays, are stored
on the Racing Post database and a profit or loss
figure for the month/year is updated on a daily
basis. Unlike tipsters who can claim big profits
on the strength of getting a certain number of
points on a selection at the best early morning
price, tipsters in the National Press Challenge
are assessed in the much harsher light of
level stakes and starting price.

You may have just had a decent-priced
winning nap at the main meeting of the day, but
if that was your only winner and the monthly
return shows you are more than £100 down on
level stakes, then you have little to crow about.

Of course, not even the most optimistic punter
would expect to make a profit betting in
every race and the chances of a tipster returning
a level-stakes profit over the 7,000 races,
Flat and jumps, that annually make up the
National Press Challenge season are very slim.

Jumping in January: Isio (left) lands the 2004 Victor Chandler Chase from Azertyuiop. January to March represents the heart of the season, when ratings perform well

Indeed, it has been achieved only once in the 13 years of the competition. Most tipsters would, given the choice, gladly opt out of giving a selection in a large chunk of the races and their ability as tipsters would probably be better assessed if this was the case.

However, the benefit of recording a selection in every race is that a vast amount of data has been built up and, thanks to the help of computer programmer Kevin Smith, we have the opportunity to examine the strengths and weaknesses of Racing Post Ratings as a tool for punting over jumps.

I certainly would not claim that ratings are the be-all and end-all, but, to my way of thinking, they are the single most important part in the selection process and a glance at table 1 appears to bear this out.

Using data accumulated in the four-year period 1999-2002 reveals a level-stakes loss of only 1.3 per cent on all selections and a strike-rate of nearly 33 per cent, results significantly better than the 12 other competitors. Looking at RP Ratings' closest pursuers, I suspect that the selections of the next five most suc-

1 NATIONAL PRESS CHALLENGE (JUMPS)

newspaper	wins	runs	profit/loss	strike-rate	profit/loss %age
RP RATINGS	3433	10472	-£138.24	32.8	- 1.3
The Express	3154	10756	-£374.59	29.3	- 3.5
The Sun	3256	11060	-£576.58	29.4	- 5.2
POSTDATA	3332	11142	-£616.50	29.9	- 5.5
The Times	3023	10626	-£606.63	28.4	- 5.7
Topspeed	2500	9358	-£546.58	26.7	- 5.8
The Guardian	3241	10632	-£646.97	30.5	- 6.1
Independent	3025	10802	-£750.52	28	- 6.9
Daily Mail	3261	11089	-£821.12	29.4	- 7.4
Telegraph	3254	11080	-£943.45	29.4	- 8.5
Daily Mirror	3288	11037	-£975.08	29.8	- 8.8
The Star	3262	11081	-£1406.05	29.4	- 12.7
SPOTLIGHT	3371	11197	-£1493.48	30.1	- 13.3

Figures for period January 1, 1999 to December 31, 2002.

cessful jumps tipsters were also largely figures-based.

CONTINUITY THE KEY Breaking down the returns into individual years (table 2) reveals a fair bit of variety. I would be the first to admit that 1999 was a freak year. A decent level-stakes profit on the back of an unusually good strike-rate resulted in a performance by some way the best in my ten full years doing the jumps RP Ratings. Similarly, the relatively poor performance in 2001 probably had a fair bit to do with the havoc wreaked by the foot-and-

2 RP RATINGS JUMPS TIPS 1999-2002

Year	wins	runs	profit/loss	strike-rate	profit/loss %
1999	987	2771	+£130.17	35.6	+4.7
2000	852	2642	-£110.40	32.2	-4.2
2001	702	2356	-£142.53	29.8	-6
2002	893	2704	-£13.85	33.0	-0.5

3 RP RATINGS JUMPS TIPS BY MONTH

Month	wins	runs	profit/loss	strike-rate	profit/loss %	position in table
January	352	1083	-19.49	32.5	-1.8	1st
February	380	1082	+44.88	35.1	+4.1	1st
March	401	1160	+56.73	34.6	+4.9	1st
April	244	867	-100.14	28.1	-11.6	11th
May	319	1035	-34.32	30.8	-3.3	3rd
June	172	538	-8.04	32	-1.5	4th
July	133	388	+9.47	34.3	+2.4	2nd
August	138	378	+1.47	36.5	+0.4	2nd
September	166	445	+30.40	37.3	+6.8	1st
October	316	935	+31.41	33.8	+3.4	3rd
November	443	1410	-84.11	31.4	-6.7	5th
December	370	1152	-64.88	32.1	-5.6	5th

4 RP RATINGS JUMPS TIPS BY RACE TYPE

Race type	wins	runs	strike-rate	position in table by s-r	profit/loss	p/l %	position in table by p/l
Non-h'cap chase	794	1856	43	1st	- 14.31	1	2nd
Handicap chase	665	2666	25	1st	- 121.61	- 5	2nd
Non-h'cap hurdle	1202	2679	45	1st	+ 266.42	+10	1st
Handicap hurdle	623	2851	22	1st	- 294.13	-10	7th
NH Flat	149	420	36	1st	+25.39	+6	2nd
Overall	3433	10422	33	1st	- 138.24	- 1	1st

mouth outbreak. It is probably significant that the two most successful seasons were the ones that suffered the fewest abandonments. From a form perspective, the fewer interruptions the better and continuity was lost in the first half of 2001.

MONTHS TO TREAD CAREFULLY The importance of continuity in the form is further highlighted when performance is broken down on a month-by-month basis (table 3). April and November are transitional months.

January through to March is the heart of the jumps season proper, there is continuity in the form and, as I would expect, this is a period when RP Ratings selections do particularly well. Similarly, the period encompassing May to October represents a chunk of the season that can be looked upon as a whole, with the same pool of horses, by and large, operating throughout. Again there is continuity in the form, resulting in a small level-stakes profit.

By way of contrast, things change in April and November. Given that my methods do not change, there must be a good reason for the abysmal performance in April.

As a rule, the ground will be getting faster, but perhaps of more importance is that April comes at the end of a long season for what I would describe as the winter horses. At the same time, the summer horses are returning at varying levels of fitness and the better novices are being held back in order to retain their novice status for the new season.

November is another month when things change. The top-of-the-ground form of the summer and autumn is often rendered irrelevant as the rains come and the winter horses return. A high percentage of novice events are won by horses untippable by RP Ratings and strike-rate falls. Like April, it is a month for punters who favour ratings to tread carefully.

COURSE STUDY A DEAD END At this point, I had prepared a table of returns for

5 NON-HANDICAP HURDLE TIPS BY SP

Odds group	wins	runs	profit/loss	strike-rate	profit/loss %
Odds-on	557	887	-33.60	62.8	-3.8
Evens to 9-4	445	981	+152.53	45.4	+15.5
5-2 to 9-2	162	615	+50.80	26.3	+8.3
5-1 to 9-1	34	180	+65.70	18.9	+36.5
10-1+	4	16	+31.00	25.0	+193.75
Evens or bigger	645	1792	+300.03	36.0	+16.7

6 NON-HANDICAP HURDLE TIPS BY CLASS

Class	wins	runs	profit/loss	strike-rate	profit/loss %
A	77	145	+57.52	53.1	+39.7
B	41	93	+6.61	44	+7.1
C	39	100	-9.06	39	-9.1
D	307	633	+112.49	48.5	+17.8
E	545	1240	+30.35	44	+2.5
F	87	207	+49.97	42	+24.1
G	106	261	+18.54	40.6	+7.1

individual courses, but on closer examination it was less useful than it initially appeared. Enthusiasm for level-stake profits of 28 per cent at Huntingdon, 16 per cent at Sedgefield and 12 per cent at Fontwell was tempered when I dug out a similar table for the years 1995 to 1997 and discovered negative returns at all three tracks. Similarly, a loss of 36 per cent at Aintree over the four seasons under examination was almost matched by a profit of 30 per cent over the earlier period. Admittedly there were courses, most notably Musselburgh and Cartmel, that showed healthy profits in both periods, but, as with so many potential punting systems, insufficient sample size looks to be the problem with a course-based analysis.

Much more informative proved to be the breakdown of results by race type, shown in Table 4.

NON-HANDICAPS PROVE FRUITFUL

Unsurprisingly, RP Ratings perform at their best in non-handicap races that feature horses of widely varying abilities. A small level-stakes loss in non-handicap chases is made up for by a reasonable profit from a selective approach to bumpers.

As with novice hurdles and chases, I will only give a selection in a bumper if a horse has shown a level of form good enough to win a typical running of that particular race. The fact that this selective approach can produce a profit suggests that bumpers, as is often the case, should not be written off as betting opportunities.

The performance in handicap chases is reasonable enough and anyone who limited their bets to Class B and C handicap chases would have shown a nine per cent level-stakes profit over the period. Although the strike-rate in the more competitive arena of handicap hurdles compares favourably with the other tipsters in the Press Challenge, the ten per cent loss on turnover is very disappointing and suggests that, for whatever reason, the selections are being overbet. Clearly there are too many people thinking along the same lines and, interestingly enough, it is the lowest-profile Class G handicap hurdles where RP Ratings perform best.

There will be good bets to have in each of the five above categories, but for anyone wishing to specialise using RP Ratings then it has to be in non-handicap hurdles.

A level-stakes profit of 10% on the best part of 3,000 races demands closer scrutiny and can be quickly improved upon with only a little fine-tuning. Table 5 breaks down the results for non-handicap hurdles by starting price and the performance is enhanced significantly by limiting selections to horses starting at evens or bigger.

7 CLASS A NON-HANDICAP HURDLE TIPS BY SP					
Odds group	wins	runs	profit/loss	strike-rate	profit/loss %age
Odds-on	30	39	76.9	+7.74	+19.9
Evens to 9-4	30	53	56.6	+19.45	+36.7
5-2 to 9-2	13	35	37.1	+20.83	+59.5
5-1+	4	18	22.2	+9.50	+52.8
Evens or bigger	47	106	44.3	+49.78	+47.0

BET-PROVOKING RESULTS Most punters would happily settle for a near 17 per cent profit on turnover, but this can again be enhanced when non-handicap hurdles are further analysed by class (table 6). Although profits are available in all except Class C races, the eye is immediately drawn to the Class A races. Logically, it is not surprising that the races featuring the cream of the horses in training running over the less-demanding obstacles should produce the best results, but a level-stakes profit around 40 per cent is certainly bet-provoking.

FURTHER PROFIT INCREASES Applying the same SP breakdown as before (table 7) further increases the profit figure to 47 per cent, although by this time the number of bets is down significantly.

CONCLUSION I prefer to judge every race on its merits and have never had a great deal of time for systems, but if asked to nominate one system based on all the returns from RP Ratings selections over the four-year period under examination, it would have to be to back the tip in Class A non-handicap hurdles at even money or bigger.

I doubt that I could ever have quite such a selective approach to punting. As stated before, the smaller the sample size, the less reliable the results and the blanket 17 per cent profit on all non-handicap hurdles at evens or bigger would more than do for me.

tackling the big races

GLITTERING PRIZES

THE BEST HORSES TEND TO WIN the best races and the best horses tend to be with the best trainers, so it is no surprise that Aidan O'Brien, Sir Michael Stoute and Godolphin dominate the Classic scene in Britain. Money talks and if you have control of the dominant Classic sire in the shape of Sadler's Wells or can buy any horse that has shown even the merest hint of ability, then you are going to win more than your fair share of big races.

However, there are regular pointers with each of the five Classic races that can give us a head start in the winner-finding search. As we all know, backing the winner of one of the Classics either ante-post or on the day is far more rewarding than some old handicap chaser at Taunton on a wet Tuesday, even if the odds are the same.

THE GUINEAS The key to the 1,000 Guineas is Group-race two-year-old form. Maybe it is because fillies tend to progress slower than the colts in the cold of the spring, making it difficult for the developing three-year-olds to catch up by early May, but it is hard to remember the last winner of the first fillies' Classic that hadn't been tested in Group company.

The two Group 1 fillies' races at the backend of the season, the six-furlong Cheveley Park Stakes at Newmarket and the one-mile Prix Marcel Boussac at Longchamp, nearly always have a bearing – 2003 first and second Russian

By TOM SEGAL

134

Fresh horse: Golan landed the 2,000 Guineas in 2001 without a prep run

Rhythm and Six Perfections came from those races. Interestingly, however, it is the Rockfel Stakes at Newmarket (once a humble Group 3 race but recently raised to Group 2) that has housed most of the recent 1,000 Guineas winners.

Musical Bliss and Lahan won both races and Wince and Ameerat were beaten in the Rockfel before going on to Classic success. It could well be that the intermediate trip of seven furlongs on the Rowley Mile course gives these inexperienced young fillies a taste of what to expect come May the following year.

Modern training methods have meant that the necessity for a previous run has lessened markedly and in the case of Sir Michael Stoute it is something of a positive if one of his horses turns up at Newmarket for either of the Guineas fresh on their seasonal debuts. His two 1,000 Guineas winners – Russian Rhythm (2003) and Musical Bliss (1989) – fell into that category, as did Golan (2001) and Entrepreneur (1997) when they took the colts' version.

Both of the Stoute colts were good examples

of the fundamental difference between the two Guineas races as they gained Classic success on the back of wins in lowly maidens or conditions races and without having been tested in top company. The Godolphin colt Island Sands (1999) fell into the same category and it could be that many juvenile colts are harder trained in their first seasons because they are still marketable stallions and those with a lot of racing behind them don't train on so well, while the fillies are allowed to develop in their own time, so the best fillies are the best fillies whatever their age.

THE EPSOM CLASSICS

There is very rarely any luck involved in the Oaks at Epsom because so few fillies actually stay a mile and a half properly and the field is always small. The big stables have dominated this race more completely than any other Classic in recent years, with Henry Cecil, Godolphin and Aidan O'Brien sharing nine consecutive winners until the run was broken by Casual Look in 2003.

The English and Irish 1,000 Guineas are key races, but traditional trials such as the Musidora and Pretty Polly Stakes seem to have lost some of their importance. As in most Classic races, anything sired by Sadler's Wells and trained by a top man makes winner-finding pretty straightforward.

There are few similarities between the Grand National and the Derby, but one common trend that has emerged in recent years is Irish domination. Kris Kin broke the mould in 2003 but that was surely only because Alamshar was not right on the day – if he had been, he would have been Ireland's fourth successive winner of the premier Classic. That domination means that the key trials have become the Ballysax Stakes and the Derrinstown Derby Trial, both at Leopardstown.

Putting a finger on why British trainers have struggled in recent years is not easy but it seems to have coincided with the emergence of Godolphin, who have taken most of the best

uncommon knowledge

Luck of the draw

The purists won't like this but the 2,000 Guineas in recent years has become like a handicap, in that the draw has played a huge part. When the stalls are placed in the middle of the track in the spring a high draw has been of vital importance, as Rock Of Gibraltar (2002) and Mister Baileys (1994) showed when winning on the far rail. When the stalls are on the stands side those drawn low tend to get in each other's way, which has allowed Golan and Refuse To Bend (2003) to win from high draws with untroubled runs up the outside. As a result, finding the winner of the 2,000 Guineas involves just as much luck as judgement these days.

Arab-owned horses from the likes of John Dunlop, Sir Michael Stoute and Henry Cecil, while the John Magnier-Michael Tabor-Aidan O'Brien partnership has raised the standard in Ireland.

Chester has provided more than its fair share of winners over the years (Kris Kin in 2003, Oath in 1999 and Quest For Fame in 1990). To win there, a horse needs similar qualities to those demanded at Epsom, with the ability to get out of a tight situation at a premium on both tracks.

In contrast, the Dante at York is on the decline as an Epsom pointer. York is very flat and it has always been difficult to come from off the pace there in small-field Group races, where the tempo is quickening the whole way up the straight. As a consequence speed is not the vital characteristic of a horse that excels at York, while the ability to grind on is, and that sort of horse doesn't win at Epsom very often these days.

THE ST LEGER The different demands of York and Doncaster help to explain why placed horses from the Great Voltigeur Stakes at York's August meeting have a much better record than the winners of that race in the St Leger a month later.

Doncaster suits the hold-up horses and it is very hard to make all the running there, which is in complete contrast to York. Silver Patriarch (1997), Mutafaweq (1999), Bollin Eric (2002) and Brian Boru (2003) are recent St Leger winners who improved on their placings in the Great Voltigeur, although Milan (2001) bucked the trend by winning both races.

Horses that have run in a Derby tend to dominate the Leger, where class nearly always overcomes stamina worries, while you have to go back to 1992 for the last filly (User Friendly) to land the spoils.

ROYAL ASCOT A few years ago it was the draw, then came the pace of the race and the new in-thing when trying to find a winner or

Johnston's goldmine: Royal Rebel (right) on his way to landing the 2001 Gold Cup, one of a stack of staying races the trainer has won at Ascot

two is trends. Most of them are absolute rubbish – just because a four-year-old carrying more than 9st won a particular race a couple of times recently does not mean that it will happen again – but the way to get ahead at Royal Ascot is by concentrating on the trainer trend.

Nearly all the races over the five days of Britain's best Flat meeting are fiercely competitive with big fields and any number of potential winners, but over the years it has always paid to concentrate on trainers who have done well in specific races.

The winner-is-a-winner brigade will lump on an Aidan O'Brien two-year-old in the Coventry Stakes, which the Ballydoyle trainer has virtually monopolised, the Godolphin older horse in the Prince of Wales's Stakes or the Sir Michael Stoute runner in the Queen Anne. However, their recent Royal Ascot successes have tended to come in the Group races and at shorter prices, so the first way to get ahead is by following the profitable trainers, especially Mark Johnston and John Gosden.

If you had backed every Johnston runner

at the meeting in the five years from 1999 to 2003, you would be sitting on a profit of more than £50 to a £1 level stake. There are a number of reasons for Johnston's success, but one which stands out is that in competitive races at the Royal meeting there is invariably lots of trouble in running and Johnston's horses are suited by racing up with the pace. Therefore they don't often lose races they could have won.

The staying races are where Johnston provides the real goldmine because as well as his terrific record in the Gold Cup, which he has won with Double Trigger (1995) and Royal Rebel (2001 and 2002), he has also landed two wins in both the Queen's Vase and the King George V Stakes (the longest race for three-year-old handicappers) since the turn of the century. There is a case for just backing Johnston blind at the whole meeting, given his thirst for winners and the improvement in the quality of his yard, which makes him as competitive as any other trainer at the major events.

Slightly less prolific but also well worth bearing in mind come the middle of June is the Gosden stable. Like Johnston, the Manton trainer only sends horses with decent chances to Royal Ascot, so do not be put off by big prices because he's far too good a trainer to be running horses just for the day out. Malhub proved that point when winning the 2002 Golden Jubilee Stakes at 16-1, while Gosden always lays out at least one horse for the Britannia Handicap, having won the race four times in the period 1996-2001.

Other trainers to keep a close eye on are the Irish shrewdies, particularly John Oxx and Dermot Weld, who only send runners that they think will win. That pair have landed a couple of good old-fashioned gambles in recent years.

The fact that the top trainers do well in the most competitive races at Royal Ascot makes it inevitable that the big-name jockeys will shine as well because they get the pick of the rides from the leading stables. However, that cannot explain wholly why it is that a £1 level stake on

uncommon knowledge

 The draw at Royal Ascot

Race position is vital

The final piece of the jigsaw at Royal Ascot is the draw because it is always best to be drawn very high or very low on the straight course. There are no hard-and-fast rules about which will come out best on the day but it seems to me that provided the ground is fast there is certainly no disadvantage whatsoever being drawn very high.

Many pundits make a big issue about the draw on the round course but race position is much more important than the draw. Provided a horse has enough tactical speed to get itself into a good position, then too much can be made of a low draw on the round track. In fact, these days jockeys are so clued up that those with perceived good draws (ie, high numbers by the rail) often find their paths blocked by those drawn less well fighting for a rail position. The outcome is that those drawn low can ride a more sensible race and don't get stopped in their runs. It is funny how many races are won by horses that are supposed to be badly drawn and it is only when something wins from what looks a good draw that everyone crows about it and tells us how clever they are.

every horse ridden by Johnny Murtagh in the period 1999-2003 would have put a profit of £142 in your pocket, or why Frankie Dettori is about £30 up to level stakes. Given the number of occasional punters at the meeting who just back Frankie blind, the fact that he is in profit at all is something of a miracle.

There are deeper reasons for their success. Murtagh and Dettori keep things very simple at Ascot and give their mounts the best chance, while some of the other jockeys are getting in all sorts of bother as they try to weave their way through from the back.

So the easy bit of punting at Royal Ascot is to stick to the best jockeys and trainers. The harder part is to dispel all the myths that have grown up over the years because, contrary to popular belief, higher-weighted horses and those that race up with the pace have an excellent record in the big handicaps.

The normal analysis of any Flat race starts with a study of the weights followed by the way the race is run. Put in simple terms, horses get lots of weight because they can run fast and are successful. That is the type of horse to look for at Royal Ascot – backing any hold-up horse in a big field at any meeting, let alone Royal Ascot, is fraught with danger. Deportivo and Attache were two examples in 2003 of how class will out at Royal Ascot and any number of the Johnston winners over the years have been raced close to the pace – therefore taking luck in running off the agenda.

THE CHELTENHAM FESTIVAL In the early to mid-1990s it was clear that the faster Flat horses were running amok in the speed tests at the Cheltenham Festival, while the number of Irish-trained winners was on the decline. If anyone had suggested that the Polish St Leger winner was going to win at jump racing's championship meeting, they would have been locked up and the key would have been thrown away.

Times are changing, however, and punters should take note of the latest trends. It seems that the advent of all-weather racing has meant that most of the good middle-distance horses stay on the Flat, where the risks are obviously lower and the prize-money greater, which has led to a number of National Hunt trainers going to France, Germany and even Poland to find good, young horses. That trend, and the re-emergence of the Irish challenge, has been accelerated by the strength of the Irish economy, which has led to many of the best store horses staying in their homeland rather than moving to England.

The results have been all too evident with National Hunt-bred (Rooster Booster) and French-bred (Hors La Loi) winning the Champion Hurdle, which had been monopolised in the preceding years by the likes of Alderbrook, Make A Stand or the mighty Istabraq. The shift in the balance of power would seem to fly in the

Best Mate: the perfect example of a horse well suited to Cheltenham

face of the fact that the ground is rarely soft for the three days of the Festival anymore after the drainage work that has been carried out, which in theory suits the faster horses off the Flat. However, so few horses make the transition from Flat to jumps nowadays that it really shouldn't be any great surprise. With National Hunt-bred horses also winning the two-mile Supreme Novices' Hurdle and the County Hurdle in recent years, it seems that their new-found dominance is no flash in the pan.

Some Cheltenham factors remain constant over the years, however, with the first and most obvious being the nature of the track. Cheltenham is one of the trickiest jumping tracks in the country and course experience is vital in the chase races. The vast majority of chase winners over the years have shown a liking for the track and the ability to jump well, while horses like First Gold and Keen Leader have never been able to reproduce their brilliant best up and down the Cotswold hills. Even the great Desert Orchid was a shadow of what we all knew he could be round Cheltenham and it was only the weather and testing ground that allowed him to beat the vastly inferior Yahoo in the 1989 Gold Cup.

Best Mate, Istabraq, Rooster Booster and Moscow Flyer are all good recent examples of horses who excel round Cheltenham and the Pillar Chase, run at the track a couple of months before the Gold Cup, was an excellent guide to the big race before Best Mate came along. It seems likely that its importance will be re-established at some point.

It is also worth keeping on the right side of fresh horses. In recent years the prize-money for conditions-race hurdles and chases has been boosted to match the level found in the big handicaps, which has meant that the best horses can be limited to a few runs throughout the season. With no huge weight differentials, these races are often less taxing than handicaps, which means that the top horses arrive at Cheltenham at the top of their game. It is very rare that a horse is able to keep going throughout the whole season and still put in a sparkling effort on the day that matters most. In general terms the fewer races a horse has had that season, the better its prospects at the Festival.

Best Mate and Istabraq are obvious recent examples but in 2003 both Royal Predica and Young Spartacus won big handicaps on their seasonal reappearances and other winners such as Xenophon and Palarshan had hardly been overtaxing themselves. It seems clear that horses who have been slogging around in the mud over the winter seriously compromise their chances of winning at the Festival.

Also worth noting are horses who have shown recent good form at a track like Huntingdon, Kempton or Doncaster. The reason is that quite often the ground isn't too bad at these tracks in the run-up to Cheltenham and the races there tend to be a test of speed rather than a test of stamina.

As speed is the key to winning at Cheltenham in big fields and on ground that is usually on the fast side, the Racing Post meeting at Kempton at the end of February is always earmarked as the best Cheltenham guide. Less well known, however, is how good a pointer Warwick had become before the abandonments of its February meetings in 2002 and 2003. The reason is that the fences come at you thick and fast at Warwick and provide the ideal warm-up for Cheltenham. The likes of Cenkos, Royal Predica, Flagship Uberalles and Monsignor have all used Warwick as their last port of call before the big meeting and all showed how useful the experience of jumping at speed was.

In contrast the slow-horse tracks like Chepstow and Uttoxeter and the soft-ground meetings at Sandown are no real guide.

In general terms the best way to win at the Festival is to stick with in-form horses who have been trained for the meeting and have proved their worth at the track and in races run at a strong pace on quick ground.

THE GRAND NATIONAL

Price, form, jockey, trainer and race conditions are what we study to varying degrees when trying to make our punting pay on a daily basis. But what if we want to get a head start on the bookmakers and have a look at the top races in advance? What type of horse should we have on the short-list before we apply the tried-and-trusted betting concepts? There is no better race to look at than the Grand National.

No event in the calendar captures the imagination of the betting public quite like the Aintree spectacular, and if we take a professional look at the race, we have a huge edge over the bookmakers. Add to that the big prices which are always flying about in the run-up to the National, and this is a race in which careful study can help us win – and win big.

First, it is worth exploding some of the myths that are trawled out year after year but simply have no foundation.

One theory says that stamina is the most important asset needed in any National winner.

uncommon knowledge

 The Aintree factor

There is no such thing any more. Recent statistics simply do not back up the theory that those who have had previous National experience are at an advantage. Back in the Red Rum era the National was more of a showjumping contest than a real steeplechase and experience of the then huge obstacles played a part. But no longer.

Red Marauder (2001) is the only recent example of a winner who had run in the National before landing the contest and he fell early on the year before, so he does not really count. Perhaps more telling is the fact that Bindaree and Monty's Pass, the winners in 2002 and 2003 respectively, had both been placed in the Topham Trophy, which is run over the big fences but, crucially, over about 2m6f.

Red Marauder (right): a rare slogger to win the National, in 2001

This is not the case. Unless the ground is heavy, the better horses with form in the high-class chases are the ones to concentrate on. This is why the Topham has become a good pointer because the shorter trip proved that Monty's Pass and Bindaree had the ability to jump the big fences at speed. This meant that, barring accidents, they were sure to travel on the bridle at the slower pace of a four-and-a-half-mile race, conserving energy.

The slow horses who win staying chases such as the Welsh National and long-distance handicaps in the mud at Haydock are simply not fast enough to keep up in a high-class race like the National, provided the ground is not bottomless. The quickest way to get any horse beaten is for them to go too fast too soon in any race and the slowcoaches are often exhausted by the second circuit of a good-ground National because they are not used to going so fast when plodding round in the mud at places like Uttoxeter and Chepstow.

However, every year such horses take out a huge chunk of the National market because stamina is still regarded as the most important ingredient in finding the winner. Perhaps the best example in recent years is Bonanza Boy, who ran in five Nationals and was well fancied on three occasions, but never had any chance because he simply could not keep up.

What we should be looking for is a horse who has shown it can travel and jump. Preferably he will have run well in the Topham Trophy, at the Cheltenham Festival or in a high-class handicap like the Hennessy Cognac Gold Cup, Great Yorkshire Chase or Irish Grand National, where more often than not the emphasis is more on speed than stamina.

Many recent Aintree heroes had good Cheltenham Festival form to their name. Papillon, the 2000 winner, had been beaten just over 20 lengths in the 1999 Queen Mother Champion Chase, Rough Quest (1996) and Royal Athlete (1995) had both been placed in the Gold Cup, while Minnehoma (1994) had won a Sun Alliance Chase. Seagram (1991) won the race now known as the William Hill NH Handicap Chase and both Monty's Pass and Bindaree had also run with credit in handicaps at Cheltenham.

However, class and speed factors are negated when the ground is as heavy as it was in Earth Summit's year (1998) or Red Marauder's (2001). The race turns into a war of attrition and it becomes a case of the last man standing.

Every year trends followers point out that horses carrying more than 11st do not win the National. On the face of it they are right, with no winner since Rhyme 'N' Reason (11st in 1988) having successfully carried that sort of burden. However, this could well be a misleading statistic because only about 12 per cent of the runners since 1990 have shouldered 11st or more and the vast majority of them had no chance.

What is probably more pertinent is that nearly all recent National winners have been trained for the race and therefore have had their handicap marks protected throughout the

uncommon knowledge

Narrowing the National field

Five golden rules

Where does all this National study leave us? Let's weigh up the evidence:

◇ Previous experience in the National is no advantage whatsoever.

◇ Provided the ground is not heavy, form in chases which are a test of speed is a must.

◇ Sloggers with form over extreme distances in the mud should be avoided, unless the ground at Aintree is very soft.

◇ Weight may not be the issue many think it is, especially now that the fences are easier.

◇ Stick to horses who have been aimed at the race all season, rather than those who are sent for the National as an afterthought.

Add all these factors together and the potential number of winners of the world's most famous chase is hugely reduced.

season, which means they are often among the lower weights. Horses who have shown their hand and won big chases that season are bound to have been clobbered by the handicapper and clearly that is going to make their chance of winning the National a lot harder. Having said that, What's Up Boys (11st 6lb), Suny Bay (12st) and Garrison Savannah (11st 11b) have all come second in recent years, while surely nobody thinks that Papillon (10st 12lb) or Red Marauder (10st 13lb) wouldn't have won even with a couple more pounds on their backs. Monty's Pass (10st 7lb) was just about the easiest National winner I've seen and he'd surely have won carrying another 7lb.

The key to staying in front of the bookmaker is to be flexible and not get stuck in one particular mode. The recent change in the handicapping system for the National, which means that the better horses are getting in lightly, suggests that in the next few years one of the better-class horses may well win the race. Those who think that the higher-weighted horses cannot win could well come unstuck.

PART FIVE

BETTING OFF-COURSE

GAMBLING MIGHT NOT BE THE oldest profession, but it has been around for thousands of years. Dice games, in particular, were popular in the ancient empires of Egypt, Greece, Rome and the Orient, and some prehistoric finds have suggested that Man's obsession with gambling and games of chance dates back even further.

By NICK PULFORD

Britain has had professional bookmakers for more than 200 years and, unlike most other major racing nations, where a totalisator system is the major forum for horserace gambling, the British betting market has continued to be dominated by off-course bookmakers. Britain has its own Tote but, although it accounts for a significant part of the market, it is not the dominant player.

This twin-track development of a strong bookmaking industry and a Tote system gives British betting its special character. And now, with the addition of more recent innovations such as spread betting and betting exchanges, British punters have more choice and opportunities than anywhere else in the world.

The most recent in-depth study of the British betting market and its regulation was conducted by the Gambling Review Group, which took submissions from the main racing and betting organisations before publishing a detailed report in July 2001. After considering the report's findings and recommendations, the Government

Shop floor: about 71% of betting-shop turnover is on horseracing

accepted most of the 176 proposals and drafted a Gambling Bill in November 2003 which, if passed by Parliament, will reform the regulatory framework of the whole gambling and gaming industry. The core of the draft bill is the establishment of a Gambling Commission to oversee all sectors of the industry, while other key proposals include the enforceability of gambling debts by law and stricter suitability tests for all commercial gambling operators.

The Gambling Review Group's report represents the most up-to-date information available on all aspects of the British betting industry, and several extracts are reproduced here as an introduction to the development, size and scope of the industry.*

*Crown copyright material is reproduced with the permission of the Controller of HMSO and the Queen's Printer for Scotland

THE MARKETPLACE The following extracts are taken from the Gambling Review Group's report and represent an overview of the betting industry at the time of the report's compilation in 2001, though some of the figures date from earlier years.

"The three largest operators are William Hill,

Ladbrokes and Coral, commonly referred to as the 'Big Three'. Between them they operate around half of all licensed betting offices (LBOs) and, based on turnover, over three-quarters of the telephone betting market. The Monopolies and Mergers Commission reported in 1998 that Ladbrokes was the largest firm in the UK off-course betting industry with a chain of some 1,900 LBOs (21%), William Hill was the second largest with 1,515 (17%), and Coral was third with 833 (9%). Figures supplied by BOLA [the Betting Office Licensees' Association, since merged into the Association of British Book-makers] suggest that there are now around 8,100 LBOs, a decrease of around one-tenth since the Monopolies and Mergers report. The Big Three operate about 53% of betting shops, compared to 47% in 1997. Ladbrokes has about 1,881 LBOs, William Hill about 1,526 and Coral operates some 868." (section 9.19)

"A bookmaker can legally offer a bet on anything other than the outcome of the National Lottery. In 1997, around 71% of LBO turnover was on horseracing, 20% on greyhound racing, 5% on other sports, mainly football, and 4% on numbers betting. The total turnover from LBOs in 1997 was estimated to be in the region of £6,190m. The Big Three had a market share of around 60% and the Tote of about 2%." (sections 9.23 and 9.24)

THE PUNTERS The Gambling Review Group's report also had some fascinating insights into punters, their gambling habits and their success (or otherwise). Using figures drawn from a Prevalence Survey by the National Centre for Social Research, the group reported in 2001 that 'in the UK almost three-quarters (72%) of the population – that is about 33 million adults – took part in some gambling activity within the past year and over half the population had gambled in the past week.' (section 5.2).

The Prevalence Survey and another survey commissioned by the Gambling Review Group both found that lotteries (more specifically, the

uncommon knowledge

 A short history of bookmaking

From small beginnings to big business

The Gambling Review Group reported: "Professional bookmakers began to make their appearance in the late 18th century. In 1845, the Gaming Act made wagering contracts unenforceable in law, thus preventing bookmakers from recovering forfeited stakes in cases where the betting had been conducted on credit terms. As a result, bookmakers insisted on receiving cash in advance and there followed a rapid growth in betting houses to meet the demand for cash betting. This was regarded as an unwelcome development and a Betting Act was passed in 1853 to suppress betting houses. The effect of the 1853 Act was simply that bookmakers operated on the streets. Consequently a further Act of 1906 made betting in the streets and other public places unlawful." (section 4.5)

"Betting continued to be conducted lawfully on-course and credit betting remained lawful off-course provided the bets were placed by post or telephone. The 1853 and 1906 Acts could not, however, suppress the demand for off-course cash betting, which consequently continued unlawfully. The Betting and Gaming Act 1960 swept away the 1853 Act and made it lawful for a bookmaker to run a cash betting office provided both he and his office were licensed." (section 4.6)

"The law on betting is to be found in the Betting, Gaming and Lotteries Act 1963. Betting is not defined by statute, but is generally regarded as entering into a contract by which each party undertakes to forfeit to the other, money or money's worth, if an issue in doubt at the time of the contract is determined in accordance with that other party's forecast. Unlike a lottery, a bet may involve skill or judgement." (section 4.19).

National Lottery (65%) and scratchcards (22%)), fruit machines (14%) and betting (13%) were the three most popular gambling activities in the UK.

The Gambling Review Group said the Prevalence Survey had found that, of those who had taken part in betting during the year under examination, 18% of men and 9% of women had bet on a horserace. Only 1% of those surveyed claimed to have made a spread bet in the week prior to the survey.

The group's report added: 'For those that had bet on a horserace in the last week, about a third said that they broke even or won and nearly half had lost less than £5. One in ten had lost between £10.01 and £50. The Prevalence Survey also found that nearly half of those surveyed who had spread bet in the preceding seven days, claimed to have won or broken even. A further 37% had lost less than £10, and 6% between £10.01 and £20. The remaining 9% had lost more than £20 although 5% had lost more than £200.' (sections 9.10 and 9.12)

TYPES OF BET The Royal Commission in 1933 described a bet as 'a promise to give money or monies worth upon the determination of an uncertain or unascertained event in a particular way. It may involve the exercise of skill or judgement.' (section 9.1)

The types of bet available with off-course bookmakers fall into three broad categories – the single bet on a particular selection (either win or each-way); combination bets, where two or more selections are combined in a single wager, with all selections having to be successful for the bet to win; and multiple bets, where a variety of bets on several selections are combined. In the case of multiple bets, not all selections have to be successful for the bet to win (at least in part).

SINGLE The simplest and most popular bet, normally a win bet on one selection in one race. The punter backs a horse to finish first, e.g. placing £10 at odds of 4-1. If the horse loses, the £10 stake is lost. If the horse wins, the bet wins £40 (4 x £10) and the total return to the punter is £50 (£40 + original £10 stake).

RETURNS Calculating returns is not always easy for the casual punter, given the differences between conventional bookmaker odds and decimal (Tote) odds and the fractions that can be involved. Things have become much simpler since the abolition of off-course betting tax, reducing the necessity for 'ready reckoner' tables to calculate returns.

CONVENTIONAL ODDS Conventional bookmaker odds are usually expressed 'to one' (as in 3-1, or three-to-one). The figure on the right represents the punter's stake and the figure on the left is the bookmaker's stake, so 3-1 places £1 of the punter's money against £3 of the bookmaker's money. If the punter's bet wins, the bookmaker pays back £4 (the sum of the £1 staked by the punter and the £3 won from the bookmaker).

One source of confusion can arise when a bookmaker puts the figure 3 against the name of a horse on an on-course board or on a betting-shop screen. This still means 3-1, as bookmakers generally bet in conventional odds, even if they may sometimes omit the 'to-one' part for their own speed and convenience.

The main complication with conventional bookmaker odds, though, is that fractions are not expressed 'to one'. For example, the fraction between 4-1 and 5-1 is expressed by a bookmaker as 9-2 (not as 4.5-1). Most 'fractions' occur at the shorter end of the betting market, where slight variations in price are necessary. The most common fractions (and their decimal equivalents 'to one') are:

Evens	1-1	9-4	2.25-1
11-10	1.1-1	5-2	2.5-1
6-5	1.2-1	11-4	2.75-1
5-4	1.25-1	100-30	3.33-1
11-8	1.375-1	7-2	3.5-1
6-4	1.5-1	9-2	4.5-1
13-8	1.625-1	11-2	5.5-1
7-4	1.75-1	13-2	6.5-1
15-8	1.875-1	15-2	7.5-1
85-40	2.125-1	17-2	8.5-1

Therefore, if a £1 bet is placed at 9-2, the fraction in decimal terms is 4.5-1. So, the £1 is staked against the bookmaker's £4.50 and, if the bet is won, the total return will be £5.50 (£4.50 + £1).

Once this principle is understood, any bookmaker odds can be converted to provide a simple calculation of returns, as follows . . .

Convert odds to a 'to one' format, by dividing left-hand figure by right-hand figure, eg 2-1 = 2, 5-2 = 2.5, 3-1 = 3, 100-30 = 3.33, etc.

Multiply resulting figure by stake, eg £10 x 2 (ie 2-1) = £20, £10 x 2.5 (ie 5-2) = £25. These are the winnings.

Add original stake to find the total return, eg £10 at 2-1 = £20 (winnings) + £10 (stake) = £30 (total return), £10 at 5-2 = £25 (winnings) + £10 (stake) = £35 (total return).

TOTE AND EXCHANGE ODDS

Unlike conventional bookmaker odds, Tote and most betting-exchange odds do not use the 'to one' format and are expressed simply as a figure (in round or decimal terms) which represents the potential total winning return to the punter. So, 4 (or 4.0) in Tote or decimal odds is the same as the conventional 3-1, as it represents a potential total winning return of £4 to a £1 stake.

Therefore, with whole numbers, it is easy to convert between the two by adding or subtracting one. With Tote and exchange figures, subtract one to find the equivalent bookmaker odds – for instance, if the Tote or exchange return is 4, then 4 minus 1 = 3-1. With bookmaker odds, add the two whole figures together to find the equivalent Tote or exchange return – e.g. if the odds are 3-1, then 3 + 1 = 4.

For odds involving fractions, subtract one from the Tote or exchange return and then convert this decimal figure to conventional bookmaker odds (e.g. 4.5 on the Tote or exchanges becomes 4.5 minus 1 = 3.5, which is 7-2 expressed in conventional terms). To change the fractions from conventional bookmaker odds, divide the left-hand figure by the right-hand figure and add one to obtain the equivalent Tote or exchange return (eg, 7-2 becomes 7 divided by 2 = 3.5, + 1 = 4.5).

uncommon knowledge

Figure it out

One key factor of betting at Tote and exchange odds is the ability to recognise quickly when a price has gone to odds-on (ie below 2.0), as it is easy to be deceived into thinking that 1.8 represents almost 2-1, when in fact it means 4-5. This is particularly vital in fast-moving markets, such as just before the off in a big horserace or during in-running betting on the exchanges (see chapter 20, page 192, for more on the pitfalls of betting on the exchanges).

Bookmakers' internet sites already offer the option of betting at conventional or decimal odds, and it may be that betting shops may also offer this facility before too long as decimal odds become more widely used and understood.

COMBINATIONS AND MULTIPLES

Returns from win doubles, trebles and accumulators can be calculated by adding one point to the price of each horse, and multiplying the new figures, then multiplying by the stake.

Take, for example, a £10 winning double at prices of 3-1 and 5-1. With a point added to each price, this becomes 4 (3+1) x 6 (5+1) = 24 x 10 (stake) = £240 (return). This is a 23-1 double.

If there are fractions, the same procedure of adding one unit can still be used, once the fractions have been converted to a decimal figure. A winning £10 double at prices of 7-2 and 5-1 becomes 3.5-1 and 5-1 – then, with a point added to each, 4.5 and 6. So, 4.5 x 6 x 10 (stake) = £270 (return). This is a 26-1 double.

The same method applies for accumulators with more legs. For example, a winning £10 treble at 3-1, 7-2 and 5-1 becomes (using the figures given above) 4 x 4.5 x 6 x 10 (stake) = £1080 (return). This is a 107-1 treble.

EACH-WAY BETTING
An each-way bet is, in fact, two bets in one. Normally the bet is split 50:50, one portion is on the win and the other is on the place – place-only wagers are not generally accepted in betting shops, so this is the only way to have a place bet on your selection with a bookmaker.

If your selection wins, the win portion of the bet is calculated in the normal way, while the place portion of the bet is settled at a fraction of the win odds. This fraction, and the number of places allowed by the bookmaker, depends on the type of race and the number of runners in the race (see table). If the selection is placed but fails to win, the win portion

EACH-WAY TERMS

Runners	Type of Race	Fraction of the odds	Places paid
5-7	Non-Handicaps	1/4	1st or 2nd
8+	Non Handicaps	1/5	1st, 2nd or 3rd
8-11	Handicaps	1/5	1st, 2nd or 3rd
12-15	Handicaps	1/4	1st, 2nd or 3rd
16+	Handicaps	1/4	1st, 2nd, 3rd or 4th

of the stake is lost but, again, the place portion of the bet is settled at a fraction of the win odds. *NB The above are the normal rules for each-way betting on horseracing, but some bookmakers differ from others. Always check the conditions of the bet with the bookmaker before striking the bet.

COMBINATION BETS

Double Consists of one bet involving two selections in different events. Both selections must be successful to get a return. To calculate the winnings on a double, add one to each of the odds, multiply them, subtract one from the total and multiply by the stake. For example, if a £10 double is placed on two horses who win at 4-1 and 8-1, the winnings are £440 – $(4 + 1) \times (8 + 1) = 45 - 1 = 44 \times 10 = 440$. The return would be £450 (including the original £10 stake).

Treble Consists of one bet involving three selections in different events. All three selections must be successful to get a return. The same method used for calculating the winnings on doubles can be used for trebles – ie, add one to each of the odds, multiply them, subtract one from the total and multiply by the stake.

Accumulator Consists of one bet involving four (or more) selections in different events. All selections must be successful to get a return.

MULTIPLE BETS

Trixie Consists of four bets involving three selections in different events. The bet includes

uncommon knowledge

**One thing leads
to another**

Related contingencies

Separate conditions apply to doubles, trebles etc when the same selection is taken to win more than one event. For instance, if a bet was placed on a horse to win the Triple Crown before the 2,000 Guineas had been run, it wouldn't simply be a case of taking the best prices on offer for the 2,000 Guineas, Derby and St Leger, and combining them in the usual way for a treble. This is because the horse's chances (and odds) for the Derby and then for the St Leger are related to its performances in the first and second legs – unlike an unrelated treble, where the winning chances of the second and third legs become no more likely because the first leg was successful. To place a bet of this type, a punter would need to ask the bookmaker for special odds, which would take account of the relation between the separate legs of the bet.

This rule caused one of the most high-profile disputes of recent years – over the 2002 World Cup double of Brazil to win and Ronaldo to be top scorer in the competition. The bookmakers' view was that it was a related contingency because if Brazil were outright winners, then Ronaldo was more likely to figure among the leading scorers. Some punters backed the double, thinking they would get the combined odds of 6-1 on Brazil and 16-1 on Ronaldo when both legs duly won. In fact, the leading bookmakers were offering a special bet at 66-1 (around half the odds the bet would have been if the double had been unrelated) or even 33-1.

three doubles and one treble. A minimum of two selections must be successful to get a return.

Patent Consists of seven bets involving three selections in different events. The bet includes a single on each selection, plus three doubles and one treble. One successful selection guarantees a return.

Round Robin Consists of ten bets involving three selections in different events. The bet includes three doubles, one treble and six single-stakes-about bets combining the three selections. A single-stakes-about bet consists of two bets on two selections (one single on each selection any to come on the other selection reversed). Any to come means that the returns from one wager are automatically reinvested on the other selection.

Yankee Consists of 11 bets involving four selections in different events. The bet includes six doubles, four trebles and a four-timer. A minimum of two selections must be successful to get a return.

Lucky 15 Consists of 15 bets involving four selections in different events. The bet includes four singles, six doubles, four trebles and a four-timer. If only one selection wins, as a consolation returns are paid at double the odds. If all four selections win, a bonus (normally 10%) is added to total returns.

Canadian (Super Yankee) Consists of 26 bets involving five selections in different events. The bet includes ten doubles, ten trebles, five fourfolds and a five-timer. A minimum of two selections must be successful to get a return.

Lucky 31 Consists of 31 bets involving five selections in different events. The bet includes five singles, ten doubles, ten trebles, five fourfolds and a five-timer. If only one selection wins, returns are paid to double the odds. If all five selections win, a bonus (normally 15%) is added to total returns.

Heinz Consists of 57 bets involving six selections in different events. The bet includes 15 doubles, 20 trebles, 15 fourfolds, six fivefolds and a six-timer. A minimum of two selections must be successful to get a return.

Lucky 63 Consists of 63 bets involving six selections in different events. The bet includes six singles, 15 doubles, 20 trebles, 15 fourfolds, six fivefolds and a six-timer. If only one selection wins, returns are paid to double the odds. If all six selections win, a bonus (normally 20%) is added to total returns.

Super Heinz Consists of 120 bets involving seven selections in different events. The bet includes 21 doubles, 35 trebles, 35 fourfolds, 21 fivefolds, seven sixfolds and a seven-timer. A minimum of two selections must be successful to get a return.

Goliath Consists of 247 bets involving eight

selections in different events. The bet includes 28 doubles, 56 trebles, 70 fourfolds, 56 five-folds, 28 sixfolds, eight sevenfolds and an eight-timer. A minimum of two selections must be successful to get a return.

FORECAST BETTING

There are various types of forecast bet. A straight forecast involves naming two selections to finish first and second in a race in the correct order. A reversed forecast involves naming two selections to finish first and second in a race in any order. A combination forecast involves choosing three or more selections in a race, with any of these to finish first and second. These bets operate on races of three or more runners. A dividend is declared according to a computer formula.

A Tricast involves naming three selections to finish first, second and third in a race in the correct order. Tricast bets are normally accepted only on handicap races where six or more horses are declared to run, and four or more runners take part. Again, a dividend is declared according to a computer formula.

MAXIMUM PAYOUTS

All bookmaking firms have maximum daily payouts for a bet, or bets, including ante-post. For horseracing bets, this is commonly £250,000, though it is sometimes raised for special events (eg, the Cheltenham Festival). The bigger bookmakers usually have the biggest maximum payouts. Punters should check the bookmakers' rules before placing a bet, especially a complicated multiple, however remote the likelihood of every leg being successful. For example, a £10 accumulator on Frankie Dettori's 'Magnificent Seven' at Ascot in 1996 would have exceeded the £250,000 maximum.

ANTE POST

This form of betting refers to wagers struck at quoted prices on named selections in advance of the day of a major event (for example, on a two-year-old to win one of the following season's Classics, or throughout the winter months in the run-up to the big races at the Cheltenham Festival). Ante-post betting is offered on about one per cent of the total number of races held in Britain each year and is normally available until the overnight declaration stage for runners in the race in question (usually the morning before the day of the race, or two days before in some cases – for example, the Grand National).

The attraction is that bigger prices are generally available months or weeks ahead of a race, due to the inevitable doubts over the final make-up of the field. The downside is that the bet is a loser if the selection fails to participate in the event. However, there are exceptions to this rule: if the race is abandoned or declared void; if the conditions of the race entry are changed prior to the horses coming under starter's orders; if the venue is altered; or if a horse is balloted out or eliminated under Jockey Club Rule 125, or prevented from running under Jockey Club Rule 1A.

If there are major doubts about whether a certain horse will run in a race, and that horse's participation will have a major effect upon the book for the race, bookmakers may opt to offer that horse 'with a run'. If the horse does not run, stakes are returned on that horse and bookmakers will usually issue a list of revised prices. Bets on other runners stand at the prices quoted at the time the bets were struck.

For more on ante-post betting, see chapter 24, page 220.

EARLY PRICES Apart from ante-post betting, there are other stages during the build-up to the more important races which offer punters the opportunity to place a bet at odds other than the starting price.

Early prices are offered on about 1,500 races a year and many are advertised in the Racing Post and other media outlets on the morning of the race, as well as in betting shops and on internet betting sites. These prices are subject to rapid adjustment according to the volume of

A new betting shop in 1961: things have come a long way since off-course cash betting was legalised, after years of underground activity

money placed on each horse – most bookmakers limit the amount of money punters can place at these prices and guarantee them only for a short period once betting starts on the morning of a race.

The next stage in the betting process comes shortly before the start of each race, when 'board' prices are displayed in off-course shops. When prices become available on-course they are returned to betting shops via direct satellite link to become what is called the opening show. From the time of the opening show all betting shops in the UK will display the same prices to their customers. Betting-shop customers can take a price at this stage, specifying the board price at the time they place the bet.

If no price is specified at the time a bet is placed (either an early or board price), bets are settled according to the official starting price, which is returned from the course once the race has finished.

There are some important differences between the rules governing ante-post bets and those placed at early prices. With the latter, place terms on each-way bets at the displayed odds are governed by the number of starters in the race and not by the number of declared runners at the time the price was taken. With ante-post bets, however, the each-way terms (one-quarter, one-fifth etc) are those advertised at the time the ante-post wager was struck.

Withdrawals are also treated differently. With ante-post betting, as explained above, a withdrawn horse is usually treated as a loser. With early price bets, stakes are refunded on any horse withdrawn before coming under starter's orders, though all winning returns on other runners in the race will be subject to deductions under Tattersalls Rule 4(c), depending on the odds of the withdrawn horses at the time the bet was accepted (see panel on page 169 for an explanation of Rule 4(c)).

For more on getting the best price, see chapter 24, page 220.

RULES AND DISPUTES The most serious problems usually arise when a bookmaker ceases trading, leaving gambling debts unpaid. There have been several well-publicised cases in recent years and most involved small firms offering seemingly attractive terms (such as unusually advantageous each-way bets). As a general rule, such offers are unsustainable in the long term and punters are advised to be wary of attractions which appear too good to be true.

Even in a case where a bookmaker is still operating, there are, at present, no statutory regulations to enforce the payment of gambling debts or to determine the validity of a particular bet (although this issue is under review by the Government). The validity of a bet is, at present, an issue between the parties involved in the wager and the first recourse for any punter with a grievance about an off-course bet is to take up the matter with the betting-shop manager or the customer services department of the bookmaker involved.

If this fails, the punter can turn to the

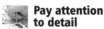

uncommon knowledge

Pay attention to detail

Betting-shop rituals

Bookmakers' rules vary, but essentially they are based on the set first drawn up in 1886 by Tattersalls' Committee, which was established under Jockey Club auspices to adjudicate on betting disputes over events held under the Rules of Racing.

Most betting-shop rituals are learned by experience and probably few punters bother to read the rules on display, but most betting disputes can be avoided by adhering to a few simple steps:

1. Use the correct betting slip for the type of bet.

2. Fill out the slip clearly, with the name of the selected horse, stake and type of bet (e.g. win or each-way), the start time of the race and the racecourse where it is being held. Enter the total amount staked in the box at the bottom of the slip.

3. If the bet is a complicated combination or multiple bet, ensure that you know the rules (especially the maximum payout) before placing the bet. Ensure that you include the correct stake and number of legs to cover the bet.

4. If in doubt, ask the betting-shop staff for assistance.

Independent Betting Arbitration Service (IBAS), which was launched in November 1998 and offers an independent, non-statutory arbitration service to settle betting disputes. Previously The Sporting Life had provided the 'Green Seal Service' as an independent arbitrator but the service ceased when the paper closed in May 1998 and IBAS was set up in its stead, being funded by Trinity Mirror, publishers of the Racing Post, and Satellite Information Services (SIS).

IBAS is supported by the main industry trade associations and is free of charge to customers of bookmakers who are registered with it – according to IBAS, over 90% of UK bookmakers have registered. Bookmakers in this scheme have to declare their intention to assist IBAS in any investigations and to abide by its decisions. Failure to do so results in a bookmaker being publicly de-registered from the scheme.

IBAS receives around 1,000 requests for arbitration each year, with the bulk of the disputes relating to horseracing and football (around 40 per cent and 26 per cent of the total respectively). The main cause of horseracing and greyhound disputes is ambiguous bet instructions.

In the event that a punter feels that they have been treated unfairly, they can contact IBAS at PO Box 4209, London W1A 6YL. Tel: 020 7529 7670/7671/7672. Fax: 020 7529 7674. Email: ibas@mgn.co.uk

Alternatively, disputes can be settled through Tattersalls' Committee, which has fulfilled that role since the 18th century, though its workload has declined in recent years and it now handles less than 50 cases a year. The committee previously charged a fee for arbitration but this was abolished for most complainants in 2001, making the process more appealing for the smaller punter. The committee is the only tribunal on betting matters recognised by the Jockey Club, which can warn off debtors from the racecourse, making the committee a powerful force in disputes involving on-course bookmakers. Punters can contact Tattersalls' Committee at PO Box 13, 19 Wilwyne Close, Caversham, Reading, Berkshire RG4 0XZ. Tel: 0118 946 1757.

THE TOTE The main alternative to fixed-odds betting is the Tote (or Horserace Totalisator Board), a system introduced to Britain in 1929 to offer pool betting on racecourses. All the stakes on a particular bet are pooled, before a deduction is made to cover costs and the Tote's contribution to racing. The remainder of the pool is divided by the number of winning units to give a dividend which is declared inclusive of a £1 stake. In other words, pool customers bet against each other, whereas in bookmaking they bet against the bookmaker. Odds fluctuate according to the pattern of betting and betting ceases at the 'off'.

For example, the win pool on a race might amount to £100,000. With a deduction of £13,500 (13.5 per cent of the pool), this leaves

uncommon
knowledge

 On-course disputes

On-course bookmaking is administered by the National Joint Pitch Council (NJPC), which was created, also in 1998, by the Levy Board. The NJPC is represented at all race meetings by its betting-ring managers, whose duties include helping to settle disputes between on-course bookmakers and punters.
Any punter with a grievance about a bet made with an on-course bookmaker should find the betting-ring manager. If the dispute is not solved on the day, punters can write to the National Joint Pitch Council, Standard House, Chord Business Park, London Road, Godmanchester, Huntingdon PE29 2WL. Tel: 01480 356589. Fax: 01480 356592.

£86,500 as the total payout. If the total amount staked on the winning horse is £8,650, this would be divided into the £86,500 to produce a dividend to each £1 unit – in this case £10 (£86,500 divided by £8,650 = £10). So the return for a £1 stake would be £10 (one £1 unit x £10), while the return for a £10 stake would be £100 (10 £1 units x £10). In both cases, the return includes the stake, so the actual odds in conventional terms are 9-1 (for a detailed explanation of how Tote odds work, see page 154).

There is a separate pool for each bet type and the deduction made for expenses and the Tote's contribution to racing varies according to bet type, but is somewhere between 13.5 and 26 per cent.

Tote betting is available at all racecourses as well as off-course at its chain of around 450 shops, through its telephone-betting arm Tote Credit Club and at other bookmakers via a system known as Tote Direct, which feeds bets into the main Tote system.

One of the main drawbacks with Tote betting is that the final odds are known only after the race has been run. TV screens with Tote information only show the approximate odds at the time of placing the bet – they are subject to change depending on the final amount bet into the pool and on the winning horse.

The Tote's off-course operation also includes a conventional bookmaking facility, offering prices on the full range of horseracing and sporting events. The main types of Tote bet are:

Win Aim: to select the winner of the race. Operates on all races of two or more runners. Minimum stake £2.

Place Aim: to select a horse to be placed. Operates on all races of five or more runners. Minimum stake £2. Place bets are settled as follows: 1-4 runners no place betting, 5-7 runners 1st or 2nd, 8+ runners 1st, 2nd or 3rd, Handicaps 1st, 2nd, 3rd or 4th.

Each-way A win and place bet on the same horse. Operates on all races of five or more runners. Minimum stake £2.

Exacta Aim: to select first and second in the correct order. Operates on all races of three or more runners. Minimum stake £2 but 50p permutations are available.

Multibet Aim: to select doubles, trebles, accumulators, patent or Yankee (see pages 156-158 for explanations of these terms). Operates at selected meetings. Bets can be placed at any course. Minimum stake £1, with permutations accepted to a minimum unit stake of 10p upwards.

Jackpot Aim: to select the winners of all six Jackpot races (usually races 1-6 on the racecard). Operates daily at one selected meeting only, though bets can be placed at any course. Bets must be placed before the first race. Dividends are declared after the last Jackpot race. Minimum stake £2, with permutations accepted to a minimum unit stake of 10p upwards.

Placepot Aim: to select a placed horse in each of the six Placepot races (usually races 1-6 on the racecard). Operates at every meeting. Minimum stake £2, with permutations accepted to a minimum unit stake of 10p upwards.

Quadpot Aim: to select a placed horse in each of the four Quadpot races (usually races 3-6 on the racecard). Operates at every meeting, except some smaller Bank Holiday events. Minimum stake £1, with permutations accepted to a minimum unit stake of 10p upwards.

Trifecta Aim: to select 1st, 2nd and 3rd in the correct order. Available on nominated races of eight or more runners. Minimum stake £2, with permutations accepted to a minimum unit stake of 10p upwards.

Scoop6 Aim: to select the winners of each of the six nominated TV races (often at more than one race meeting). Operates on Saturdays only.

For Jackpot, Placepot and Quadpot bets, dividends are declared after the last applicable race. On Placepot and Quadpot bets, any horse on which a place dividend is normally declared counts towards a winning line, but in races of

New face of the Tote: shops were rebranded early in 2004

four or less runners the winner must be selected.

BETTING OVERSEAS Outside Britain and Ireland, most betting is conducted at tote (or pari-mutuel) odds. For some of the major overseas races, such as the Group events at Longchamp's Prix de l'Arc de Triomphe meeting in October, British bookmakers usually declare 'industry' starting prices. Punters have the choice between these prices (either an early price, a board price or the SP) and pari-mutuel odds but, if no price is taken and pari-mutuel odds are not requested, bets will be settled according to the industry SP.

The difference between British industry prices and the local pari-mutuel odds can be significant – the basic rule of thumb for most punters is to back a British horse at overseas odds and the foreign runners at British prices.

For overseas races where no industry prices are issued, bets at starting price will use the official pari-mutuel dividends in the country where the race takes place. For races in most countries on continental Europe, only win and

uncommon knowledge

**It's good
to talk**

Telephone betting

While the traditional betting shop still dominates the off-course market, there has been significant growth in more 'user-friendly' means of placing a bet, notably via the telephone and internet.

Telephone betting played a role in the off-course business throughout the 20th century but until recently required customers to have credit accounts.

On this sector, the Gambling Review Group reported: "The bulk of turnover is now accounted for by debit cards, which were first used in 1991.

"Turnover from telephone betting is said to be around 10% of the turnover in licensed betting offices (LBOs). In 1997, the market share of the 'Big Three' was reported as 78%, which equated to a turnover of around £412m. The Tote was said to have a market share of around 13% and a turnover of £70m." (section 9.22)

The group's report also found that, "telephone betting appears to be more weighted towards horseracing, football and other sports and less so towards greyhound racing and numbers betting, such as betting on the outcome of the Irish lottery.

"There is a much higher proportion of customers from the higher socio-economic groups than for LBOs. The average stake of around £50 for Ladbroke and Coral telephone customers is far higher than that in licensed betting offices." (section 9.11)

The growth of new media such as spread betting and betting exchanges is covered in chapters 19-23 (page 191).

---

place bets are accepted by British bookmakers.

For races in the United States, most British bookmakers accept win and show (1-2-3) bets, while each-way bets are settled in accordance with the 1-2-3 show pool.

SPs are returned on races in South Africa and normal each-way terms apply.

In some countries, horses can be 'coupled' in the pari-mutuel win pools, usually where the horses have the same owner. This means that a single price is offered for the two horses and a win bet is successful if either horse wins. Coupling usually shortens the price of the better-fancied horse, while offering no value about the longer-priced runner (which also will be sent off at the shorter price).

Coupling does not normally extend to place or forecast pools, although in some races, particularly in the United States, coupling sometimes applies to all pools.

British bookmakers usually open an ante-post book on the major overseas races, such as the Arc and the Breeders' Cup events, with the normal ante-post terms applying.

SOME KEY RULES

Tattersalls Rule 4 (c) One of the most commonly invoked rules (often referred to simply as Rule 4), as it deals with deductions from winning bets in the event of any withdrawn runner(s) from a race. Adjustments are necessary in such cases due to the fact that the book on a race becomes unbalanced if horses are withdrawn – the more fancied the horse, the more unbalanced the book becomes. The rule applies to winning bets struck at prices (eg, morning prices) laid before a withdrawal (other than ante-post bets, which are unaffected by Rule 4(c)) and to starting-price bets where, after a late withdrawal, there is insufficient time to reform the market.

The rate of deductions is in proportion to the odds of the non-runner(s) at the time of the withdrawal, as shown in the panel below.

RULE 4 (C) DEDUCTIONS

On the left is the price of the withdrawn horse at the time of withdrawal; on the right, the amount deducted from winnings under the rule

1-9 & shorter ..90p in the £	5-4 to 6-4............40p/£
2-11 to 2-17........85p/£	13-8 to 7-4..........35p/£
1-4 to 1-5............80p/£	15-8 to 9-4..........30p/£
3-10 to 2-7..........75p/£	5-2 to 3-1............25p/£
2-5 to 1-3............70p/£	10-3 to 4-1..........20p/£
8-15 to 4-9..........65p/£	9-2 to 11-2..........15p/£
8-13 to 4-7..........60p/£	6-1 to 9-1............10p/£
4-5 to 4-6............55p/£	10-1 to 14-1.........5p/£
20-21 to 5-6........50p/£	Over 14-1 ....no deduction
Evens to 6-5 ....45p/£	

In the case of two or more horses being withdrawn before coming under starter's orders, the total deduction shall not exceed 90p in the £

Dead heat In the event of a dead heat for first place, when a winning bet has been made, half the stake is applied to the selection at full odds and the other half is lost. If more than two horses dead-heat, the stake is proportioned accordingly.

In the case of each-way bets where the selection dead-heats for a place, stakes are applied in full unless the dead heat is for the last available place (eg, second in a race with 5-7 runners, third in a race with 8-15 runners, or fourth in handicap races with 16 or more runners). In these cases, half of the place stake will be applied to the selection at full place odds and the other half is lost.

Non-runners Stakes are returned on single bets where the selection is a non-runner – except with ante-post bets (see pages 159-160 for the rules on ante-post betting). In combination and multiple bets, the stake on the non-runner is allowed to run on to the other selections. A double which includes a non-runner, for example, becomes a single on the remaining selection, while a treble with a non-runner becomes a double on the remaining two selections.

The rules on multiple bets are more complicated and differ according to the type of bet, but the basic principle is the same – the stake on the non-runner is re-invested on the other selections in the bet.

MAKING A BOOK Fixed-odds betting, whether on- or off-course, involves a process known as 'making a book', in which the bookmaker determines the likelihood of each possible outcome in a race and presents this in the form of odds or prices.

The principle behind bookmaking is to deliver a profit in the long term, through a built-in margin known as the overround. In the simplest example, if a bookmaker were to offer odds on the outcome of the toss of a coin, he might offer 4–5 heads and 4–5 tails rather than even money, thereby giving himself a margin that the punter does not have. Over time,

Making a book: fearless layer Freddie Williams at his racecourse pitch

the bookmaker must win; the punter must lose.

Taking this principle a step further, consider a three-runner race where all the horses have the same theoretical chance of winning. The true chance of each of the three runners is 2-1, and if a punter were to have £10 on each of them at 2-1, he would neither win nor lose (a £10 bet at 2-1 returns £20 profit plus the original £10 stake). But, in this scenario, the bookmaker would not cover costs or deliver a profit margin, assuming the same amount is placed on each horse.

The actual odds offered, therefore, might be 7-4 for each of the three horses. This time, assuming that there is equal support for all three runners, the bookmaker will make a profit. If £100 in stakes is taken on each horse, the total payout would be £175 plus the £100 staked against takings of £300, giving a profit of £25. The size of the bookmaker's profit margin, or overround, can be translated into percentages. There are a number of ways of expressing odds as percentages, but the simplest is to work out how much needs to be staked at the given

ODDS AS PERCENTAGES

Odds against	Price	Odds on	Odds against	Price	Odds on	Odds against	Price	Odds on
50.00	Evens	50.00	26.67	11-4	73.33	11.11	8-1	89.89
47.62	11-10	52.38	25.00	3-1	75.00	10.00	9-1	90.00
45.45	6-5	54.55	23.08	10-3	76.92	9.09	10-1	90.91
44.44	5-4	55.56	22.22	7-2	77.78	8.33	11-1	91.67
42.11	11-8	57.89	20.00	4-1	80.00	7.69	12-1	92.31
40.00	6-4	60.00	18.18	9-2	81.82	5.88	16-1	94.12
38.10	13-8	61.90	16.67	5-1	83.33	4.76	20-1	95.24
36.36	7-4	63.64	15.39	11-2	84.61	3.85	25-1	96.15
34.78	15-8	65.22	14.29	6-1	85.71	2.94	33-1	97.06
33.33	2-1	66.67	13.33	13-2	86.67	1.96	50-1	98.04
30.77	9-4	69.23	12.50	7-1	87.50	0.99	100-1	99.01
28.67	5-2	71.43	11.76	15-2	88.24			

odds to return £100. At 2–1, it is £33.33 or 33.33 per cent; at 9–1 it is £10 or 10 per cent.

The most commonly used betting odds are shown expressed as percentages in the table above. A perfect book, like the example above with all three horses at 2–1, comes to 100 per cent. The bookmaker's profit margin (or overround) is the amount by which the percentage exceeds 100 when the prices of all the horses (expressed as a percentage) are added together. In the example, with the horses all at 7–4, the book totals 109.08 per cent (ie 36.36% + 36.36% + 36.36%) and the profit margin in favour of the bookmaker in such a theoretical race would be 9.08 per cent.

The overround tends to vary with the type of race and number of runners, but typically ranges from 108 to 145 per cent. As a broad generalisation, there is two points overround for each runner in a race with up to 12 runners, and one point for each runner thereafter. Theoretical profit margins only produce the 'perfect' result when the amount placed on each horse is in direct proportion to its price, ie,

uncommon knowledge

 **It's a matter
of opinion**

The true odds

One major difficulty with making a book on a horserace or other sporting event is that, while the odds may represent the likelihood of each possible outcome in a race, they can never be the 'true' odds. To return to the toss of a coin, the true odds on each of the two possible outcomes is evens – ie there is an even chance that the coin will land heads and an even chance that the coin will land tails, and the probability (or odds) will not change however many times the process is repeated.

Horseraces are influenced by so many different factors that there is no such mathematical probability about the outcome. The so-called 'true' odds on a horserace are a matter of opinion – first of all, the opinion of the bookmaker or the professional odds-compilers he appoints and, later, the view taken by the punter on whether those odds constitute a fair bet.

the bookmaker has balanced his books.

In practice, this never happens because setting a margin is a far more difficult process than the examples suggest, with the law of supply and demand crucial. For example, suppose all three runners are 7-4 and the bookmaker takes just three bets, £200 on horse A, £100 on horse B and £20 on horse C; the bookmaker's total takings on the race are £320. Although the theoretical margin has not changed, the actual margin depends on the result of the race. If horse A wins, the bookmaker has lost £230, or 71.9 per cent, rather than making a profit of just over 9 per cent (returns on horse A would be £350 winnings plus £200 staked).

The bookmaker will attempt to offset an imbalance by changing his prices, shortening better-backed horses and lengthening the odds on unfancied runners in an attempt to deter more bets on the former group and encourage bets on the latter. He may also 'lay off' part of his liability, which would involve betting on Horse A with another bookmaker in an attempt to cover losses if that horse wins.

best to stay single

BETS TO CONSIDER

THE MODERN-DAY PUNTER IS

By RICHARD BIRCH

confronted with an enormous – sometimes bewildering – selection of bets. They range from singles, doubles and trebles to forecasts, accumulators and yankees. Tote clients are offered placepots, jackpots and exactas, while the more intrepid speculators who thrive on the adrenalin rush and buzz created by high-risk spread betting are also well catered for. Throw in the spectacular growth in betting exchanges over the first few years of the 21st century and it's crystal clear that the choice of bet for punters to invest their money has never been wider.

Ask 99 per cent of professionals, however, which type of bet forms the core part of their business and the reply will be instant: singles.

Common sense, isn't it? The people who make a consistent living out of betting – or a useful second income to supplement their wages – don't wager in every race, every day of the week. In fact, it's highly unlikely that many will have more than two or three bets a week – let alone in a day. If a punter sits up half the night thoroughly researching the next day's card and comes up with one gilt-edged opportunity, he won't frantically try to find another two horses to make up a hasty treble – he will have a single on the day's 'good thing' providing it represents reasonable 'value'. And that's the way professionals play.

Speak to any high-street bookmaker and ask

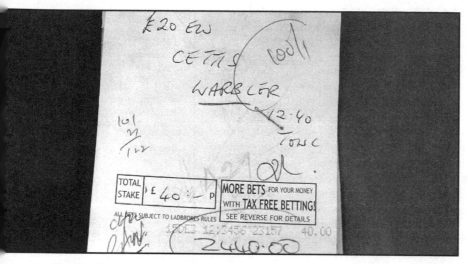

Not all your singles will be as successful, but it's still the best way to bet

which bet they hate the most. No offers they will reply, 'the single'. Bookies loathe singles because the profit margins are so much lower than on all the other bets that they advertise so vigorously.

How many times have you seen pictures of scantily clad, drop-dead gorgeous models smiling from the windows of betting shops promoting yankees, patents and canadians? Every day of the week. Yet how often do bookies advertise the delights of singles? Never, I would wager with the utmost confidence.

Basically, singles should form the nuts and bolts of any serious punter's betting toolkit. Punters who bet singles are making the point that they fully expect to win – perhaps not an extraordinary amount of money, but welcome profit nonetheless.

Players of multiple bets bear comparison to National Lottery mugs who are merely dreaming of winning a large, life-changing amount. Once in a lifetime or never. What a waste of life!

Each-way betting forms a vital component of

singles. There is an archaic view among some punting dinosaurs that 'you should never bet each-way because the fact that you are introducing a place element into the bet suggests that you don't really expect the horse to win'. What blinkered, dated rubbish!

On a personal level, 80 per cent of my betting at odds of 3-1 or more is carried out on an each-way basis. Betting win-only is high-risk, often unnecessarily putting all your eggs into one basket. Each-way betting has a ready-made built-in allowance for jumping mistakes, jockey error or just sheer bad luck, which happens to us all from time to time.

The key to successful each-way punting is finding the right races to play in. Obviously big-runner handicaps paying a quarter the odds 1,2,3,4 fall into this category, but arguably the best medium for 'sharks' to punt in are eight- or nine-runner maidens in which there is a bad-value favourite – often a much-hyped animal from a fashionable stable – against two horses with reasonable, if not, comparable form, and six or seven others who couldn't win if they started yesterday!

Each-way punters should focus on this type of contest, with prices such as 4-6, 3-1, 5-1, 20-1 bar, and back the 3-1 or 5-1 shot each-way.

From a psychological point of view, too, each-way betting is superior to win-only wagering in that you are far more likely to get a return from your investment – even if it is sometimes less than the money you laid out.

There is nothing more depressing than a sequence of win-only bets that come second or third, thus taking a huge portion out of a punter's betting tank – and with it, denting confidence, often to irreparable levels.

Doubles and trebles – sometimes of the each-way variety – are also popular bets among some professionals. Obviously the potential for a big payout is much greater than on win-only bets, but if one of the selections loses, the entire stake is lost.

Bookmakers willingly accept doubles and

trebles, particularly when lazy punters perm two or three odds-on favourites in their bets. Basically the punter wouldn't dream of backing a win single at 4-7, but would put three 4-7 shots in a treble to obtain odds-against on the payout. Nine times out of ten they come unstuck, leaving the bookies grinning like Cheshire cats.

TAKING A VIEW The advent of betting exchanges has made ante-post betting infinitely more attractive.

Nowadays the shrewd speculator has the opportunity of taking big odds about a horse weeks or months before a race – and then laying off part or all of the bet at much shorter odds nearer the time of the race to guarantee a profit.

For instance, shrewd people who fancied Best Mate to win his first Cheltenham Gold Cup in 2002 backed the horse at 33-1 some 15 months in advance of D-day. Two weeks before Cheltenham, Henrietta Knight's star was available at a best-price 6-1 with the major firms, so, to ensure a profit on their ante-post investment, Best Mate's backers could have laid off part of their bet at, say, 8-1.

When steeplechasing's blue riband finally dawned, those shrewd punters could be relaxed in the knowledge that whether Best Mate finished first, third or fell, they would make a profit – a wonderful position for anyone to be in.

Ten years ago, ante-post betting was viewed by many with cynicism. Not any more. It's a thriving, 'must-play' activity for people with foresight, where big profits for much lower risk than in previous eras of gambling are readily available.

Another form of betting to have gained in popularity is spread betting, although it remains very much a niche activity confined to backers with more 'city-type' mentalities than your archetypal betting shop punter.

Spread betting, whereby the punter bets on a 'spread' of numbers relating to a particular event – for instance, the number of lengths between named horses at the end of a race –

and either 'buys' or 'sells' depending on whether he expects the amount to be higher or lower than the spread, is particularly suited to the 'high-roller' type of punter. The attraction of spread betting is the more right you are, the more you win – and by the same token, the more wrong you are, the more money you can lose.

BAD VALUE

What are the chief culprits among bad-value bets? Patents, yankees and canadians figure highly on any list. A patent is a bet combining three horses in different races in seven separate wagers: three singles, three doubles and one treble. A £1 patent costs £7.

A yankee is a bet combining four horses in separate events in 11 bets (a £1 win yankee costs £11 and a £1 each-way yankee £22). The bets are six doubles, four trebles and one fourfold.

A canadian (also known as a super yankee – not so super, I'm afraid!) comprises five selections combined as ten doubles, ten trebles, five fourfolds and one fivefold – 26 bets. A £1 canadian would cost £26.

This type of bet is popular among betting-shop punters who have neither the self-confidence nor the bravery to invest significant sums in single wagers, or the time or inclination to sit around all afternoon watching the action unfold.

Canadians, yankees and patents generate high rates of profitability to bookmakers, and are quite rightly regarded by professionals as 'mug bets'. Punters who place these bets don't really expect to win, but just occasionally might pick three out of four winners, which gives them the will to continue doing this bet and thus makes sure the bookmakers' gravy train stays firmly on the rails.

Backers who lump four odds-on shots in yankees are the biggest mugs of all. Basically they need three winners to get their money back, and the chances of getting all four for a profit are slim. It's like jumping off Beachy Head – just occasionally there might be one survivor.

NO FUN Many Tote clients, both on-course and off-course, view the Jackpot and Placepot as 'fun' bets. However, no bet is 'fun' when it's a loser and Jackpots and Placepots are hard to win by their very definition – the fact that they involve six races at a meeting.

For the Jackpot, the punter is required to pick the winner of the first six races at a designated meeting; for the Placepot, the six selections must all be placed to qualify for a payout.

These bets were designed to give punters the option of having an interest – without having to open the wallet every half hour – in every race. Ask yourself this question, though. How many professional punters bet in every race at the principal meeting each day? Exactly.

Other Tote bets such as the Trifecta (punters must predict first, second and third in the correct order in the day's designated race) and the Quadpot (requires the selection of horses to be placed in the last four of the Placepot races) have their band of loyal followers but, from a professional's point of view, they are best left alone.

The Tote Scoop6 was designed to give the small-staking punter the same opportunity of winning a life-changing sum of money as the bigger, more professionally run syndicates. It's a weekly bet which every Saturday involves picking the winners of six designated races, all of which are normally shown live on Channel 4.

Money bet is pooled and distributed among that week's successful punters, who are then eligible to increase their winnings substantially by predicting the winner of the designated 'bonus' race the following Saturday.

Once again, it's a 'National Lottery' type of bet. Those people who bet to supplement their wages won't be interested, but the dreamers will. Let's leave them in dreamland and get on with the task of winning consistently – with singles.

PART SIX

BETTING ON-COURSE

THE RACECOURSE BETTING RING

By NICK PULFORD

is one of the most colourful aspects of the British racing scene. While its rituals can seem confusing to the novice racegoer, the daily battle of wits in the ring is, to many, the very essence of the sport's attraction. In contrast to the uniform prices generated by the faceless tote system which dominates in most other major racing nations, the on-course betting rings of Britain (and Ireland) offer a one-to-one, face-to-face interaction between punter and bookmaker that is fast-moving, exciting and almost gladiatorial.

The on-course betting market is a vital component of the UK horserace gambling machine, as the odds set at each race meeting also determine the starting prices (SPs) available to betting-shop punters around the country.

The importance of the on-course market is not in direct proportion to the sums invested there, as turnover is relatively low on-course compared to the massive sums generated off-course. Roughly £20,000 is staked on-course on each bread-and-butter race, but the betting patterns produced by that money determine the odds at which £1 million of bets are settled off-course.

The wider picture was provided by the Gambling Review Group's 2001 report, which said: "On-course betting is not subject to duty and there is no requirement to keep

In the ring: the on-course market is a vital part of the betting industry

official records but on-course betting turnover in 1997 at horseraces and greyhound tracks is estimated to have been around £700m, less than a tenth of overall betting turnover."

However, most observers agree that a robust on-course market is vital to the overall health and integrity of the whole betting industry, mainly because of the need for SPs to be independent of the major off-course chains.

ON-COURSE BASICS There are three main places to bet at a racecourse – with a bookmaker in the ring or on the rails; with the Tote; or in a betting shop.

The biggest players by far are the ring and rails bookmakers, who are believed to account for about 78% of on-course betting turnover. A further 18% is spent on the Tote and the remainder in on-course betting shops. (Gambling Review Group report 2001, section 9.34, from figures given by the Monopolies & Mergers Commission in 1998).

There are restrictions on where the various betting organisations are allowed on course – for instance, rails bookmakers are so-called because they operate alongside the fence, or rails, dividing the Tattersalls enclosure (the main ring at each racecourse, where most of the betting activity takes place) and the members' enclosure, where betting is prohibited. According to the National Joint Pitch Council, which is responsible for the administration of the betting rings on all racecourses, an estimated 90% of all public areas on-course are available to the Tote, 8% to racecourse bookmakers and 2% to betting shops. (Gambling Review Group report 2001, section 9.34.)

Ring bookmakers display their prices on boards, usually from about 15 minutes before the start of each race, though they may offer prices on the day's big race from the start of the race meeting. These prices are subject to rapid fluctuations according to the amount of money placed on each horse – one major influence on the market is money placed by the off-course betting-shop chains, who may hold large liabilities on a certain horse and therefore 'lay off' some of their potential losses with the on-course bookmakers, thereby contracting the price and reducing the amount they will have to pay out to SP punters in the shops if the horse wins.

The boards also display each bookmaker's terms – for example, the minimum stake and the each-way terms available on a particular race.

Most on-course betting is straight win or each-way and punters (having found the bookmaker showing the biggest odds on their selection) place a bet with the bookmaker by stating the horse they want to back, the amount to be staked and the type of bet. The bookmaker then repeats the name of the horse, the stake and the odds at which the bet has been accepted. This information is usually recorded on tape (in case of any later dispute) and the punter, after handing over the stake, receives a computer receipt confirming the details of the bet. If the selected horse wins the race, the punter should wait for the 'weighed-in' announcement confirming the result before

uncommon knowledge

**Betting away
from the ring**

On-course alternatives

Like the betting ring, the on-course Tote can be a sensitive mechanism and bigger-staking punters often prefer to bet with the bookmakers due to the likelihood that investing a large sum into the Tote pool will shorten the odds dramatically (no prices can be taken at the time of the bet with the Tote, which declares the winning dividend only after the race has finished). As a rule of thumb, Tote odds tend to compare more favourably with SPs at bigger meetings such as the Cheltenham Festival, where pools are larger and stronger, in bigger fields (more than 12 runners) and on long-priced outsiders.

The on-course betting shop operates like any off-course establishment and, along with the Tote, offers the facility to bet at other race meetings. The other option for a bet at another racecourse is with an 'away' bookmaker in the main ring, though their odds are often seen as offering poor value.

Another variation is that, in races with a long odds-on favourite, ring bookmakers may offer betting 'without the favourite', which is a book based on all runners in the race apart from the favourite. A 'without the favourite' bet is a winner if the selection wins or finishes second to the favourite.

returning to the bookmaker's pitch to collect the winnings. The winnings are paid out in cash, along with the returned stake money.

The Tote has a considerable on-course presence, though its turnover is only a fraction of the amount that passes through the betting ring. The bets on offer with the Tote are detailed in chapter 16, page 148.

THE ON-COURSE MARKET One of the attractions of on-course betting is the price competition between the individual bookmakers. The initial prices 'chalked up' on the boards may be fairly uniform, as they are compiled from the 'tissue' or betting forecast in the Racing Post, but variations quickly appear between bookmakers, who will have different liabilities on the horses in each race. Even seemingly small variations, like 3-1 and 7-2, can make all the difference to a punter's profitability.

On-course punters always have the chance of securing better than the generally available price – they are always on the lookout for the one bookmaker who offers 11-4 when all the rest are displaying 5-2 on their boards. This is not an option open to off-course punters close to the off, as the prices relayed from the racecourse to the betting shops are a reflection of the general odds – 5-2 in this case. The off-course punter would not even know 11-4 was on offer in a place and would not get the opportunity to take that price.

However, just as the daily on-course betting market can be highly volatile, so the 'value' available there has been subject to some major shifts in recent years. In December 1998, there was a big shake-up in the system of allocating and transferring bookmakers' pitches, which until that point had been viewed as something of a closed shop. The first public auction of bookmakers' pitches took place that month, bringing new faces into the betting ring.

Margins quickly went down as the newcomers offered better prices in an attempt to secure a bigger slice of turnover, which was to the advantage of on-course punters, though betting-shop customers also benefited due to the knock-on effect on starting prices.

In October 2001, however, the on-course market's major advantage was wiped out when off-course betting duty was abolished. From 1987 (when on-course betting tax was abolished) until that point, the betting-shop punter had been subject to a tax rate of up to ten per cent on all bets, while the same punter could have the same bet on-course and pay no tax.

The immediate effect of the October 2001 tax change was to push margins back up – a trend that was assisted, according to some observers, by a settling-down of the on-course betting rings as a number of the new pitch owners left the business and something like the old order was re-established.

Around the same time, however, the betting

exchanges started to have an effect on the market both on- and off-course. On-course bookmakers began to lay off their liabilities with the exchanges, instead of within the betting ring, leading to claims that this practice was weakening the on-course market and distorting starting prices, leading to lower margins and, in turn, damaging off-course bookmakers.

Those hostile to the use of exchanges claimed that, if a racecourse bookmaker offered 3-1 when 7-2 was available on an exchange, he could back the horse at 7-2 and perhaps even push his own price out to 100-30. If there was money for the horse, whereas he would previously have cut its odds to below 3-1, he could now keep it at 3-1 or even 100-30, because he could still make a profit.

It was alleged that this practice contravened the National Joint Pitch Council rule forbidding bets being laid off "other than with an authorised bookmaker". However, in April 2003, the Levy Board decided to give on-course bookmakers the freedom of the market by allowing them to hedge with betting exchanges and off-course layers for the first time.

This was seen as a victory for the exchanges and for punters, who could expect better prices through lower margins, but some claimed that it was another nail in the coffin of the SP system. There was concern that any further fall in margins would lead the major off-course bookmakers to press for reform of the SP system, or even to come up with an alternative pricing model (the so-called 'industry SP') which would reflect their own liabilities.

THE STARTING PRICE The system of deciding the prices on which billions of pounds and millions of horseracing bets are settled in Britain each year had, until the turn of the 21st century, been relatively unchanged for almost 150 years. Essentially, the starting price of each horse was taken on-course by at least two independent returners, who agreed the SP from their observations of prices on racecourse bookmakers' boards. Radical change is afoot, however, with the traditional manual system due to give way to a computer-assisted process by April 2004. The principles will remain the same, but the time-honoured method of using independent returners will be replaced by prices taken from on-course bookmakers' computers. These prices will be turned into SPs for each horse, according to the existing formula.

The SP Executive, the body responsible for collecting and administering SP returns, is also set for major reform. Traditionally, administration has been under the auspices of major media outlets (after 1998, this comprised the two organisations responsible for gathering the information – Trinity Mirror, publisher of the Racing Post, and the Press Association – with Satellite Information Services (SIS) acting as observer). The 21st century model, however, is a five-member panel of independent people with experience of the racing and betting industries. The Press Association will take on a managerial role, with Trinity Mirror ceasing to play a part in the day-to-day operation, though it could have a place on the executive.

THE HISTORY OF SPs From an article by Howard Wright in the Racing Post on November 6, 2003: In the early 19th century, up to half a dozen starting prices were returned by different newspapers, but some time after The Sporting Life was founded in 1859, it and The Sportsman produced a single accepted price, determined through agreement by one reporter. A disagreement in 1905 led to their producing separate SPs for seven years, but eventually the two newspapers merged.

In the late 1920s, The Sporting Chronicle, which was first published in 1872, took up the joint SP operation with The Sporting Life. That arrangement ended in 1983, when The Sporting Chronicle closed. For a time Mirror Group Newspapers was solely responsible for returning prices, until owner Robert Maxwell gave way to complaints from bookmaking organisations and agreed to a joint arrangement with the Press Association.

When MGN bought the Racing Post from Sheikh Mohammed, and The Sporting Life ceased publication on May 12, 1998, the system for returning SPs through the deliberations of two or more men, employed by MGN (later Trinity Mirror) and PA, survived. Meanwhile, SIS, which like the Racing Post came into being in 1986, had entered the fray, using racecourse reporters to produce betting shows for its shop customers while having no input to the finalisation of the SP.

The biggest change to the PA/MGN operation came less than two years ago when, after a study by auditors Arthur Andersen, criteria for deciding which and how many bookmakers should be used as the sample from which to obtain SPs were laid down. Reporters were given less discretion over the prices they should return.

Now the system faces its most radical shake-up ever, in which machines will replace men and validators will replace determiners.

THE ON-COURSE PUNTER

As several experts point out in this book, serious punters should watch as much racing as possible and there can be advantages in seeing the sport live. Aside from the excitement of a day at the races, the on-course punter is perceived to have more information at his fingertips when he places a bet, having been able to assess the weather and going, the fitness and well-being of the runners, and the state of the betting market.

Professional punter Alan Potts says going racing plays an essential part in his betting. He says: "Categorically, the biggest benefit is being able to see things in three dimensions instead of two – you get a much clearer picture of a race from seeing it live than you do from watching on TV, especially nowadays when producers seem to prefer arty camera angles or focus only on the leaders, instead of showing how the whole race is unfolding. At the racecourse, you decide what you want to watch.

"When I'm on course, I never bet a horse on the Flat without watching them going down. I'm looking for athleticism, a horse that wants to stretch out. So many horses make it look like an effort, and they're the ones to avoid."

In the race, Potts says: "I'm looking for a horse on the Flat with the power to stamp his authority on a race a couple of furlongs out. Others may close in the final furlong and get noted as unlucky fast finishers, but those tend not to represent value as future bets in the long term. Over jumps, I'm looking for sound jumpers, those who can accelerate into a fence or hurdle and land running."

Two horses Potts picked out early on were La Landiere and Kingscliff, both of whom went on to win at the 2003 Cheltenham Festival.

"I saw La Landiere win a mares' novice chase at Wincanton and followed her through the winter [she won four more races on the trot after that, including the Racing Post Chase and the Cathcart at Cheltenham]. She did everything so fluently. She jumped straight at every fence, which is rare for a jumper."

Potts also recalls seeing Kingscliff when he won his first hunter chase at Wincanton in February 2003, before landing the Cheltenham Foxhunter the following month and going on to make the grade in the top chasing ranks.

He says: "With Kingscliff, it was his pure presence in the paddock. It's always hard to put into words what you mean, but with experience you develop a feel for these things. He was also the best jumper I'd seen in a hunter chase since Double Silk [the Cheltenham Foxhunter winner in 1993 and '94] and he was a big bet for me at Cheltenham."

MARKET MOVES The off-course punter's reading of the market depends on the quality of information supplied in the betting shops and on television, but in theory the on-course punter

uncommon knowledge

 Steamers and drifters

Mark Coton, in his book One Hundred Hints for Better Betting (Aesculus), is quite clear about the approach to 'steamers' – horses who become popular gambles and contract rapidly in price. "Don't follow the herd and join in these gambles," he says. "If you have taken the best price all well and good. If not, stay out. The value will nearly always have gone."

Coton argued that if the horse you have backed drifts in the betting, back it again: the selection has not become a bad bet because the betting market appears to be against you.

Alan Potts says the best punters rely on their judgement and form study. "I don't follow market moves because I'm betting my opinion and nobody else's," he says. 'If the horse I want to back shortens up, I might walk away because the value has gone. But I've backed plenty of winners who have drifted on-course."

is able to see – and react to – changes in the market much more quickly.

However, while market movers are heavily touted on TV and in the newspapers, most serious punters would take little note of them, even on-course. There are too many nagging questions – who is backing the horse? Why? Is the money a reaction to outside influences, such as the horse being a Pricewise selection in the Racing Post, or inside information? Punters generally cannot know all the answers but most experts would say that the reply will be no to the most important question: is there any value in backing a market mover?

Two high-profile examples from 2003 illustrate the difficulty of knowing when to follow the market. In the 1,000 Guineas, Russian Rhythm drifted on the day from 6-1 to 12-1 after reportedly working unconvincingly in the run-up to the race. She won by one and a half lengths, however, and many punters might have asked: how could a filly beaten only once in four outings have been allowed to go off at 12-1?

The opposite happened in the Derby. Kris Kin, virtually unconsidered a month before the Classic, had come down to 12-1 on the morning of the race after an impressive win in his previous race at Chester. He was the subject of a wholesale gamble on Derby Day, tumbling to 6-1 after being selected by some high-profile tipping services, before running out a one-length winner.

The only common theme in this tale of two Classic winners was that both horses were trained by Sir Michael Stoute and ridden by the champion jockey, Kieren Fallon.

Market moves, then, appear to be a flimsy basis on which to make a selection. Where they might prove more profitable is as one of the planks from which to build a future selection – if a horse was backed last time, then perhaps there was some confidence behind the horse even if it didn't win. It pays to be wary of such information for the reasons already outlined, but it can be of some use in assessing a horse's chance.

PART SEVEN

NEW
MEDIA

By NICK PULFORD

ONCE UPON A TIME THERE WERE only bookmakers and punters. How times have changed. The advent of spread betting, and more recently betting exchanges, has redrawn the traditional boundaries of the betting landscape. We can all be bookmakers and punters now.

This section looks in detail at this fast-growing sector, offering practical advice on how to get the best out of the new opportunities available on the exchanges and spreads.

Leading Racing Post tipster Nick Fox, who writes the highly successful Trading Bureau column, offers a survival guide to the exciting, yet risky, new world that has opened up to punters over the past decade. He explains how to read the market and its various players, and how to make a book and get the best odds.

Matt Williams of the Racing Post provides a punter's view of the turnaround in betting fortunes which can be gained from the new betting media. He offers tips on how to make a success of betting in running and the skill involved in placing the right bet at the right price.

Some sobering thoughts, however. Nick Fox estimates that only 15 per cent of exchange punters are in profit, while the opportunity to play bookmaker by laying horses is no guarantee of riches. Betfair, the leading exchange, has said that less than one per cent of its clients make more than £15,000 a year.

up close and personal

EXCHANGE OF VIEWS

THE BETTING EXCHANGES HAVE By NICK PULFORD
transformed the UK horserace gambling market
since their introduction in the late 1990s. Peer-
to-peer (P2P), or person-to-person betting,
as it is also known, has proved one of the success
stories of the dotcom era, being conducted almost
entirely via the internet.

Turnover is still relatively small in comparison
with the huge amounts generated off-course by
the Big Three bookmakers (Ladbrokes, William
Hill and Coral Eurobet), but the rise of the
betting exchanges represents a remarkable
cultural shift in a business previously regarded
as being in the pocket of the major bookmaking
firms.

The exchanges themselves are now major
companies within the betting industry, with
Betfair claiming the bulk of the market share
and most of the rest taken up by Betdaq, GGBet
and Sporting Options. However, they differ from
traditional bookmakers in that they have no
direct financial interest in the result of a race
or other event. Unlike traditional bookmaking,
the odds on the betting exchanges are formed
entirely by the players, who can choose to
bet (as with a traditional bookmaker) or lay
(effectively 'crossing the fence' to become a
bookmaker). The exchange operators operate
as 'middle men' in the transaction, taking a
commission (normally five per cent) from the
winning player's profit, whatever the outcome.

Betting exchanges have transformed the picture for punters and bookies

The betting exchanges are widely expected to grow exponentially, though accurate predictions are difficult as they are still in a honeymoon period and it is possible that their fortunes could dip if they encounter bad publicity or a fall in punter confidence due to some of the drawbacks outlined later in this chapter. Another limiting factor could be the market dominance of Betfair, which has become almost a generic name for betting exchanges and therefore attracts most of the business.

Another question mark is the future attitude of governments to this 'new' industry. Betfair's planned expansion into potentially lucrative markets such as Australia and Hong Kong has met resistance amid concerns about the financial and 'integrity' risks, and it is possible that similar worries could take root in the UK. The tax position of exchanges, and in particular layers, is also under review

Each betting exchange holds a bookmaker's licence in the UK, though technically they do not make a book, but it is the status of individual 'layers' on the exchanges that has aroused

uncommon knowledge

 On the exchanges

The simple rules

When you back a selection, you are betting that it will win. When you lay it, you are betting against it winning. In essence, therefore, the exchanges boil down to the age-old principle of two people having a wager on the outcome of a race or event.

All betting exchanges use a similar layout. A line is drawn down the centre of the page, with the odds for backing on the left-hand side and the odds for laying on the right-hand side. The best price in either category (back or lay) always appears in the column nearest the centre and is highlighted in colour. The prices are displayed in bold, usually in decimal odds, though one or two firms offer traditional odds. In the decimal odds format, 2.5 = 6-4, 3 = 2-1, and so on, and underneath is the stake available at that price (eg, the price 3 with the figure £250 underneath means that you can stake a maximum of £250 at odds of 2-1). You do not have to take all the stake available – you can usually set your stake anywhere from £2 up to the maximum.

If you back a selection at 3 (ie, 2-1) with a £100 stake, your gross return (including your stake and less 5% commission) would be £290 (£200 winnings less 5% commission = £190 + £100 stake = £290).

Alternatively, you could lay a selection at 3 for £100. If the selection loses, you receive the backer's stake of £100, less 5% commission on your profit, making a total return of £95. If the selection wins, however, you must pay the backer £300 (ie, £200 winnings + the returned stake). In this case, you do not pay commission (always paid by the winning party). Once the odds offered by a layer are accepted by a backer (or vice versa), the bet is 'matched' by the exchange and cannot be altered or withdrawn, although you can continue betting as the market moves to increase or decrease your liability.

the greatest controversy. Bookmakers have argued that, because individuals are acting as bookmakers, they should also hold a licence.

HOW EXCHANGES WORK When betting with a conventional bookmaker, it is the bookmaker who either compiles the odds himself or takes the market prices, and the individual bets against the bookmaker. Although it is often said that punters are effectively playing against each other when they bet with a bookmaker

uncommon knowledge

On the exchanges

A licence to win money?

On the vexed issue of whether exchange punters should have to hold bookmakers' licences, the Racing Post's Nick Fox says: "We can bet legally, quickly and efficiently on the shares of British companies falling as well as rising. We don't need a licence for that, so why should we need one to bet against a horse at Fontwell?" Currently, the government has not appeared minded to impose regulation on betting exchanges but future policy is uncertain in a rapidly changing environment.

Expanding on the argument that exchanges and the punters who use them are not of themselves a threat to racing's integrity, Fox adds: "Backing two horses in a three-runner race is no different to laying the third horse. The exchanges allow us to do this more efficiently and cheaply. Nobody from the Jockey Club asks for names and addresses of punters who back more than one horse in a race, so why should they be any more worried by layers on the exchanges?"

due to the in-built profit margin in the book, this is literally the case with betting exchanges as the operator acts only as a go-between for two bettors with opposing views.

On one side is the backer, who wants to put money on a selection in the conventional way. On the other side is the layer, who will offer odds to other punters. The operator facilitates this 'exchange' by providing the medium for odds to be displayed (usually an internet site), providing the means by which the money involved in any bet is transacted, and by taking a commission from the winning party's profit.

There is no 'welching' on bets as each player must lodge money in their account, at least enough to cover the potential loss on any bet. Once a bet is completed, the betting exchange transfers the appropriate amount of money from the losing party to the winner's account.

One of the key attractions of the betting

exchanges is the opportunity to name your own price. If you want to back or lay at better odds than are currently available, you can place an order for a better price. For example, if your selection is shown at 5-2 {3.5} and you want 3-1 {4.0}, you can lodge an 'order' for 3-1 {4.0} at your designated stake. If a layer wants to accept your stake at those odds, the bet will be matched. If not, it will remain unmatched. Or, if you decide against the bet before it is matched, you can withdraw it. There is a certain skill in setting your own price as it requires good reading of the market and a sense of realism because there has to be somebody prepared to lay the bet at those odds, and vice versa.

Another exciting innovation with betting exchanges has been the introduction of 'in-running' (or 'in-play') betting, which means players can back or lay once a race has started. In-running betting operates as normal, but as a separate market to any previous markets (eg ante-post) on the race.

Betting continues as normal prior to the race, but at the 'off' all unmatched bets are cancelled and the market is turned in-play. This allows you to leave an order on the system, say two days before the race, and know that it will be cancelled automatically when the race starts (if it has not already been matched). There is no further intervention by the betting exchange until the end of the race, at which point betting is suspended and all unmatched bets are cancelled. If a photo or a stewards' inquiry is announced, betting is usually re-opened as a new market.

Apart from straightforward odds betting, the exchanges also offer variations on spread betting with line and range betting. One of the most common lines on horseracing is the aggregate of the winning distances at a race meeting. In this case, the number in bold is the predicted aggregate and punters have the option of buying (ie betting that the aggregate will be higher) or selling (ie betting that the aggregate will be lower). This is always a bet at evens and so, unlike spread betting, there is reduced scope for big gains or losses.

THE ADVANTAGES

The advantages of betting exchanges are the ones which for years punters wished they could have had with bookmakers, but for business reasons were never offered. The exchanges take the principle of betting your opinion against another to its logical conclusion.

Value Odds on the betting exchanges are set by individuals, not by professional odds compilers, and this leads to more price variation than can be found with the high-street bookmakers. According to Betfair, the over-round of a race with a conventional bookmaker is typically 120%, whereas with betting exchanges the average over-round is 102%. This makes betting exchanges very appealing from a 'value' point of view.

Opposing bad-value favourites Previously the sole preserve of the bookmaker, this is now an option for all players on the exchanges. Every experienced punter has the ability to spot a bad favourite in a big 20-runner handicap; now, rather than having to find the winner, their bet on the race can be to lay the favourite. If they can find the winner at the same time, so much the better, but it is no longer the essential part of horserace betting.

Choosing your own price If you don't get that price, no bet is matched, but at least you have had a realistic opportunity to strike a bet at a price you believe is value.

One of the biggest perceived advantages of the betting exchanges is the possibility, often in conjunction with other betting media, of backing horses and laying others in the same race to gain an arbitrage position (ie, one in which you cannot lose whatever the outcome). While arbitrage can be achieved sometimes due to the variation in prices on the exchanges, it is by no means always possible and may be an overrated advantage.

THE DISADVANTAGES Most of the media coverage on betting exchanges has been so favourable that it appears there is no downside to the phenomenon. While the exchanges are presented as a medium for ordinary punters with opposing views to pit their wits against each other, without the edge enjoyed by conventional bookmakers, this is not always the case.

Many of the layers on the exchanges possess at least a high level of expertise (in the case of professional punters looking to exploit their advantage), inside knowledge (in the case of those connected to racing stables) or bookmaking skill (in the case of on-course bookies now allowed to lay off via the exchanges). While the bookmakers have always enjoyed the same advantages over punters, it pays to be wary of prices that look too good to be true. If an ante-post favourite is available at very attractive odds two days before a race or a hot favourite drifts markedly on the day of a race, it pays to ask: does someone know something about this horse?

When comparing prices available on the exchanges and elsewhere, punters must factor in the commission on winning bets. Effectively the commission brought a return to betting tax, at a time when it had just been abolished in betting shops, and perceptions of value can be coloured if the commission element of the price is ignored.

Most importantly, it pays to bear in mind that the magic number 2 (evens) is effectively odds-on if a successful bet is placed, due to the commission taken from the winnings. The real figure to look for on the exchanges is 2.05 (which represents evens once the commission on winnings is taken into account).

Mistakes Although the exchanges all offer a step-by-step guide to the facility, their 'newness' has undoubtedly contributed to punters making elementary errors. Among the most common are selecting back instead of lay (or vice versa), entering the wrong stake (eg £100 instead of

Delayed reaction: the fastest TV pictures are vital for in-running betting

£10) and entering the wrong odds (33 instead of 3.3 to lay a favourite, for instance).

The downside of in-running punting In-running betting is one of the most attractive features of the betting exchanges but it can be a high-risk market, requiring quick-fire decisions on the horses to back or lay and the odds available. The speed at which the market changes in the course of a five-furlong sprint, run in less than a minute, can be bewildering and increases the likelihood of bets being taken or laid in error.

Also, it has become well known that the transmission delay in TV pictures differs between the various providers such as Attheraces, SIS and the terrestrial channels, giving some viewers a time advantage over others and therefore an edge in seeing how a race is unfolding.

'Con' tricks Because exchange punters make mistakes, a whole sub-culture has developed in an effort to exploit them. The golden rules are: make sure you're betting in the right event and make sure you understand the price.

making the right move

SPREAD THE RISK

SPREAD BETTING BROKE THE

By NICK PULFORD

mould of conventional fixed-odds gambling when it emerged into the mainstream in the early 1990s. Until then, the concept had been popular in the City for around 20 years as a means of betting on the ups and downs of the stock market as well as sporting events, but was little known beyond the financial dealing rooms.

Spread betting quickly took off as it presented the first large-scale opportunity for punters to bet both for and against a particular outcome – ie in horseracing, for horses (particularly favourites) to perform well or badly.

Like the betting exchanges, this opened up the possibility of betting on a race without necessarily having to find the winner. Another key attraction was that some spread bets provided the punter with an interest in the whole day's racing, rather than just one horse in a particular race.

The leading spread-betting firms now offer a range of markets on horseracing and general sports, though the high level of risk and the perceived complexity of the concept have limited its appeal mainly to high-rollers and more experienced punters.

In addition, the Racing Post's Nick Fox points out, "spread-betting firms are under fire from the exchanges. They need to take more risk themselves by lowering margins if they want to revive sports-betting business."

On the job: trading room at Sporting Index, one of the main spread firms

HOW DOES IT WORK? The basic premise is simple. The spread-betting firm sets a range which it believes covers the likely outcome of a race or other event. The punter has to decide whether the result will be higher or lower than the spread – if he thinks it will be higher, he 'buys' the spread at the higher quote. If he thinks it will be lower, he 'sells' at the lower figure. In both cases, the punter decides on the stake and the profit/loss on the bet is calculated by multiplying the stake by each point the result finishes above or below the buy/sell figure.

This means that the more right you are, the more you win. But, equally, the more wrong you are, the more you lose. Placing a £10 bet with a traditional fixed-odds bookmaker means all that can be lost is £10, but with spread betting you can win and lose many multiples of your £10 stake because the stake is not the limit of your financial risk. This makes spread betting both more exciting and more risky for the punter.

THE MARKETS There are three basic types of spread markets – total bets, supremacy bets

On the spreads

The simple rules

Take the Favourites Index – one of the most popular horseracing spreads. The question with this market is: how will the favourites perform overall at a particular meeting?

A winning favourite is awarded 25 points, with 10 points for a second place and five points for a third place, with the result calculated on the points accumulated by all the favourites at the meeting. In the event of a race starting with joint favourites, the favourite is usually taken as being the horse with the lower racecard number.

The opening spread might be 44-47 points. The punter must decide whether to sell (go low) at 44 if he thinks the favourites will perform worse than predicted, or buy (go high) at 47 if he thinks the favourites will fare better than predicted. If, at the end of the meeting, two favourites have won and another has finished second, the points make-up will be 60 (2 x 25 = 50, + 1 x 10 = 60).

With a stake of £10, a buyer's winnings would be £130. This is calculated from the difference between the final make-up of the market (60) and the buy figure (47), so 60 – 47 = 13 x stake = 13 x £10 = £130.

If, on the other hand, the punter sold the favourites at 44, the loss to a £10 stake would be £160. This is calculated from the difference between the final make-up of the market (60) and the sell figure (44), so 60 – 44 = 16 x stake = 16 x £10 = £160.

and index bets. Total bets are decided by the totals of certain numbers such as the aggregate winning distances at a race meeting. Supremacy bets mean that the interest is not on who will win, but by how much. Bets are generally on the margin of victory, or supremacy, of one performer over another (eg two horses in a race). Index bets mean that where, for example, lengths are not suitable to measure success, an index can be created which allows prices to be offered. A different number of points will be awarded to the winner, runner-up and third-placed horse – the Favourites Index is an example of this type of bet (see panel).

Spread betting is far more volatile than fixed-odds betting and spread quotes are fluctuating all the time on 'in running' markets, giving the punter the option of closing the bet before the end of the event.

Take the Favourites Index. The spread will change after each race depending on the finishing positions of the favourites up to that point of the race meeting and whether the favourites still to run are proving popular or not. If the favourites are performing better than expected, the spread will move upwards to reflect the likelihood of a higher points total – if the first two favourites have won, for example, the score will already stand at 50 and the opening spread (perhaps 44-47) will have risen considerably.

Buyers will be sitting pretty at this stage with a guaranteed profit of three times their stake even if the remaining favourites are unplaced – the final make-up will be at least 50 (three points higher than the buy price of 47).

But the seller of the spread at the opening 44-47 is already certain to lose six times their stake, and probably much more – the final make-up will be at least 50 (six points higher than the sell price of 44). The seller, however, has the chance to 'get out' of the market and limit his losses. If, after two races, he decides the new spread is likely to be exceeded, he can close the bet and take a loss. If, however, he thinks the remaining favourites will perform poorly and the total will not reach the lower end of the new spread, he can let the bet continue. Although he will still lose on the bet, his losses will be smaller if the final make-up is only 60, but much bigger if the final make-up reaches 100 or more.

On the other hand, the Favourites Index spread may move downwards if, say, the first three favourites are all unplaced. The seller would then hold the aces and be able to decide whether to close the bet at a profit – if the spread moves down to 30-32, the seller could close the bet with a guaranteed win. This is calculated by the difference between the original sell price (44) and the new (buy/sell) price.

In this scenario, it would be the buyer of

the original 44-47 spread who would be worrying about whether the final make-up would be sufficient to cover the spread. Again, the buyer could get out at this stage with a guaranteed loss or let the bet continue in the hope that the remaining favourites would perform better.

The Favourites Index is an example of a market with a maximum make-up – at a six-race meeting, six winning favourites would make up to 150 points (25 x 6) while six unplaced favourites would make up to zero. This means that the final make-up must fall between 0 and 150 and punters can know the maximum profit/loss on a bet before placing a bet.

The main horseracing spread bets have a maximum make-up but some markets in other sports (eg total runs in cricket) do not, which raises the possibility of a substantial loss if events turn against the punter. For this reason, spread-betting firms operate a stop-loss policy on some markets and offer the same facility to punters on other markets.

A stop-loss means that your bet will stop once the make-up of a market reaches a specified figure. For example, on the Favourites Index spread of 44-47 a seller could have a stop-loss of 120, meaning that the maximum loss on the bet is 76 (120 – 44) x stake. Some spread-betting firms will offer special accounts or markets where a spread bet is automatically subject to a maximum stop-loss. This means you will know the most you can win or lose every time you place a bet.

THE ADVANTAGES Spread betting is exciting, fast-moving and offers possible massive returns for a low investment – because the odds are not fixed, a punter can win a lot more than in traditional betting if he is able to predict the outcome of an event better than the bookmaker.

Flexibility As with betting exchanges, punters have the opportunity to back horses to do well, or to do badly. You don't even have to be exactly right, either – as long as you are in the right direction, you will make a profit.

In-running betting Some markets offer betting 'in running', which means bets can be closed before the end of the event, enabling you to 'lock in' a profit regardless of the final outcome.

Security Spread betting is regulated by the Financial Services Authority (FSA) and, unlike with a traditional bookmaker, debts on both sides are recoverable by law.

No tax Betting tax is absorbed by the spread-betting firms and there is no commission on bets.

THE DISADVANTAGES Spread betting is a high-risk form of gambling and the spread-betting firms all carry prominent warnings about the dangers involved. Many spread-betting markets are very volatile and, while there is the potential for a massive return, there is also the risk of a big loss if the punter fails to predict the outcome of an event better than the book-maker. One misjudged bet can make huge inroads into a punter's account. Punters should always be aware of the maximum downside and the fixed-odds equivalent they are betting at, in order to evaluate the risk and 'value' involved in any bet.

Spread betting is not considered suitable for smaller, low-risk punters who are unwilling or unable to absorb big losses. However, punters can guard against big losses by placing a 'guaranteed stop-loss' on their account or by opening a limited-risk (or shield) account. With these accounts you will know the maximum you can win or lose on each bet.

TYPES OF BET Spread betting has developed a new range of bets on a race or race meeting, with the main types outlined below. The guide includes the most common points-scoring systems used by the spread-betting firms but there are variations, so punters should always check the rules of a market before placing a bet.

Favourites index The spread is an estimation of how the favourites will perform in each race at a particular meeting. A favourite earns 25 points for a win, 10 points for a second place and five points for a third place. In the event of a race starting with joint favourites, the favourite is usually taken as being the horse with the lower racecard number.

Racing Post favourites index This is based on the same principle as the Favourites Index but the favourites are those listed in the betting forecast below each racecard in the Racing Post. The advantage of this bet can be that the punter knows which horses he is basing the bet on before the meeting starts, rather than having to wait for the betting market to determine the SP favourite. Points are awarded on the same basis as the Favourites Index.

Racecard double numbers The make-up is double the total racecard number of the winners of each race in a meeting. So, for example, if horse number 6 wins the first race then 12 points are allocated.

Starting prices (SPs) of winning horses The aggregate sum of the starting prices of the winners at a race meeting. A maximum SP is normally set, such as 50-1, even if a horse wins at a greater price.

Stop at a winner How many races on a card will elapse before a favourite wins? The make-up will usually be a multiple of the number of that race, such as ten times.

Winning distances The spread is an estimation of the total winning margins at a race meeting. A maximum winning distance will normally be set, for example 15 lengths for a Flat race and 30 lengths for a National Hunt race. This also applies should only one horse complete the race. Distances under a length will be given fractions of a length: short head = 0.1 of a length, head = 0.2 of a length, neck = 0.3 of a length, half a length = 0.5 of a length, three-quarters of a length = 0.75 of a length.

Jockey index The spread represents a jockey's performance, where selected jockeys are awarded various performance points based upon their results, usually at big meetings such

Short heads: betting on winning distances is a popular spread market

as the Cheltenham Festival. The points allocated for finishing positions in each race may vary between spread-betting firms, but often a jockey earns 25 points for a win, 10 points for a second place and five points for a third place.

Race index A bet may be offered about the performance of horses in individual races, awarding points according to official finishing positions. This market allows the punter to back or oppose a horse, something which traditional fixed-odds betting does not offer. The points allocated may vary between spread-betting firms and depends on the number of runners, but often a horse earns 50 points for a win, 25 points for second place and 10 points for third place in races with up to 12 runners, and 50 points for a win, 30 for second place, 20 for third place and 10 for fourth place in a race with more than 12 runners.

Match bets The distance between two nominated horses in a race at the finish. A maximum distance will normally be applied – for example, 12 lengths in a Flat race and 15 lengths in a jumps race.

exchanges and the odds

A SURVIVAL GUIDE

THE TERM 'PUNTER' IS OUTDATED.
Trader or investor might be a better term for those who bet on sports in the 21st century. And whatever those who seek to profit from predicting the outcome of sports events are called, they have never had it so good.

Over recent years, the choice facing old-time punters has never been clearer. Those who want to profit from sports betting now have an excellent opportunity to do just that, with margins slim to non-existent for those willing to give up the delights of the betting shop for a lonely day in front of a PC.

With no betting tax and internet betting exchanges joining traditional fixed-odds book-makers and spread firms, the days when the only real decision was to back win or each-way are happily in the past.

Betfair, the leading exchange, would not give the precise proportion of their clients whose accounts are in profit. But my feeling is that a figure of around 15 per cent would not be far off the mark. Of course, the exchange system means that for every winner there has to be a loser. It is up to us all to decide how much effort we put in to make sure we are one of the 15 per cent.

For new-breed punters – let's call them bettors – there are new skills to be learned. An Excel spreadsheet has become as indispensable as the form book. This is the program that will crunch

By NICK FOX

uncommon knowledge

 The spoofer

This guy wants to lay a horse but he tries to make you think he wants to back it, or vice versa. He'll take the chance and put up a very large bet at a price big enough to put you off taking it, but not so big that you won't notice. "Look at that, someone wants five grand on this horse, it must be well fancied and I'll back it," thinks the novice. Those who think like that have fallen into the spoofer's trap – doing precisely what he wants and taking his bet on a horse he thinks will lose.

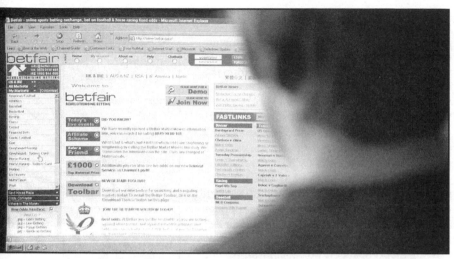

Home work: forget afternoons in the betting shop and compute for profit

uncommon knowledge

The cheat

Gets to know market-sensitive info in advance, such as the selections of the most popular tipsters. He'll back them and wait for the crowd to catch up. When they do and start to back the horse, he'll either lay it back or content himself with being on at a far bigger price than everyone else. There are also those who find out that a horse won't turn up for a big race and lay it ante-post.

the numbers for you in milliseconds and ensure you are making the most of the new opportunities.

Set up in advance, the spreadsheet will tell you in an instant whether you would be better off backing that 7-2 good thing at fixed odds or buying it on the spreads. It will help you compute a 'true' odds book easily and it will keep a record of where you are going right and where you are going wrong.

The majority of my exchange turnover is on football, not horseracing. The reason is simple: while the racing is on, I am usually ploughing through the form of the following day's runners for my Racing Post column. But while my racing turnover is lower, my Betfair history shows it provides more bang for the buck; a higher percentage of profit than the football bets provide.

When I do get the chance to spend a day betting on the exchanges, I have a ready-made advantage. I've already studied the form for the Post the previous day and got paid for the pleasure. Even so, with so much racing, it is impossible to keep up with every race.

The answer, especially for those with proper jobs, is to specialise. Why look at the maiden race when there is a good chance that someone on the exchanges is going to know a lot more than you about the unraced youngster from the big yard?

If you want to make your own book – essential if you want to turn into an exchange winner – then you have more chance of producing decent prices in a race for older horses with plenty of form than in a two- or three-year-old maiden. Making a book is not difficult, especially when you become familiar with decimal odds. These are simply the old prices +1, so 2-1 becomes 3.0, 5-2 becomes 3.5 and so on.

Using a spreadsheet, put in column A your decimal-price estimation for the chance of each runner in a race. Start in space A1. In column B1 enter the formula '=1/a1' and copy this to all the rows for which you have runners.

In cell C1 enter '=1/(sum (B1:B?)). Replace the question mark with the number of the last row in column B. Cell C1 will show a percentage book, 1.0 being a fair book. You can change any price of any horse and cell C1 will show the percentage over or underround.

Remember the market is very efficient. It is not usual that a horse who is a true 3-1 chance will be offered at 8-1. If this happens, it is almost certain that the market is more right about the horse than you are. So be realistic. If there is a big discrepancy between your price and the market, check to see what you have missed.

A decent set of prices to work with is your armour as you battle on the exchanges. You will be able to bet with far more confidence than those who have not done the groundwork.

When you are betting on the exchanges you are facing two barriers to making a profit. One is the exchanges themselves because they charge you commission. But without commission there would be no exchanges and there is not much you can do about it anyway (except by winning or losing more), so this is not something

uncommon knowledge

 On the exchanges

You've got to understand the market

As the race gets close the action on the exchanges starts to heat up. You might see a horse available at 3.5 when, according to your spreadsheet, it should be only 3.1.

A decision to be made then is whether to play straight away or wait in the hope of getting even better value – a decision which might have a better chance of being right if you understand how exchanges and racetrack markets work these days. Many players make the wrong assumption that the exchange follows the track market.

The wonderful cricket broadcaster Brian Johnston used to tell a great story about his early days commentating on the Boat Race. From his position above the Thames, both boats went out of his view for a proportion of the race and, during this period, he used to have to improvise on his radio commentary. He did, however, know which team was in the lead because there was a flag system on the course. One flag raised meant that Oxford was in the lead, the other Cambridge.

This seemed to work fine for several years until one day he met the man who operated the flag system. "Tell me, how do you know who is in the lead? They're out of view from where I am," Johnners asked.

"Oh, I can't see them either," said the flag man, "I find out who's leading by listening to the radio."

Something similar seems to be happening on the betting exchanges when the markets open on course. More frequently, the on-course bookmakers are framing their books according to what is happening on the exchanges. This is especially true at the smaller midweek meetings. When you realise that it is often the exchanges leading the track and not the other way round, you will get a better feel for the way the market is moving.

When placing a bet on the exchanges you are bartering with others about the price for a commodity. Be realistic but firm about the price you want to trade. Horserace betting is a lot more volatile than other financial markets.

Expect the 3.5 chance to hit both 3.4 and 3.6 in a short space of time. That's a good reason to show some patience and not be panicked into taking the first price that is available.

You will find that if you have made a sensible offer the bet will usually be taken even if at times it looks like the price is going against you. Even if it seems that a 3.5 chance is shortening and your 3.6 is not going to be matched you might be surprised how often the market goes back the other way and your bet disappears from the table. Those who chase the price down, panicking that they are going to miss out, often end up with a worse price than a more relaxed player.

we should worry about unduly. The other barrier is the people you are betting against, the rascals trying to take your money!

A newcomer to consider is binarybet.com from the IG Index stable. It is really fixed-odds betting in disguise, in which 100 points are offered for being right and 0 for being wrong.

Here is a snapshot of a soccer market on November 3, 2003, Birmingham v Charlton.

Spot the opportunity? There was £4,060 available for the draw on Betfair at 3.3. If

	Betfair	Binarybet	IG Index (25 win, 10 draw, 0 loss)
Birmingham	2.12/2.14	47.4/52.4	15/16.5
Draw	3.25/3.3	26.5/29.9	–
Charlton	4.5/4.6	21.6/25.1	7/8.5

you took the lot you would stand to lose £9,338 if the match ended in a draw. But if at the same time you had £135 per point buying the draw with Binarybet you would win £9,463.50.

If the match didn't end in a draw you would lose £4,036.50 with binarybet but would get the £4,060 from Betfair. This does not take into account commission but perfectly illustrates the opportunities of exchange and other internet betting.

From the above, you can also work out what the true value of the IG win index ought to be. Say you thought the Betfair prices for Birmingham and the draw were spot on. The chance of Birmingham winning is the mid-price 2.13, which is 46.94 as a percentage (100 divided by 2.13). There are 25 points to the winning team, so Birmingham is worth 25 x 0.4694, which is 11.73. There are 10 points for the draw and the chance of the draw is 3.275. Turn this into a percentage, 100/3.275= 30.53. So 10 x 0.3053 =3.05. Add this 3.05 to the 11.73 for winning and the right mark for the 25-10-0 index should be 14.78, which is slightly below the quote. If you believe the Betfair prices

Overshadowed: opening shows on the on-course market are nowadays often driven by earlier action on the exchanges

uncommon
knowledge

 The hedger

They have backed a horse ante-post at bigger odds and want to take their profits. They are not into haggling – by laying it back at shorter odds than they backed it at, they can guarantee a profit. In my opinion it's wrong to take a profit unless you are sure the second bet is a good one. If the horse you backed is still overpriced, why lay it? If anything, you should be having more on.

to be right there is a bit of profit in selling at 15 with IG.

Betfair have a football market on the half-time score for televised games. The price that the betting public seems anxious to lay is 0-0. This is the price that often ends up bigger than it should based on statistics of the scoring records of each team.

So why is 0-0 a popular lay? My theory is that those who lay the bet know they can actually win at any time during the 45 minutes of the half. One goal and the money is theirs. If a team scores in the first or second minute they can sit back and feel smug about their winnings – and they will win more often than not. Backers, in contrast, have to sit out the whole 45 minutes and any stoppage time, enduring extra stress every time the ball goes near one of the goals. The backers will lose more often than win but will make a profit in the long term if the tendency to lay bigger than true prices on 0-0 continues.

Although I cannot speak for the present as most of my betting has switched to the exchanges, another market that used to be out of touch with reality was cross-corners from the spread firms.

This is where the make-up is the number of corners in the first half multiplied by the number of corners in the second. Even though the price was pitched artificially high, it still used to attract more buyers than sellers. The reason was fear and greed. Fear and greed gives shrewd players the opportunity to make money even in the most efficient of markets, like the stock market.

Fear, in the cross-corners case, was driven by the worry that there would be eight corners in the first half and another eight in the second, to make up 64, which would cost the sellers a packet. Greed is that sellers can look forward to only small profits.

The maximum profit is the selling price, usually around 28, and that requires no corners in one of the halves, an unusual occurrence. Buyers, though, might get up to something above 70 in a good game, giving them a profit of, say, 40 times their stake.

It is a bit puzzling why the exchanges have attracted so much controversy in racing when long before Flutter and Betfair opened, punters already had the opportunity to bet on horses performing badly by selling them with the spread firms. Cynics might suggest that the spread firms did not pose such a threat to bookmakers as the exchanges but let's not get into that argument.

Apart from the pre-exchange opportunity of being able to oppose dubious favourites directly, spread betting for horseracing has long disappointed me. The spread firms rarely take a view against the fixed-odds market and their prices are usually just a mirror image of prices offered by Ladbrokes and chums. Betting both ways and taking a profit before the race starts is near impossible as the margin is too big.

And now, with no tax to pay on fixed odds and the advent of the exchanges, the early attractions

uncommon knowledge

The cheat

With two minutes to play in a Cup game, Manchester United go 4-0 up against Leyton Orient. When the market reopens, the cheat sticks up a £10,000 bet on the Os at 1.02 in the hope that someone clicks the wrong button. He'll offer 1.02 against seven goals or more when it's 0-0 and four minutes to play in another game. He'll also try to lay fallers in running in jumps races. It should be said that one day one of the cheats got his comeuppance when the other horses fell too and the one he'd laid was remounted to win!

uncommon knowledge

On the exchanges

Spotting a mug

Mugs watch the way the market is moving and join in, usually when the bubble is about to burst. In 17th century Holland a speculative frenzy in the sale of tulips led to bulbs changing hands at astronomical prices.

Good on the way up, not so good for those foolish enough to swap their house for a few bulbs just before the market crashed. Spurred by a tipping line, there was an example of a horse traded on the exchanges from 13.0 to 3.7.

It returned 4-1 SP and whether it won or not is irrelevant (it didn't). Those who backed it at 3.7 have no hope.

The mugs back 1.01 chances in the belief that such bets never get beaten and like to bet on the horse or soccer team that everyone else wants to back. I always seek the advice of a betting enthusiast in my local. He rarely has an opinion different from the crowd and gives a good indication of where the mug money will go that day.

of spread betting on horses are not nearly so obvious.

Those who do not have the time or inclination to make their own prices have another option: get the bookmakers to do it. One friend simply adjusts Ladbrokes' early prices to 100 per cent – this gives him his tissue for the big races. He knows what prices to lay and what prices to back and the nice oddsmakers at Ladbrokes do all his work for him.

On the racing spread markets you can take the mid-price of all the quotes and buy or sell when you can trade outside this number.

IG, Spreadex and Cantor might be trading the Favourites index at an average of 69, suggesting this is their opinion of the fair price. If you can sell at 70 with Sporting Index you have a potential bet. Remember, though, the spread firms do not price up solely on what they believe the true price to be but also the way they think people will bet. Rarely in betting is anything quite as it seems.

epiphany on the internet

A FAIR EXCHANGE

NAMING BETFAIR AS MY EXCHANGE

By MATT WILLIAMS

of preference will not come as a surprise to regular online punters, as it is by far and away the best site available and quite rightly stands head and shoulders above its main competitors at the moment. From site navigation through to sheer volume of choice, everything you need from an exchange is provided by Betfair and, as they are the patriarch of this whole concept, I feel my affairs are safe in the hands of a reputable outfit.

Before you start wondering if this writer is sponsored by Betfair, I would like to think I make Betfair work for me rather than the other way around. They are getting the plug because they have done most to bring exchanges to the fore in what is a rapidly expanding betting medium.

Life before the betting exchanges was laborious to say the least. I love a bet, always have, and regretfully admit to frittering away thousands over the years. Those closest to me have even suggested I was a gambling junkie and, though I would vehemently deny it at the time, I secretly knew I was in trouble.

It was easy for me to figure this out because I would find myself betting on things I knew nothing about. A score on the 'one dog' at Catford, followed by a nifty on the favourite at Greyville (South African racing, for goodness sake), and I had the cheek to look down my

uncommon knowledge

**Stay in touch
with reality**

It's live, but not as we know it – so watch your horse feed

In-running betting is difficult at times and you need everything to go right. However, you would not believe the number of people who sit in front of their television screens on a Saturday afternoon watching, and betting, on what they believe to be a live horserace, when in a large number of cases they are watching a feed that can be as much as seven or eight seconds behind real time.

Attheraces provides the slowest feed, and punters betting while watching those pictures are in for a rough ride, as the SIS feed is marginally quicker. Normal terrestrial television is quicker than both, but it is also worth remembering that we live in a highly technical world nowadays and, believe it or not, there are people betting on the exchanges using laptop technology, watching the races unfold in front of their eyes direct from the track. It's a dog-eat-dog world, but to me the clowns operating on the in-running markets from the track are not clever and should be treated with disdain. Maybe that is a bit strong; I'll just label them conmen instead.

nose at the one-armed bandit mugs who continually feed a machine in the desperate hope of scooping the paltry 15 quid jackpot.

There is no real moral to this story, or indeed an ending. I am just trying to rationalise my actions and come up with a plausible reason why I suddenly became good at gambling. The answer is simple, really: I discovered Betfair.

All of a sudden I had a vehicle through which to prove I could make money at gambling. To my mind, I was brilliant with the form and the thought of operating on a person-to-person exchange stimulated me much more than betting with the high-street bookies. So, after 13 years of doing my moolah in cold blood, I stopped and turned my attentions to Betfair.

The exchanges have empowered punters and traders alike to be in control of their money, thus providing bettors with the opportunity to trade a position during a race. In the past,

I would have had to watch and suffer as my selection got chinned a short-head, thus costing me the price of my bet and leaving me with the emotional hangover of having a large amount of money snatched from my grasp.

Nowadays, using the exchanges, I can place my bet and watch a race safe in the knowledge that if my horse looks like it is going finish there or thereabouts I am in a position to trade – so it doesn't really matter if my horse wins or not. I win either way.

Trading is not really my bag. However, plenty of people make a decent living from laying a book on any given race or event, and playing the online bookmaker can minimise the risks associated with gambling. Certain people will argue that taking a guaranteed profit, however small, is a worthwhile exercise and, while they have a valid point, I see the whole process of trading for a positive position a bit time-consuming and the rewards are often meagre.

My first year on Betfair cost me a grand, but it was a learning experience and, looking back, I can say categorically that it was the best grand I have ever spent. It took me a year to suss out that betting in-running was the way forward. If you want to make money using this method then you have to ask yourself a couple of things. Do you have an extensive knowledge of the form book? Can you read a race? If the answer to both questions is yes, then you should be following a path similar to mine.

Take the time to study colours. There is no point looking down at the cards in the Racing Post to identify a beast that, a furlong from home, is cruising to certain victory. Forget it – exchange punters are like vultures, they know the colours of every runner and the chances of grabbing the available 2s are slim.

A common problem I hear about all the time is people moaning about failing to gather up a price in-running. There is no point asking for the apparent 4-1 on show because you very rarely get it. Why don't you ask for evens? The system is trying to give both sides the best deal, and by design it will match the bettor asking for the shortest price with the layer offering the biggest odds. Eureka. Such a simple finding, but it has been the single biggest factor in my success and the difference between doing well, and doing exceptionally well.

An example. I was watching a maiden race from Doncaster one day and wanted to lay the favourite. My liabilities added up to a couple of grand. With less than a furlong to go I could see my lay switching to the outside, gearing up for a serious challenge. Somebody was offering a monkey at 35-1 about the horse, so I decided to cover my position on the race and try to make a bit on the same horse because now I could see it was going to win.

I am no genius and, as always, I could be sure there were plenty of other Betfairians reading the race the same as me. They would be asking for much shorter odds in the hope of securing a bigger price through the system. I quickly priced up the horse as a 1-3 shot and asked for a monkey at those odds. Sure enough, I got my monkey matched with his, and the rest is history – except to say I got the 35-1 ahead of all the other players. Examples like this are not singular; in fact, they happen every day.

I would imagine laying horses is the most popular way of betting on the exchanges. I do it all the time. But it is a mistake just to lay a horse, watch it run and then hope it gets beat. Over a period of time you will lose money by laying one horse in a race. The mathematics do not add up, as you are invariably offering over the odds on the exchanges and a 5-1 starting price probably equates to a 7-1 exchange price. If you are steadfast about laying the odd horse here and there, always give yourself the opportunity to bail out.

I don't want to paint too rosy a picture with regard to betting exchanges, as it took me over a year to work out what strategy works best for me. Nobody should expect to hit the ground running with their exchange accounts and a bedding-down period is advised.

PART EIGHT

GAINING AN EDGE

MANY LEADING TIPSTERS AND professional punters will tell you that the approach to betting is just as important as finding the winner of an individual race. The mechanics of betting – how to pick the right race, right bet and right price – can provide that all-important advantage over bookmakers and other punters.

By NICK PULFORD

Professional punter Alan Potts, whose approach is clear from the title of his 1995 book Against The Crowd, says his edge comes from an analytical approach. "The successful punters I know come from similar backgrounds – they've worked with computers, data, in the City – and they've all got an analytical approach. The key for punters is to avoid the vague. You'll hear people say on TV that you need a horse with a high draw in the Stewards' Cup, but it's not enough to say that – you've got to have a good idea of what a high draw means in terms of probabilities or odds.

"That kind of approach is not difficult, but most people don't do it that way because they're not analytical enough."

PICKING THE RIGHT RACE The cards in the Racing Post normally include at least 20 races a day, and regularly as many as 50 on Saturdays. No punter can hope to assess every race, so it is important to scale down the choice and quickly find the races with the best betting opportunities. To a large extent, this is a matter

Opportunity knocks? No punter can hope to study every race in detail

of preference and one approach is to specialise in a certain form of racing – two-year-olds, for instance, or the all-weather. This limits the number of races for study and, over time, allows the punter to get to know the horses involved and spot form patterns. A punter using this approach might well have an edge over others with less intimate knowledge of the subject.

Alan Potts says: "The sheer volume of racing nowadays means that specialisation is essential. I have limited my Flat bets to eight leading tracks, plus a few at my local courses, and I cut out all the moderate stuff – 0-70 and below. I used to have a personal preference for races over longer distances, but sprints have served me well in recent years. Over jumps I tend to avoid races of less than two and a half miles."

Another approach is to home in on races with the right 'shape' for betting. This phrase is open to different interpretations, but Racing Post Ratings expert Steve Mason gives one view: "There are various approaches. Sometimes you might have a horse that's massively progressive and so you're not too worried about the strength of the opposition. Other times you could have a horse who has good recent form and might be progressive in a race where there are doubts about some of the main rivals. It might simply be that a horse is just massively overpriced in a competitive race. Or you might find an even-money shot you fancy but you don't want to back it at evens, so you look to get 2-1 or 3-1 by coupling it with another in a forecast."

The 'shape' of the race may indicate quickly that the favourite can be taken on, or equally it may indicate that the favourite is strong and most of the other runners are weak, providing the opportunity for an each-way bet or a forecast.

Professional punter Dave Nevison says: "The route to success is finding a weak market leader. If you find one, it's Christmas. You rub your hands and get stuck into backing perhaps two or three against the favourite."

Simon Turner, of the Racing Post Ratings team, looks especially for each-way opportunities (his philosophy is explained on page 229). With experience, he says, punters can easily find the races they are looking for.

"I can quickly look at a race and see if there is a place bet to be had – if I can't see it quickly, it probably means it isn't there. If you have a method to your betting, whether it's going for the best-rated, best last time, or whatever, that's the best start to finding the right races to bet in. Bookies detest people who bet methodically."

While it is a vital skill to be able to find the right races, it is equally important to be able to avoid the difficult ones. As Tom Segal says: "The kind of races I struggle with can be summed up in one word: Goodwood. I can't stand the place and very rarely bet there."

THE PSYCHOLOGY OF PUNTING "Stick with what suits your temperament because, to my mind, that is the most important factor for any winning punter."

That is the view of Tom Segal and he is not

uncommon knowledge

 Learn to specialise

Know your horses and be aware that less is more

"With the best part of 8,000 races in Britain each year it is impossible to be an expert on all of them. While the types of bets available to punters have exploded with the advent of spread betting and more recently the exchanges, it still makes sense to specialise," says Racing Post Ratings expert Steve Mason.

"You could focus on novice hurdles, two-year-olds, two-mile handicap chasers, all-weather performers or even sprinters. There are plenty of options, but the more you know about the form of the horses you are betting on, the better.

"Concentrating your efforts on more specific areas gives you a real chance to get to know the patterns of form and the way that certain trainers tend to work. Does a particular horse go well fresh? Is it at its best giving weight away to inferior animals in smaller fields or does it thrive in a strongly run race off a low weight? Is this horse better going right-handed or does it need a sharp left-handed track to show its best form? Does a particular trainer target a particular race or run his lesser lights at a certain course?

"These are just a few of the questions that a punter should be considering before he even gets into the vexed issue of whether a horse represents 'value' at a certain price. As a punter I have found it is better to know more about less than less about more."

alone, because most betting experts agree that the right temperament is high on the list of the ingredients that make a successful punter.

Segal adds: "For example, if you hide behind the sofa after having £50 on a 10-1 shot, then looking for big prices clearly doesn't suit you. Finding big-priced winners is not the only approach – if you want the thrill of winning regularly, you'll probably be looking at shorter prices. The important thing is to be in it for the long run. The people who aren't ideally suited to betting in any form are those who are so money-orientated that they just want to win. Whatever approach they take, they are likely to lose in the end because they haven't the temperament to take the losers and end up chasing their losses."

Steve Mason, another Racing Post Ratings expert, says: "The options for gambling nowadays are immense and there are lots of different ways of making a profit – there is a wrong way to go about betting, but there isn't one right way. For instance, some of my biggest successes have been multiple bets.

"Some people want to back as many winners as possible, but others back more longshots and accept the possibility of a long losing run, knowing that when they have a winner, it will make up for the losses. It's a question of finding the approach that suits you best."

Alan Potts adds: "Most people look for positives when they are working out their bets, but it's just as important – if not, more so – to look for the negatives. I tend to look for reasons not to back a horse, that's another edge for me."

VALUE ADDED Value has been the in-vogue concept in betting for well over a decade, stretching back to the 1987 launch of the Pricewise column in the Racing Post. However, even now, the term often appears misunderstood and misused, with many pundits associating value only with big prices. But is that right?

The theory of value is that every runner in a race has a chance of winning, and for each horse that chance can be translated into odds that represent its true chance of winning. The horse with a 50 per cent chance of winning a race, for instance, should be offered at odds of even money, while a horse with a 25 per cent chance of winning should be priced at 3-1.

Bookmakers are adept at translating chances into odds, but even their prices must have an element of subjectivity – it is impossible to verify the true chances of runners in a horserace. An experienced punter, therefore, might find variations between the price he makes each horse in a race and those set by the bookmaker.

A value bet, according to the theory, is one

uncommon knowledge

 Dealing with a losing run

'As Scarlett O'Hara said, tomorrow is another day'

Losers are inevitable for any punter, even the professionals, and the reaction is all-important. Alan Potts says: "The one thing I will do during a losing run is to cut down on the number of bets. You don't go looking for more bets to try to get the money back. I'm more likely to take a break, have a few days off and try to clear the mind.

"After every season I will review my methods and consider what improvements can be made, but once that is done all I can do is keep on working and wait for the results to turn in my favour. It's easier to maintain confidence when you've got years of records that show that you do beat the game."

Dave Nevison, another well-known professional punter, adds: "You just have to cope with a bad run – the important thing is not to panic, especially if you've got a track record of getting it right. If you haven't got that history behind you but you're convinced your method is right, then you should carry on – if you run out of money, then you'll know your method was wrong!"

On the subject of individual losers, Potts says: "You get irritated about results occasionally, like when the one you've backed in a jumps race is cantering along and looks a 1-4 shot after passing halfway, then it falls. But within five minutes I've calmed down to the 'oh well, it happens and you've got to expect it to happen' point of view. Look at it the other way – there will be times when your horse has only won because something else has fallen, not necessarily at the last but out in the country when it was going well."

On a similar theme, Mason says: "If you do find something that has worked for you over a long period of time, don't be swayed from principles that have served you well just because of a bad run.

"You are never as good as you think you are when things are going well, but neither do you suddenly become useless when things are going badly. Don't chase when things are going badly – because, as Scarlett O'Hara famously remarked, 'Tomorrow is another day'."

where the punter believes the true odds about a horse are shorter than the price being offered by the bookmaker. A horse might be considered a 7-1 chance by the punter but is priced up at 10-1 by the bookmaker – the 10-1, by definition, is a value bet.

The theory goes that value betting is the only

way to beat the bookie in the long run, but it is not as simple as that – the main reason being that finding the value in a horserace is one thing, but it is not the same as finding the winner.

Tom Segal on value, chapter 25, page 234.

THE BEST PRICE Four in every five bets are settled at starting price, so it follows that any punter who can beat the SP consistently must have an edge over the majority of punters.

As outlined in the section on value, the first step is to have an idea of the price each horse in a race should be. Then it is a question of finding that price and, in today's market, there are various methods available to the punter.

For the bigger races, the Pricewise tables in the Racing Post provide a handy comparison of the major bookmakers' prices, including the total percentage for the best odds available on the race. A more wide-ranging service is available online via Smartbet (part of the Racing Post website), which shows up-to-the-minute odds for all horseraces and major sporting events, and provides a link to bet with the major book-makers featured. Similar services are online at oddschecker.com and easyodds.com.

A punter needs to be an account-holder with the bookmaker to place a bet online or over the telephone, and the general advice would be to register with as many bookmakers as possible to guarantee being able to obtain the best prices available in the market.

The betting exchanges are included in the online packages but, as well as showing the prices on offer, they also provide the punter with the facility to name his own price.

This gives the punter the option to nominate the price he considers value and see if anybody is willing to 'match' it. The betting exchanges often claim to beat SP by 20 per cent, though this is disputed in many quarters.

With all the activity off-course, especially after the abolition of betting duty in 2001, many have feared for the future of the on-course market. But, according to many betting-ring regulars,

uncommon knowledge

 Check the early prices

Another way to try to beat the SP is to check the early prices available on the bigger races with the major bookmakers. This market used to be a very important guide, both to punters and bookmakers, but its significance has been diluted by the fact that prices have become available earlier on the betting exchanges, which means the market on a race is often set before the release of the bookmakers' early prices. The response from William Hill, who promised to offer early prices on every TV race from early 2004, has further increased the options open to punters.

these fears are largely unfounded and on-course betting still offers tremendous value.

Professional punter Dave Nevison says: "The on-course backer will get prices that the Teletext punter never sees. You'll often get 12-1 about a general 10-1 shot, and that difference could pay the expenses for a week. When you see '20-1 in a place' in the Racing Post, and you were in that place, while everyone else took 14s, that's a hell of a difference – £600 on a £100 bet."

Fellow professional Alan Potts has some invaluable advice for getting best price on- and off-course. "Generally, you'll get the best price on-course three to four minutes before the off, when the race will have been priced up for several minutes and the early action has taken place. If a horse is going to drift, it will probably have done so by then.

"For the betting-shop punter who wants to get best price, I'd say the best time to step in is when the signal comes up that the horses are going behind [on the Flat] or the equivalent stage over jumps. That's the key moment – if the office boys are going to step in and back a horse, that's when they'll do it."

WHAT'S YOUR WAGER? As detailed in chapter 16, page 148, bets come in all shapes and sizes – singles, multiples and the more complicated combination bets, either with bookmakers or the Tote.

Most experts agree that the win single has to be the mainstay bet and, for any punter who believes there is value in any of the 'specials' that are heavily promoted in betting shops, professional punter Alan Potts has this answer: "If bookmakers wanted you to back the win single, you'd see posters and special coupons for the 'Lucky One' bet. They don't want you to have singles, they want you to waste money on all those other bets."

Potts is even mistrustful of doubles. "Think about it. Say the first leg of a double wins at 4-1, then you are effectively putting five times as much on the second horse. Do you fancy it five times as much? No."

An alternative view comes from Dave Nevison, another professional. "I have absolutely no rules for betting – if I did, I expect I'd break them pretty quickly," he says. "I go for whichever bet I think is appropriate for the race or the card. Certain cards are suited to trebles or a Jackpot, or I might have three or four horses in one race. Often I'll have a mix of all those bets in one day."

Steve Mason agrees: "The options for gambling nowadays are immense and there are lots of different ways of making a profit – there is a wrong way to go about betting, but there isn't just one right way. For instance, some of my biggest successes have been multiple bets."

In chapter 17, page 174, Richard Birch takes a closer look at the types of bet and the reasons why some are better than others.

WIN OR EACH-WAY? These two common types of bet are often seen as going hand in hand, with each-way betting regarded as a fail-safe against the win portion, but equally they can be regarded as mutually incompatible.

The mathematical arguments about each-way betting are long and tedious, but many books on punting strategy favour win singles over any other bet – why, the theory goes, increase the risks on a good bet by opting for multiples? In the case of each-way betting, the opposition points to the fallacy of taking a win and place bet on the same horse. If the horse finishes first, they say, the value on the win portion is diluted by the place bet; if there is enough doubt about the win to bring the place bet into consideration, then is the bet sensible in the first place?

The mistrust of each-way betting goes back a long way – Timeform founder Phil Bull's famous Ten Commandments of Betting included: "Thou shalt not bet each-way in big fields, unless thou art well satisfied as to the value of the place bet."

uncommon knowledge

 Each-way betting

'Bookies despise those who specialise in this discipline'

Racing Post Ratings expert Simon Turner says: "Each-way betting is an excellent punting medium in the right circumstances.

"A long odds-on favourite is usually a turn-off for many punters, but it needn't be. Often in races where the favourite is very short the next few in the market have better chances of placing than their odds suggest. Next time you see a race with a long odds-on favourite, check the place prices for the next one or two in the betting on the exchanges and then work out the price of the place portion of an each-way bet on them. You will see that the place odds on the exchanges are much nearer the true odds (perhaps 1-3), but the same runner in an each-way bet might be 7-10 to place.

"Another angle is to consider those horses who, for win purposes at least, are best avoided. An example is Torrent. He runs a lot (67 times from 2001 to 2003), rarely wins (just once in that period), but regularly makes the frame (20 times in the same period).

"Layers often field against horses such as Torrent for win purposes because they have plenty of ability but are not easily persuaded to use it in the finish. This type is ideal for place betting as they have a much better chance of placing than their place odds suggest, due to their place odds lengthening as win backers turn against them.

"I like to punt each-way in multiples. Finding three 5-1 shots that make the frame returns a 3-1 winner to total stake. Opportunities to bet like this usually only occur two or three days a week and it is important to wait for the right opportunities.

"Betting with a view to getting horses to place only can sometimes offer very nice surprises when all the selections manage to win. The above example of three 5-1 shots would make a 215-1 win return.

"Many frown on each-way betting but, if practised with patience, it is a decent addition to the punting armoury. One thing's for sure – bookmakers despise punters who specialise in this discipline."

Mark Coton took the same line in his seminal book Value Betting (Aesculus), first published in 1990, saying that if value was lacking in an each-way bet, "you are striking two bad bets, one for the win and one for the place".

Professional punter Alan Potts agrees: "Very occasionally I'll have an each-way bet, but I have to be satisfied that there is value in both the win and the place portions. In fact, when I record my bets, I separate an each-way bet into a win bet and a place bet – that way, I can see whether there was any value in the place bet.

"The huge weakness of each-way betting is that most punters are backing the horse because they think it's going to be placed, not because they think it's going to win. In other words, they're only betting each-way because they don't have the confidence to back the horse to win."

There is a school of thought which holds that there are instances when each-way bets could prove worthwhile due to a certain lack of control bookmakers have over each-way odds, which are always a fixed proportion of the win price (usually one-quarter or one-fifth depending on the number of runners in a race). The theory here is that, in some uncompetitive races (e.g. with a long odds-on favourite, a solid second choice and a host of no-hopers), the place chance of the second favourite would be underrated in his win odds, therefore making an each-way bet a steal.

The problem is that opportunities for these 'each-way thieves' are few and far between. But if you're prepared to wait, the rewards can make the patience worthwhile.

WISE BEFORE THE EVENT?
While the main risk with ante-post betting is that your selection won't even give you a run for your money, many other factors can come into play between the bet being struck and the race being run. Chief among these are injury or loss of form by your selection, but it is also important to understand that an ante-post book is not 'closed' (ie, the horses quoted at the time of making a bet can alter), so other contenders can emerge through race performance and/or by being added to the race unexpectedly (for example, by being supplemented at a late stage to a major Flat race).

It does not always follow that a horse will

---

uncommon knowledge

 Get your timing right

Ante-post bets generally carry more risk the earlier they are struck, and prices will reflect that. For those who want to speculate with more information in hand about the race in question, there are periods on which to concentrate – the publication of the Grand National weights in February, for example, or during the spring Classic trials, or after a major Cheltenham Festival prep race.

The bookmakers react to these events, too, so it can pay to stay one step ahead by betting in advance of such staging posts. For instance, if you fancy a horse for a Classic trial and believe that it will be a major contender in the Classic, it can make sense to have an ante-post wager before the trial as the price is sure to contract if it wins.

be a bigger price ante-post than it is on raceday. Some of the potential pitfalls and benefits of ante-post betting were illustrated by the long-range prices available on the 2003 editions of the 1,000 and 2,000 Guineas. Russian Rhythm, the eventual 1,000 winner, was 3-1 after her dramatic York win more than eight months before the Classic, 5-1 by the end of the season, and started 12-1 on the day after adverse rumours about her wellbeing.

Refuse To Bend, the eventual 2,000 Guineas winner, was 12-1 second favourite the previous autumn after his National Stakes success, a price which held steady over the winter before contracting in the fortnight before the Classic. His winning SP was 9-2.

Of the eight horses quoted at under 20-1 for the 2,000 Guineas at the turn of the year, only Refuse To Bend and three others made it to the race. The 1,000 Guineas was a different story, however, with four of the five fillies quoted at under 20-1 early in 2003 eventually lining up at Newmarket. In fact, that quartet filled the first four places in the race.

The difference in the withdrawal rates from the two races emphasises one of the most important factors in ante-post betting – the ability of the punter to pick the right race in which to speculate. It is not unusual for most of the principals in the 1,000 Guineas betting to get to Newmarket for two main reasons: they are aimed at the race through the winter, while less-exposed fillies generally do not come to the fore early in their three-year-old season, leaving the race to those who performed well as juveniles. This means that punters who bet ante-post on the 1,000 Guineas can be reasonably sure they are looking at a true market – one in which all potential runners are quoted and most will run.

The 2,000 Guineas is different because the late-maturing colts seem more able to catch up quickly in the spring of their three-year-old season – 2001 winner Golan being the most recent example, landing the Classic after just a maiden success on his only start as a juvenile.

Of course, a race with a high dropout rate might also leave the shrewd punter with a better bet on his hands. For instance, Galileo was quoted at 16-1 for the 2001 Derby after his winning debut as a juvenile, but of the other nine quoted at under 33-1, only two made it to Epsom. Anyone who thought at that stage that Galileo would be Aidan O'Brien's number-one Derby hope had a good bet because three of those other nine quoted were also from his stable – Galileo ended up as O'Brien's only representative at Epsom, started 11-4 joint-favourite and won by three and a half lengths.

It is important to keep a close eye on the news – the Racing Post is the most comprehensive source – to stay up to date with the latest running plans and injury news for the top horses. Another key factor with ante-post bets can be whether a trainer or owner has shown a preference for targeting certain races in the past, as this can indicate the likelihood of a bid for the race where a bet is being considered.

Tom Segal, who writes the Racing Post's highly successful Pricewise column, says: "Ante-post is a good betting medium, but you've got to be able to take the knocks because it's inevitable you will end up with some non-runners. But people shouldn't be scared to have a go – there's nothing like getting the winner of a big race like the Grand National at 50-1 or 66-1."

The Grand National has become Segal's speciality – in recent years, he has backed the 2000 winner Papillon at 66-1 (SP 10-1), Red Marauder (2001) at 50-1 (SP 33-1) and Monty's Pass (2003) at 33-1 (SP 16-1).

Segal's approach to ante-post betting is to read between the lines of the information in the public domain, combining elements of form, a horse's big-race entries and comments from connections, in order to assess a horse's profile. "I pay close attention to what the trainers say – in features like Stable Tour in the Racing Post and Straight From The Stable in the Weekender, and in their post-race comments.

uncommon knowledge

 Follow the form

Look for early signs of a horse's big-race potential

One approach to ante-post betting is form-based, as Steve Mason, the Racing Post's jumps handicapper, explains: "I'm always on the lookout for ante-post bets for the Cheltenham Festival and the trigger point is usually when a horse demonstrates, on ratings, a level of form that is good enough to win an average running of the race in question. Rooster Booster was a good example when he won at Cheltenham [the Rehabilitation of Racehorses Handicap Hurdle in November 2002]. On that form, he was clearly good enough to win the Champion Hurdle and he was 10-1 at that stage."

Rooster Booster went on to win the 2003 Champion Hurdle (SP 9-2).

Trainer Philip Hobbs's comments wouldn't have deterred anybody from backing Rooster Booster at that stage, either, so it is clear that both form and 'information' are valuable assets.

It's all about trying to get inside the trainer's mind but, quite often, the signs are there, either from things they've said, or the career path that a horse is taking.

"Quite often a trainer will give an indication of a horse's merit before it has the form in the book – they might compare a younger horse favourably with one of the yard's big-name horses, or say it is being aimed at a big race. I only believe it with top trainers, though – people like Paul Nicholls, Nicky Henderson and Sir Michael Stoute, who have the track record."

The key, says Segal, is the price. "I wouldn't go for anything under double figures. You've got to be looking at big prices – if the horse is likely to be 3-1 on the day and you're only getting 5-1, it's not worth it. But how many times do you end up backing a horse for a big race on the day, when in fact you've fancied it for weeks, and you think, why didn't I back it three weeks ago when the price was much bigger?"

v is for victory, as well as value

ANORAKS ARE BACK

JUST AS THERE ARE HUNDREDS OF

By TOM SEGAL

ways to skin a cat, so there are many ways to win at gambling on horses and no one way is necessarily better than any other. Over the past decade most people have got sucked into looking for value as a way to win at the game, but what actually is value and is it really what every winning punter should be looking for?

The first thing to say is that if you are constantly obtaining a bigger price than you believe any horse's realistic price to be, then you are obviously on to a winning formula from the start. Theoretically you are likely to come out on top if you keep backing horses at bigger prices than they should be.

However, over the last few years obtaining prices has become more important than backing winners to a lot of people and surely all of us are guilty of backing horses just because they are a big price rather than believing they will actually win.

That may sound over-simplistic but think back to the times when you've stood at the races and gone along the bookmakers' line with the intention of backing a horse only to see it a shorter price than you've wanted and as a result you've gone and backed something else just because it's a supposed better-value bet.

It seems to me that value has become an excuse for backing lots of losers or trying to be too clever and, as all the enjoyment in betting

Limited choice: you won't get far shopping around for best prices at Southwell on a winter's day

comes with the winning, you really do have to have a temperament of steel to adopt a value-betting strategy. In any case, what is value to one man is surely the opposite to someone else, as the backers and layers on Betfair and the other betting exchanges are proving day in, day out.

As the Pricewise columnist of the Racing Post over the past few years, my attitude to value has changed. To begin with, it was all about bagging a couple of 33-1 shots a year to make yourself look clever – and if you threw enough darts at the target at that sort of price, then a few would hit the bullseye.

However, it soon became very evident that, for me and most punters, this approach was not value or enjoyable betting in any shape or form. Yes, I may have come out of any given season with profit, but if nobody trusted the horses I'd suggested it made no difference whatsoever.

The best feedback I get from punters is when I make a very good case for a fancied horse. A 4-1 shot that starts and wins at 2-1 is a real value bet, not one that is 14-1 in the morning and gets beaten at 8-1.

Ten years ago, when Ladbrokes were 10-1 and Coral 4-1 over any horse in the big race, it didn't take a rocket scientist to work out where the value was. Nowadays that sort of divergence is very rare and so trying to obtain any perceived value is that much harder. Of course there are going to be occasions when the bookies get it wrong because pricing up any horserace is fraught with danger, but the ricks of a few years ago are few and far between these days and so maybe the days of value punting are numbered.

The exchanges are taking over and, while there is no doubt that they have been the best thing that has ever happened to punters, I'm not totally convinced that they assist any value-betting approach.

Every time I look at an exchange it seems that about three horses are very short prices and the rest are very big. Since the exchanges have started, the average price of the favourite has come down for the simple reason that on-course bookies are following the exchanges and everyone now knows which horses are fancied and which are not.

Occasionally you are going to get massive prices about winners, especially in running, but before any race all the money is for one or two horses while the rest can be backed at any price you like. It doesn't seem to me that too many people are greatly interested in the value-betting approach on the exchanges.

The best punters are those who are totally open-minded when it comes to any race and do not go in with any preconceived ideas or betting strategies. For me, the art of winning is to be pragmatic about everything and never to stand still.

Value was the watchword for punting of the 1990s and, as with any in-vogue idea, it worked for a while, but everything evolves with time. Now that everyone has all the information, the exchanges have made the betting market much more streamlined and those 12-1 shots of ten years ago are around the 6-1 mark and no longer

uncommon knowledge

Choose your races

'Nobody can be a jack of all trades'

The racing authorities seem hell-bent on adding to an already jam-packed fixture schedule, which will result in more and more average horses running in more and more average races.

It is physically impossible to take in all the information gleaned from every race run, and so the way to increase your chances of making a few quid is to specialise. Concentrate on the races that you enjoy the most, the ones you are most interested in, and forget about the rest. If you have a punting mentality like me, then the races you like best will coincide with the ones that over the years have made you the most money.

For example, over the years I've been exceptionally lucky in staying chases, especially the Grand National, and, as a consequence, I'm prepared to put much more time and effort into solving that type of race.

In stark contrast, I can't back an all-weather winner for love or money and have stopped betting on the sand. The only reason I could find why I lost money on the sand was because I didn't watch or take in enough races – I can't remember seeing an enjoyable all-weather race, which resulted in not enough effort on my part.

Specialisation is the key – be a jack of one trade and a master of one. Nobody can be a jack of all trades, not in this day and age of wall-to-wall racing. And it is only going to get worse.

the value – if they were in the first place.

That means that another horse in the same race is going to be a bigger price than it should be, but those tend to be the non-sexy ones, the ones who can win on a piece of form from a few runs ago rather than the ones with the good speed figures or the track form or the draw.

Consequently, perhaps the next decade of winning punters are going to go back to the way it used to be before the clever boys got involved, days when solid hard work and formbook study paid dividends. Could it be that the anorak is about to make a comeback and everyone is going to concentrate on finding the winner rather than studying the prices?

how to make it pay

A WINNING FORMULA

THERE IS NO BETTER FEELING ON

By RICHARD BIRCH

earth than backing winners – and then counting out readies. It's deliciously addictive. Great for the ego and self-esteem. It keeps the brain active, the bank manager happy, and, I honestly believe, not even a daily two-mile jog can beat it for maintaining good health.

What's more, the present-day punter has never enjoyed so many benefits. Bookmakers are offering tax-free betting and more early prices and concessions than ever before as they compete with their rivals – and, of course, the betting exchanges, led by Betfair. The margins on horseracing are hugely attractive. Compared to other countries, deductions of 13.5 per cent from a win bet on the British Tote offers outstanding value for money, and Britain's trade paper, the Racing Post, is packed with stats, tips and punter-friendly information to guide you – every single day.

A disciplined, long-term approach towards betting in the current climate can pay handsome dividends. But what are the basic steps punters must take in order to do so? What sort of strategy will enable them to have the best chance of beating the old enemy?

In my opinion, winning money from betting is 60 per cent skill, 20 per cent psychological factors, and 20 per cent luck. Obviously the last category is difficult to quantify, but let's provide some simple guidance on the other two.

What it's all about: backing a winner is good for your pocket – and health

SKILL How can we improve our winner-finding skills? Any moron from Land's End to John O'Groats can pick a winner, but unless he has a long-term strategy, which revolves around looking for value, he will not last the season.

Value is the most important concept in betting. Ever since the Racing Post's revolutionary Pricewise column was launched in 1987, value betting has become the greatest single preoccupation of punters. Value is usually associated with big prices, but this remains the biggest fallacy in 21st century gambling. You will meet plenty of good judges who sneer when told of a 5-4 favourite that rates 'great value'.

Of course, we would all like to back 12-1 winners every day – but it's just not possible. Getting stuck into shorter-priced good things which offer value, though, is certainly achievable.

Value is intimately personal. Before placing a bet, the punter must know the price he will accept. If he makes a horse 5-4 and the bookmakers offer 2-1, then he has a value bet. Combining regular wins on value short prices with the occasional value big-price touch is the key to profitable punting.

What about odds-on betting? Can that be profitable? Think logically for just one minute. If merely backing odds-on shots was a passport to prosperity, every factory, office and industrial estate nationwide would lie empty. Why work when you can lump £1,000 on a 1-2 shot and win a week's wages in the process? Sadly, it's not that easy. Most professional odds-on backers I've encountered can now be smelt huddled under blankets in shop doorways, muttering "gambling stinks".

That's not to say punters should avoid all odds-on shots. If you price up a horse at 4-7 and the bookmaker offers 4-5, it's obviously value and might be worth playing at that price.

It's the staking 'plan' adopted by odds-on punters that sends the vast majority skint. Individuals who risk £500 on 2-5 shots must ask themselves the following vital question: would they invest £500 – or an equivalent £250 each-way – on an equally fancied 5-1 shot?

If the answer is no, as sure as night follows day, they have less chance of making money in the long run than an ice-cream salesman at the North Pole. In fact, bank robberies aside, they'll be broke within three months.

Numerous odds-on shots get turned over. Of course, even more 5-1 chances are beaten. But how will a punter recoup the £500 odds-on stake if his next bet is £50 at 5-1? Financial suicide. By all means back the occasional odds-on shot, but don't increase the stake purely because of the short price. That's nuttier than a Madness video!

How do punters decide whether a horse represents value? In a nutshell, they need to have an extensive knowledge of form. Remember revising for exams at school? Students who graduated with A and B grades were invariably those who allocated plenty of time to study – and, just as importantly, enjoyed it.

Gambling is no different. To make long-term profits, form books must be dissected, races analysed, videos re-run and contacts phoned on a daily basis. Make full use of the Racing

Post website for horseracing form and both smartbet.co.uk and oddschecker.com to discover where the best prices lie.

Punters must possess a fundamental enjoyment of research as the foundation of punting profits. If you cannot allocate a couple of hours a day to study, then, rather than gamble halfheartedly – and lose – select a favourite tipster from the Post and follow their advice.

Once you've acquired a sound knowledge of form, decide in which aspects of racing you are going to specialise. There has never been so much racing in Britain. Flat, jumps, all-weather, handicaps, conditions races, two-year-old races, hurdlers, chasers, stayers, sprinters . . . so many categories from which to choose. It's impossible to analyse them all, particularly during the long, hot months of midsummer madness when there are often six or seven meetings per day.

My own particular policy during the summer is to choose racetracks that offer draw biases – such as Windsor, Goodwood and Beverley – and never attempt to analyse more than two cards per day.

Remember that bookmakers are compelled to lay bets on every race every single day; punters can choose when to play. It's our biggest weapon. Be professional; specialise; limit your bets; be competitive; utterly ruthless. Next time you enter a betting shop to pick up £100 winnings, walk straight out the door with the cash firmly pocketed. Don't even contemplate having a 'fun fiver' on something. There is no such thing as a fun bet. It's never any fun losing money. People insist that alcohol and adultery can wreck lives. Take it from me, relying on out-of-form horses to return to their best comes a close third in the life-ruining stakes!

Recent form – up to two months old – is of paramount importance in picking winners. Never rely on six-month-old form. It can only offer a one-way ticket to Skint City. Stick with in-form horses from in-form stables who have delivered career-best performances in their recent outings. Following progressive performers is the right route to take.

There is one other important variable in this 'skill' category. To maximise long-term gains, punters must take the best early prices each morning. This is confirmed by research undertaken by Easyodds.com, the odds comparison website, whose survey into results at Newmarket's July meeting for the ten years up to 2002 discovered that a punter betting £100 on every winner over the three days annually in that time period, would have increased his profits by £6,670.83 had he taken the best early price available instead of the starting price – a hugely significant increase of 10.5 per cent on turnover.

Similarly, a punter backing every winner at Royal Ascot in 2003 to a £100 level stake would have seen profits soar from £23,624.64 (SP) to £32,872.50 at early price, a wallet-fattening difference of £9,247.86 – or 39.1 per cent.

That's why it has never been so important to operate in the early-price market – particularly at the big horserace meetings. Whether you are a favourite backer or a long-odds merchant, the most important time of the day is the morning, when early prices become available.

PSYCHOLOGY Self-control is the hardest lesson of all to learn. Keep your focus. Gambling, drinking and socialising at the same time is a recipe for financial disaster. Pretty obvious, isn't it? After all, when have you seen a bookmaker sipping alcohol between races?

From the moment a punter walks into a racetrack or betting shop, he should remain solely focused on winning money from bookmakers. Leave the bars, girls and meeting up with friends until after the last race. How many times have you been put off your well-researched fancy by loose talk among brainless muppets at the bar? Have faith in your own opinion.

The biggest threat to long-term profits is the inevitable losing run. How punters react when seemingly cursed by ill-fortune makes the difference between a winning or losing year.

It is those psychological factors that determine

uncommon knowledge

 Don't play mind games

How many times have you gone racing to back a horse, changed your mind at the last moment and driven home in a rage? Too often to count, I would wager.

A friend of mine turned up at Newbury in the summer of 2003 to back a Marcus Tregoning four-year-old. "The missus has only let me out because I told her it was a certainty," he said. However, when 11-10 was chalked up, all sense of sanity and reason disappeared. "Too short – I'll back Stoute's at 8-1 instead."

You know the rest. Tregoning's hosed up, my pal lost, and slunk off to tell his Teletext results-watching wife that things had unexpectedly gone pear-shaped! If you change your mind at the last minute, split the stake on the original selection and the new one – or just walk away.

how you deal with a losing run. Do you (a) carry on as normal (b) chase losses (c) back everything each-way (d) reduce stakes (e) rob a bank and increase stakes (f) file for divorce because "it's the wife's fault" (g) take a holiday.

Enjoying a foreign holiday (not British, where the temptation to walk into a betting shop will prove too strong) is the best option. You'll forget the nightmares and return refreshed and focused to start again. But how many people can decide instantly to bail out for a couple of weeks without sending the credit card balance spiralling out of control? Not many.

The best advice I've ever been given to combat a losing run came from racecourse bookmaker George Reed. I'd lost over £4,000 in three weeks and my confidence was in tatters. I was displaying a more vivid imagination than Steven Spielberg in making cases for no-hope 12-1 shots. My average stake was £250. George told me: "Wait until you really fancy a 2-1 shot and then just have £50 on."

I did. It won. My confidence and spirits rose, and six weeks later I had recouped the £4,000 with £1,500 interest. Of course, the natural inclination after a loser is to 'chase'. Succumb to this bank account-draining madness and the bookies will have a million reasons to smirk all over their suntanned faces.

Only bet when the odds are in your favour. If the price is wrong, don't bet. How many people would purchase a car for £3,500 if they felt it was worth only £2,000? The same applies to gambling. If you want 5-2 and are offered 6-4, walk away and wait for the next opportunity.

So that's it, then. Making it pay by skill and psychology, while acknowledging that luck – both good and bad – plays a vital part during the punting year. Punting is fun; all-embracing; exciting. Always bet with cash, if possible, rather than on the phone – because being paid out in crisp notes feels so much better than receiving a cheque through the post seven days later! The moment it stops becoming fun is the time to walk away – before it's too late. ■

there's more than just form

MAXIMISE YOUR EDGE

THE KEY TO SUCCESSFUL PUNTING

By MEL CULLINAN

is to adopt an assiduous, methodical, painstaking approach and frame this willingness to pull a race apart within a set of general maxims – the dos and donts of betting. If fun bets are your bag, fair enough – I have never seen much fun in losing. If you are interested in making betting profitable, hopefully this chapter can offer some pointers.

Later we will examine some of the cardinal sins backers can commit and discuss some of the many avoidable pitfalls. First, though, it makes sense to outline how a punter can get geared up to start betting profitably.

A concentrated approach is the only way to make betting pay, unless you happen to be the best friend of Martin Pipe or Aidan O'Brien. There is no alternative to the analytical dissection of a race. The volume of racing is so great nowadays that it also makes sense to be selective; time constraints make it an absolute necessity to cut out much of the legwork and home in on a pool of horses, be they two-year-olds, Flat horses rated 80 or above, or two-mile hurdlers. It simply is not possible for most punters to keep fully abreast of the whole picture, so home in on a specific set of horses.

Common sense is needed to decide what set of horses to concentrate on. Following top sprint handicappers may be appealing initially

Revise your opinions: the 2002 Queen's Vase in which Mamool (left) beat Mr Dinos (centre) turned out to be better than it had seemed

because of the prices at which winners start, but the workload in logging the minutiae of the characteristics of up to 30 horses a race might well be too much.

Because horses are priced up primarily on account of collateral form, it can give us an all-important edge if we take an overview, spot early trends and gain more generalised insights to contextualise a horse's form and characteristics. These insights into our chosen pool of horses will complement the nuts and bolts of the particular form and characteristics of a horse.

For example, it was clear early in the autumn of 2000 that the previous season's novice chasers were mopping up an inordinate number of top handicaps. The first three in the Thomas Pink Gold Cup and the first four in the Hennessy Gold Cup that year were all second-season chasers. Yet the bookmakers were not factoring this into their prices, so here we had an edge that was to pay dividends all winter.

Similarly, when the Italian Derby winner Morshdi split Galileo and Golan in the 2001 Irish Derby it was a strong clue that the Capannelle Classic that year was well above average. The subsequent exploits of Falbrav and Vinnie Roe, second and fourth in Italy, confirmed that, but many were very slow to cotton on, taking the lazy, uninformed view that because the race was run in a 'second division' racing nation, the race could not be up to much.

Be revisionist when necessary. When Mamool beat Mr Dinos in the 2002 Queen's Vase, the consensus was that it was a substandard renewal, but a quick revision was required. In particular, Mr Dinos's subsequent efforts that season (let alone in 2003) suggested that both colts had shown marked improvement at Ascot. The betting market is often not flexible enough to accommodate such shifting viewpoints. By taking a more detached, sometimes revisionist overview, we can profit.

Twice in particular in recent seasons, such an approach has quickly identified that the perceived gulf between Group/Listed-class sprinters and handicappers was close to non-existent, as horses such as Eastern Purple, Ivory's Joy, Repertory and Rushcutter Bay – all Listed or Group winners – showed in 2000, while the first six in the 2003 Wokingham went on to Pattern-race success later that year.

With regard to a pool of horses, it is strongly advised to use a favoured ratings service as a foundation for form assessment (unless you are confident enough and have time to compile your own). And of all the positive points to ponder when backing horses, one in particular would be very close to top of the list: concentrate on horses who have very little (if anything) to find on form.

It is very difficult to watch all the races we need to, so it is worthwhile to read press comment on the relevant contests, whether in the Racing Post analysis section, Raceform, Chaseform, or your favoured service. Generally speaking, backers will do well always to be ready to stand out from the crowd, think independently and be prepared to modify their views over time as trends emerge. For example, in 2002, the seemingly well-proven adage that three-year-

uncommon knowledge

 Foreign raiders

Swim against the tide of parochialism

It used to be the case that more or less any foreign-trained runner was worth close attention – racing is parochial in many ways and punters were (and still are) no different, so that, for instance, the likes of Sinndar and Namid were underestimated in the betting before European Group 1 wins in 2000.

Things have changed since then, though, so that Aidan O'Brien's runners and, to a lesser extent, those of trainers such as Andre Fabre, tend to be sent off shorter than their form warrants nowadays. Backers need to be more discerning nowadays and the time when more or less any foreign-trained horse was underestimated, especially on the Flat, is gone.

There is still mileage in swimming against the tide of parochialism,

however. Look how long it took in 2003 for most people to realise that ex-Italian horses Falbrav and Rakti were seriously good. And, while European Flat racing is moving into a more international phase, the betting market has not been that quick in cottoning on. Some horses from other racing nations are often underestimated.

An example of this has been the big prices at which some Japanese-trained horses have won major races in France in recent years. And remember how Choisir, a Group 1 winner in Australia, went off at 25-1 for his King's Stand Stakes win at Royal Ascot and then was 13-2 for the Golden Jubilee Stakes four days later – even though his Australian form showed a regular ability to put in two good runs close together in top races.

olds find it extremely hard to beat their elders in handicaps in the first half of the year did not stand up as well as usual – from early in the year, starting on the all-weather, the younger horses did much better than might have been expected. Whatever the reason, it made sense to adapt your viewpoint to the changing evidence.

That said, it is worth citing some enduring trends which seem as relevant as ever and which can help provide insights and give some guidance when analysing a race. Horses who run well in valuable, big-field handicaps, on the Flat in particular, are well disposed to do so again.

There is mileage in backing good apprentice jockeys on the all-weather; a good claim can be a huge advantage, particularly since many of the very best jockeys disappear to sunnier climes over the winter, so competition among riders is not what it is in the turf season.

Races over seven furlongs on the Flat require a peculiar blend of speed and stamina, yet the realisation that being a seven-furlong specialist is a particular advantage is often ignored by the betting public. Specialists over the distance, such as Salse, Decorated Hero, Arkadian Hero and, more recently, Nayyir, can be profitable to follow.

Try to be aware of changing patterns in the betting market. A few years ago, there was a big backlash against first-time headgear, many punters seeing it as a complete negative. However, the market overreacted to such horses; high-profile, big-race winners such as See More Business (16-1 Cheltenham Gold Cup), Royal Rebel (10-1 in the Ascot Gold Cup) and Enzeli (15-2 in the Doncaster Cup) all confounded the prejudice against horses in first-time headgear.

As well as having a set of positive ideas in mind when betting, disciplined punters will save plenty of money if they also adhere to a set of 'must not do' maxims.

There is so much racing nowadays that specialising is the only viable option for most backers. Bookmaker Victor Chandler has said that the one major advantage punters have over bookmakers is that they can choose when to bet. Yet many backers lose their head with so many options to choose from, and bet willy-nilly on far too many races.

Leave a sizeable number of races alone, principally because they are of a type which defies rational form analysis. Results over the years have often been so incomprehensible that we can impose a blanket ban on them as betting mediums. Into this category come Listed fillies' races - especially in the autumn - and low-grade nurseries on the Flat. Over jumps, juvenile handicap hurdles, bumpers and most

Second can be first

Be prepared to support what are apparently stable 'second strings'. With the rise of the betting exchanges and their tendency to help create a market built around a few key horses, perceived second strings can start at artificially big prices. History suggests that trainers are often unsure as to which horse is the better – hence the decision to run two (or sometimes more) horses in the same race. There are many examples which spring to mind from recent years of a stable's 'second string' winning, including many from pre-exchange days – Rock Of Gibraltar, 9-1 winner from stablemate Hawk Wing (6-4 favourite) in the 2002 2,000 Guineas, is as good as any.

marathon chases (over three and a half miles-plus) are best avoided.

As a general rule we should be very suspicious of collateral form as an accurate guide when stamina is at a premium – the distances horses are beaten by in testing conditions are notoriously unreliable. Similarly, races run in very bad ground under either code are a no-go.

History has shown that a handful of tracks are so idiosyncratic that they should be written off for betting purposes unless a horse is proven either there or at a similar track – if there is one. Chepstow over jumps, Wolverhampton on the all-weather and Brighton top this list, with Hexham and Towcester not far behind. Conversely, the substitution of Polytrack for Equitrack at Lingfield seems to have made races there much more comprehensible and punter-friendly, again showing how things change.

Next for the chop are those races run over a peculiar distance. Royal Ascot's Jersey Stakes is a good example of this. Seven furlongs is a specialist distance and, as the race is for three-year-olds, there is not a lot of form over the trip to go on; it's hardly surprising that the race has thrown up some seemingly unfathomable winners over the years.

There is a strong case for not betting on three-year-old races until May at the earliest, due to a lack of recent form and the fact that so much guesswork is required as to how these young horses have progressed over what – in terms of their racing career – is the most crucial, influential winter of their lives.

Developing hard-and-fast, unbending ideas about certain horses is a bad move. Have an opinion about a horse's going and distance requirements by all means, but take an overview. A horse may have run badly over a certain trip but in conditions to which it was ill-suited. And again, be prepared to revise previous assumptions – one good example is to consider the number of occasions on which a horse has been castigated for being 'ungenuine' but has just been unlucky and has confounded the critics by winning plenty of races.

Even if a horse is quirky, do not dismiss it out of hand. Such types seem to win an inordinate number of races, often at nice prices, because most punters will not go near them. A good example from recent years is Bhutan, derided left, right and centre but, for all of his quirks, the winner of a stack of races. The over-hasty would have found him a costly horse to back against many times in the recent past.

Bookmakers and punters alike can sometimes be obsessed with collateral form and ratings, when betting is every bit as much about exercising some common sense on other variables, such as jumping or stamina.

On the Flat, it is not 'after timing' to cite Refuse To Bend's 11-4 starting price for the 2003 Derby as failing to take account of stamina doubts; over jumps, an inexperienced horse of potential will often be put in at far too short a price when jumping could well be an issue against much more experienced horses. Not only should we take a common-sense approach that includes more than just collateral form, but if we can thereby identify a falsely priced horse, we can home in on something that must be at reasonably generous odds against it.

Wide-margin winners are best treated with extreme caution, as the betting market tends to go completely overboard about this type of horse. Hawk Wing's Lockinge Stakes win in May 2003 meant he went off a silly price next time when beaten in the Queen Anne Stakes, while arguably better examples still are Royal Anthem, runaway winner of the Juddmonte International in 1999 but beaten at short odds next time, and Zero Tolerance, an eight-length Beverley winner but beaten next time in a Sandown handicap, in May 2003. Again, punters failed to take an overview of the overall record of the horses, going into premature raptures on the strength of one more-than-likely flattering performance.

Horses perceived as unlucky losers should also be treated with extreme caution because

uncommon knowledge

 Don't chase big winners

Many people will feel very self-satisfied if they back the winner of one of the big handicaps on the Flat, but these can be very tough to work out and require an awful lot of time and effort, so have the strength to let them pass you by if need be.

There are punters who take the view that the bigger the race, the more compelled they feel to bet, while others are 'scared' of missing a nice winner. However, though they may back the odd big-race winner now and again, punters who try to unpick these races on the back of a cursory analysis will lose bucketloads in the long run.

uncommon knowledge

 Go against favourites

A large number of favourites are best avoided nowadays because of the tendency of the betting market to overreact. Developing this point further, it is worth identifying those stables associated with a large number of short-priced horses.

Stables go in and out of fashion to some extent, but David Loder, Aidan O'Brien and Paul Nicholls are three trainers whose runners we should be wary of, purely because the betting market is often too cautious when assessing the real chance of their representatives. Follow the racing results closely for a few weeks and other trainers will make their way on to the list.

they tend to start far too short in the betting next time. High-profile examples from 2003 include Norse Dancer and Yesterday in the Derby and Oaks. Some punters commit the cardinal sin of allowing sentiment to affect their judgement; backing a horse because it 'deserves' to win is irrational.

A willingness to think laterally and not be taken in by what seems to be the obvious, can be an important asset. Lazy backers may see a series of 1s next to a horse's name and be tempted into supporting it. But we should always assess the class of those victories to put the quality of the performances into perspective. Horses boasting impressive-looking form figures can be interesting in that they help make the market for something else in the race.

Another important 'don't' in betting is that punters should not be seduced by the 'class horse' factor. If a smart – but perhaps long-absent – horse is dropped sharply in grade, ask why the trainer has taken this drastic step. It will often be because the horse has deteriorated.

In my 'Mel's Maxims' feature in the Racing Post, I pointed out that once-raced maidens and maiden winners, especially those from fashionable stables, should be viewed with considerable scepticism by backers. These horses are priced up according to potential, rather than on what they have achieved. Win, lose or draw, they offer no mileage in the long run.

Finally, keep a watchful eye on the results on a day-to-day basis and certain hard-and-fast maxims will become apparent. Some of the more obvious ones which spring to mind include: never back selling-race winners in good-quality nurseries, oppose older horses (aged ten and upwards) in top handicap chases at up to two and a half miles, and be very wary of supporting recently gelded (say, in the past four months) horses on their first run back.

That concludes a longish list of 'don't's. Put together with the positive maxims and a methodical, patient approach, they should provide a firm foundation for more profitable betting. ◼

putting theory into practice

SYSTEMS ADDICTS

EVERYONE INTERESTED IN BETTING

By PETER MAY

on horses either uses a system or knows someone who does. This may seem an over-generalisation but it is nonetheless true. Systems are a very popular betting method. As opposed to form study, they are easy to employ and take very little time to check each day, which is a major advantage for those who do not rely 100% on the sport for income.

The bulk of the work is undertaken during a period of system development resulting in one or several systems which can then be employed during the season. Another advantage with this approach is that systems can be precisely structured.

This rigid style allows them to be tested against known race results and thus provides the bettor with invaluable information about their likely performance. Unfortunately this level of rigidity can be a drawback since it does not allow the system to develop and adapt to changing circumstances.

Like many things in life, systems are based on past experience. The developer either uses their personal knowledge of the sport to generate a system, or a more structured technique based on an analysis of previous results. This latter approach is often referred to as back-fitting since it requires the fitting of a system (or rule) to historical results. The method is very effective but, like any form of retrospective analysis, it needs to be conducted and validated in an unbiased manner to achieve the best results.

HORSERACING SYSTEMS A requirement of a horseracing system is that it should be able to be written as a rule that is unambiguous and straightforward to apply. The system should also generate an acceptable success rate and return a profit. But, most importantly, the system should be likely to reproduce its good historical performance in future races.

To satisfy the first objective the system should rely on quantifiable variables, such as the number of days since the horse last raced or its position in the betting market. Qualitative variables, such as suitability of the going, or race distance, should be avoided unless they can be defined precisely. These opinion-based variables are always difficult to validate and often their assessment does not remain constant over time.

Simple systems are always preferred to highly complex ones. A simple system consisting of just a few conditions is easy to implement and hence more likely to be applied correctly. Furthermore, these systems tend to be more general, requiring less data to validate them and are less prone to over-fitting. Though highly refined systems map the historical data more precisely, they may not perform as well in the future.

Ideally, the system will also be unique. Using the usual data items in a conventional fashion is unlikely to return a long-term profit. However, a new relationship between the data and the odds is more likely to return a profit since it will not already have been accounted for in the prices on offer.

Finally, the system must be structured so that the bettor is able to implement it. It is no good developing a highly profitable system that cannot be implemented. For instance, someone who is employed full time may not be able to monitor the betting shows closely and so would not be able to run a system with such a requirement. This may appear to be obvious, but it is surprising the number of systems that are developed without thought for how they are going to be run.

DEVELOPING SYSTEMS

Although it is possible to identify specific combinations of variables which return a long-term profit as a result of general form study, the most common approach to systems development is by data mining.

Data mining methods require a data set containing historical results which include all of the critical factors. This is a key step in the whole process. It is necessary for the systems developer to base their work on a data set that is representative of the domain, accurate and unbiased. This may seem obvious, but it is not necessarily a straightforward task to undertake, especially when extracting the data manually from a form book. Furthermore it is important to use data from more than a single season. Seasonal variations need to be accounted for in any system, thus a data set covering three or more seasons is desirable.

The data mining process then requires the analyst to search the data for profitable relationships between the data elements. Consequently, the search is driven by the profit variable. With form study the result is generally the horse with the highest chance of success – the bettor can then convert these findings into acceptable prices before considering a bet.

However, with systems development the target is profit from the outset and this changes the way the variables need to be viewed. When analysing a race with the aim of determining the most likely winners, the factors considered generally have a linear relationship with the outcome of the race. For instance, the higher the speed rating, with respect to the other runners, the greater the chance of success; the higher the trainer's success rate the more likely the horse is to win and so on.

With systems development the relationships

that need to be considered change from linear to non-linear simply because the target variable is not chance of success but profit.

The betting market mirrors the horse's chance of winning and the more likely a horse is to win the shorter the price on offer will be. Consequently, a horse with ideal credentials is unlikely to be on offer at a value price. This also applies to horses at the other end of the market, where again the odds will understate the chance of success. The aim of a system is to find a combination of factors which generate a profit in the long term. This may require the bettor to invest in horses which are far from the most likely winning candidates.

Although the combination of variables that constitute a system may not match the idealistic view of horserace analysis, they must still be logical. However, this logic is not based on conventional approaches, but with respect to the profit/loss statistics. In other words, a profitable system may have as a condition that the horse has been unraced for over 100 days This defies the conventional logic which dictates that horses returning from a long course absence are less likely to be fit and hence less likely to win. However, the system view is that these horses are more likely to be over-priced by the market simply due to this factor and the general assessment of its importance by the betting public. So although it may at first seem illogical to include such a condition, it is in fact a sensible factor to include when considered in the context of the profit/loss variable.

DEVELOPING A SYSTEM: EXAMPLE USING SENSITIVITY ANALYSIS

The easiest way to develop a horseracing system is to identify an initial key variable (or base factor), and then build the system around it. This initial factor may be something as simple as a rating, or it may be more complex, such as good horses running below par. Once identified, the race results should be analysed with respect to this key variable to determine a benchmark profit/loss value, and then the other factors considered in turn to determine whether they make any significant improvement to this benchmark figure. However, with detailed databases examining the other variables is a time-consuming task, and the simplest method is to use sensitivity analysis.

Sensitivity analysis is used in many different numerical disciplines, and essentially it monitors how one system reacts to changes in its influencing variables. For horseracing systems, the initial condition is fixed and the other critical variables allowed to vary across their entire range with profit and loss figures calculated for each value. Naturally the easiest way to present this analysis is in graphical form.

As an example consider the following system which takes the top-rated horses, based on speed figures, in novice and maiden hurdle races as the base factor. Over the four seasons 1998/99-2001/02, these horses returned a level-stake profit at starting price of 7p for every £1 staked on the 2,014 races. This is an excellent starting point, and in fact could be used as the system itself since a 7% return is not insignificant and a success rate of 31% is more than acceptable. However, it is always desirable to check other influences in case the system can be improved without losing any generality.

Sensitivity analysis produces the graphs presented here. The graphs show the performance of the top-rated horses with respect to each of the other critical variables. Interestingly, the effect of the non-linearity is immediately visible. Conventional form study states that recent winning form is preferred – however, from graph 1 it is apparent that horses who finished unplaced on their latest start are favoured over winners, simply based on the level of profit. Applying this one condition reduces the number of races to 625 but increases the profit to 25p for every £1 staked. The overall success rate does drop to just over 20%, though, which may be too low for some bettors, so this condition is reset and ignored at this

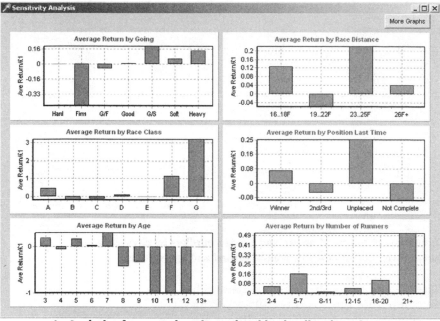

1: Analysis of top-rated novice and maiden hurdlers by going, race distance, race class, position last time, age and field size

stage of the process.

A more interesting influence is weight carried (see graph 2). The profit increases as the weight increases and setting a lower limit of 11st produces a profit of 16p per £1 staked for 1,124 races with a success rate of 38%. Leaving this condition as part of the system and reapplying the sensitivity analysis produces graphs which show that, although horses unplaced on their latest start return the best profit, all previous race positions now return a good profit. However, the profit is low for horses making a quick return, and negative for those off the track for over 84 days, which is again evidence of the non-linearity involved with this type of analysis. More importantly the profit is negative for all horses aged eight or more (see graph 3). Restricting the system to horses aged between three and seven produces 412 winners from 1,047 bets and a profit of 21p for every £1 staked.

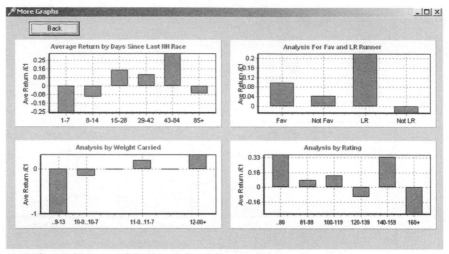

2: Analysis of top-rated novice and maiden hurdlers by days since last jumps race, market position, weight carried and speed rating

This is now a reasonably general system with an acceptable success rate (39%) and an excellent profit margin. The conditions are sensible and not overly specific, and though the addition of a maximum-days-off-the-course condition would improve the return, the level of improvement would be only minimal. Consequently this system would appear to be worth following and could be validated against a new data set, and analysed by season as final checks before implementation.

UNDERLYING INFLUENCES – HIDDEN FACTORS

In 1936 the Literary Digest published the results of a poll designed to forecast the result of the forthcoming American presidential election. The poll indicated that Alfred Langdon would win the election with 370 votes; his opponent, Franklin D Roosevelt, was expected to receive only 61 votes. In fact the election results produced 523 votes for Roosevelt; Langdon secured a paltry eight. Clearly the poll was misleading. The error here was far from intentional and lay in the incorrect method of sampling employed. As opposed to sampling the views of the public in a

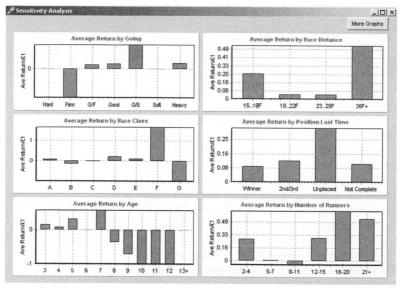

3: Analysis of top-rated novice and maiden hurdlers set to carry 11st or more by going, race distance, race class, position last time, age and field size

conventional way, the pollsters decided to conduct a telephone poll. In 1930s America the telephone was a rare commodity and only the very rich normally had access to one at home. These tended to support Langdon, which resulted in a bias in the poll results.

There are very often connections, in statistical terms, between sets of information which are not fully realised. In the previous example, the company conducting the poll had not appreciated that people that owned telephones were not representative of the country and that they were likely to provide a biased sample.

The same can happen in horseracing systems, with third-party variables affecting the outcome of the system for reasons the system developer does not fully understand. This can lead to invalid systems which suddenly under-perform for no apparent reason. A change in race structuring may not appear to have any bearing on a system, yet this apparently unrelated variable could be affecting the results. Furthermore, an understanding of the relationships can produce more meaningful analyses of the races and produce more reliable systems.

As an example, consider the novice hurdle system developed earlier: all novice and maiden hurdle races; top-rated on speed figures; age of horse less than eight; weight carried 11st or more.

This simple, four-condition system generally produces around 250 selections per year and returns a profit of about 20p for every £1 staked at starting price.

The four conditions of the system seem relatively straightforward, using variables that are very common in system development. Speed figures can be very useful when applied to jump racing, providing they are based on accurate time and distance information. In this instance, speed figures are used to identify the horse with most proven ability in the race.

The age condition eliminates older horses who tend to underperform in these race grades. Though a few older horses can run well in these races, in general an eight-year-old with ability should no longer be qualified for a novices' event, having won hurdle races previously. Those who are tend to be either poor or unreliable animals.

Eight-year-old Ad Hoc is the obvious exception. After a period running over fences, winning such races as the Whitbread Gold Cup at Sandown, he returned to hurdle racing in the 2002/03 season and showed he still possessed the speed and ability to win over the smaller obstacles. However, horses such as Ad Hoc are very much the exception, in fact horses aged eight or more win less than 4% of all novices' hurdle races at a success rate of about one in 20.

While the age requirement is easy to justify, the weight condition affects the system in more subtle ways. In handicap races horses carrying more weight tend to win more often and this variable can be an important discriminating factor in systems. However, novices' and maiden hurdle races are not handicaps, and horses are not assigned different weights based on their ability. The weight each horse carries is dependent on such factors as the race conditions, the age of the horse, jockey's allowance, gender and, in the case of novices' events, previous wins. Though maiden hurdle races feature only horses that have not previously won a hurdle race, novices' events can include runners that have won several similar events. These are awarded penalties depending on the value of the races they have won (as opposed to ability) and can increase the weight they need to carry by up to 14lb.

The weight condition would not exclude previous winners since, in most cases, the penalty they are set to carry would increase their weight above the 11st limit. However, it does bias the selection against younger horses when they compete in all-aged races, also mares would be less likely to be selected when racing against geldings and in many cases it would rule out horses ridden by conditional jockeys. So although the condition relates directly to weight, its effect is due, in the main, to other conditions.

Consequently the system could be revised with each of these factors analysed in detail. For instance, the races could be partitioned into those where mares race against geldings and separate analyses performed, the results of which may improve the performance of the original system.

However, this will make the system more complex to apply and could result in over-fitting. In other words, the system becomes too specific and, although it produces good results historically, does not continue to perform well in the future. This is the main drawback using back-fitting to generate profitable systems. Whilst a system may work well, it is important to be aware of the effect of underlying variables and, although it may not be necessary to modify the system, such variables need to be considered carefully with respect to other changing conditions that could affect the results of the method.

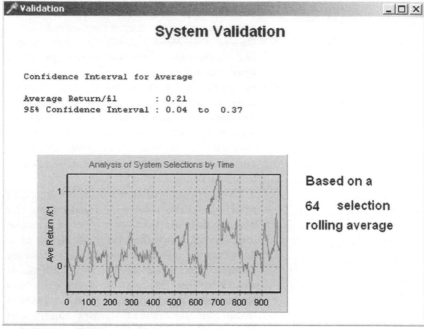

4: Validation of a horseracing system

VALIDATING SYSTEMS Back-fitting is a biased approach to generating systems and, as a result, can produce inappropriate rules that do not perform well in future events. For instance, the system could be very specific, producing rules that refer to small areas of the data which, in the past, were profitable but are highly likely to be unprofitable in the future. Also, the system may rely on a few large-priced winners to generate the positive return that have been found by repeated refining and filtering of the data. Such systems are unlikely to continue to produce a profit and should be avoided. Given this weakness in the systems development approach, it is necessary to validate any system carefully before implementation.

If back-fitting has been used, the best way to validate the system is by using a new data set. Before developing the system it is necessary to partition the data set and use one part for

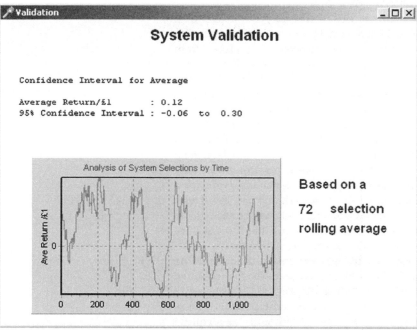

System Validation

Confidence Interval for Average

Average Return/£1   : 0.12
95% Confidence Interval : -0.06 to 0.30

Analysis of System Selections by Time

Based on a 72 selection rolling average

5: Validation of an unreliable horseracing system

development and another for validation. Normally this partition is performed randomly. However, given that horseracing is time-dependent (ie, races, training methods and so on change over time) a more effective partition is achieved by simply using the most recent data for validation. With five years of data, the usual approach would be to use the first four years to develop the system and the fifth year to validate any rule.

There will be cases where, due to lack of data, it is not possible to reserve a complete season for validation. Under these circumstances, other approaches to validation are required. The most common method would be a statistical approach, specifically a confidence interval. If applied to a randomly selected sample, the confidence interval provides a range in which the average of the population from which the sample was selected will fall. For instance, the results of opinion polls are normally supplemented with a confidence interval, such as 38% ± 4%, that shows the degree of error associated with the estimate. However, for this method to work well, the sample needs to be selected from the whole population – not possible for horse-racing, since this would need to include the future races in which we would like to support the system's qualifiers. Consequently this approach should not be relied upon to provide a guarantee of the system achieving a predetermined level. Its value is to determine systems that are unlikely to perform well. Any system that has a confidence interval with a lower limit close to zero should be viewed with a degree of doubt and, if followed, stakes should be kept to a minimum until sufficient data are accrued that support the system.

Another form of validation that should be applied in addition to the methods mentioned previously, is an analysis of the performance of the system over shorter time periods. This is easily represented graphically as a rolling average. The data on which the system was developed together with the test data form the population on which the rolling average is based.

To calculate the rolling average it is necessary to set a sample size, s, for instance. The average return for the system based on the first s qualifiers is calculated and plotted on the graph. The first qualifier is then dropped and the s+1 qualifier added to the sample. The average is again calculated and the point plotted on the graph. This continues until all of the qualifiers have been used. The resulting graph illustrates how the performance of the system has varied over time and shows the highs and lows that can be expected to be repeated.

A further advantage of this approach is that it highlights potentially important patterns in the data which are not apparent from the statistical measure of confidence. For instance, the system may have worked well for a period of time, then deteriorated significantly. The confidence interval may still indicate a profit, but from the graph of the system's performance it would be clear that the system was unlikely to perform well in the future.

As an example, graph 4 shows the various methods of validation for the novice hurdle system discussed earlier.

Graph 4 shows the average return for the system, in this case 21p/£1 staked; the confidence interval 4p to 37p and the rolling average graph for the 1,047 system qualifiers. The lower limit of the confidence interval is relatively close to zero and indicates that this system may produce a negative return in the future. The graph shows the average return for each consecutive set of 64 bets.

The low point, around bet 850, was during the foot-and-mouth crisis of 2001 and showed that the system did not perform well under these unusual circumstances. (Again this illustrates how systems can be susceptible to changing circumstances not previously considered.) However, the majority of 64-bet samples produce a profitable outcome, so on this alone I would consider the system to be worth following. Graph 5 shows the validation output for a less reliable system.

Though the average return at 12p for every £1 staked is reasonable, the confidence interval ranging from -6p to 30p is not particularly encouraging. Furthermore the graph shows that for a vast number of 72-bet samples the return would be negative, consequently there would be too many occasions through the season when the system was appearing to perform poorly. Under these conditions the bettor is unlikely to continue with the rule and losses would be sustained. Given this information I would not be prepared to follow this particular system. However, the cyclical nature of the graph suggests that a time-based factor may be unduly influencing the system's performance, so further analysis might be useful.

IMPLEMENTING SYSTEMS When developing the system, success rate may not appear to be important. After all, the main aim is to return a good profit, so providing this is achieved the rate at which the system identifies winning bets is irrelevant. However, once a system is running its success rate becomes a crucial factor.

The problem facing most system followers is whether to continue with a system that is performing poorly with long losing runs. Naturally this is more likely to happen if the system has a low success rate. For instance, a system with a 10% success rate is very likely to produce a losing run of over 20 during a run of 200 bets.

The worst response to a losing run is to stop playing the system. Providing the system is well founded, and adequately tested, there is no need to doubt that it will return a profit at the end of the season providing other conditions remain stable.

Systems have good and poor runs, this is only to be expected, so unless there are significant changes to the conditions that directly impact on the system it should be followed for the pre-determined time period.

During the foot-and-mouth crisis, system players were well advised to stop following their methods, simply because this unexpected outbreak had a significant impact on the structure and results of races, but under normal circumstances this action should be avoided in order to give the method a chance to recover.

In order to avoid long losing runs, it is preferable to follow systems that possess a high success rate. As a guide, a 20% success rate is considered a minimum, and one method to ensure this outcome is to restrict the system to qualifiers that are priced nearer the front of the market. As an example, a maximum price of the qualifiers can be set to a relatively low figure, such as 9-1.

Other methods include staking plans that reduce the stake for the longer-priced qualifiers. However, these staking methods need to be fully accounted for in the system development and validation phases.

INDEX

Page numbers shown in italics refer to illustrations.

Ad Hoc 260
Against The Crowd (1995) 220
Against The Odds (2003) 65-66
Aintree 14, 131 *see also Grand National*
Airwave 80
Alamshar 120, 136
Alderbrook 141
Allen, Professor Twink 52
Ameerat 135
Anabaa 57
ante-post betting 159-160, 177, 230-233
Ascot 45, 70, 76, 85, 138 *see also Royal Ascot*
Ascot Gold Cup 138, 139
Ashkalani 57
Attache 84, 85, 141
Attheraces 41, 107, 199, 217
Ayr 78, 85-86
Azertyuiop 127

Ballysax Stakes 136
Barathea 54, 56, 67
Bath 86
Berry, Jack 75
Best Mate 142, 143, 177
bet, types of 152-159, 227-228
  see also Tote
  canadian 158, 178
  combination 152, 155, 156, 176-177
    related contingencies 157
  double 227-228
  multiple 152, 155, 156-159, 175, 176-177
  patent 157, 178
  single 152, 174-175, 175, 227

  yankee 158, 178-179
Betfair 191, 192, 193, 197, 208, 209, 212-213, 216-219
bets, bad-value 178-179
bets, returns on 152-153
bets to consider 174-179
betting
  'don'ts' 251
  history of 148, 151
  key rules 169-170
  not changing mind 243
  rules and disputes 162, 164, 165
betting, gaining an edge 220-266
  ante-post betting 230-233
  best price 226-227, 234-237
  dealing with a losing run 225
  each-way betting 228-230
  getting timing right 230
  how to maximise 244-251
  making it pay 238-243
  picking the right race 220-222
  psychology of punting 222-224
  specialising 223, 237
  systems *see systems, horseracing*
  types of bet 227-228
  value added 224-226
Betting Acts (1853/1906) 151
Betting and Gaming Act (1960) 151
betting-exchanges (P2P – person-to-person/ peer-to-peer betting) 184-185, 191, 192-199, 193, 209, 226
  see also Betfair
  advantages 197
  aggregate of winning distances 196-197,

    206, 207
  best price 196
  disadvantages 198-199
  football matches 212-214
  how they work 194-197
  in-running betting 196, 199, 199
  laying-off bets 192, 194, 195
  and licences 195
  odds 154-155
  simple rules 194
  survival guide 208-215
    arbitrageurs 210
    bookies 210
    cheats 209, 214
    contrarians 212
    Excel spreadsheets 208-209, 210
    hedgers 213
    spoofers 208
    spotting a mug 215
    understanding the market 211
Betting, Gaming and Lotteries Act (1963) 151
betting industry, overview 149-150
  see also book making industry, history of
betting off-course 148-179
  market moves 188-189
betting offices (shops), licensed (LBOs) 149, 150, 161, 221
  rituals 163
betting on-course 171, 180-189, 181, 213, 235
  advantages 184
  alternatives 183
  basics 181-183
  market 183-185
  starting price *see starting price*
Beverley 63, 86-87, 121
Beyer, Andy 22, 37
Bhutan 250

binarybet.com 212
Bindaree 144, 145
Birch, Richard 174-179,
    228, 238-243
blinkers 38, 79, 81, 248
Blowing Wind 143
Boat Race 211
Bollin Eric 137
Bonanza Boy 146
book, making a 170-173,
    171, 210
bookmaker's profit margin
    (overround) 172-173
bookmakers, on-course 171,
    181-185, 181, 213, 235
bookmaking industry,
    history of 148, 151 *see
    also betting industry,
    overview*
Brazil national football
    team 157
breeding 50-57
    the Derby 57, 68-69
    distance, assessing best 67
    Dosage system *see
        Dosage system*
    heritability of racing
        potential 51-52
    nicks 50, 54-55
    Northern Dancer-line
        sires 54-55, 56-57
    precocity 55-56
    stamina 52-53, 68
Brian Boru 137
Brighton 63, 87
Brisbourne, Mark 75
Britannia Handicap 139
British Horseracing Board
    11-12, 18, 39
Bull, Phil 228
Butler, Gerard 77

Caribbean Coral 96
Carlisle 87-88
Cartmel 131
Casual Look 136
Catterick 88
Cecil, Henry 80, 136, 137
Cenkos 144
Cesarewitch 83, 84, 97
Champion Hurdle 141
Champion Stakes 120
Chance, Noel 143
Chandler, Victor 248
Charles II, King 69
cheekpieces 38, 79, 81, 248

Cheltenham 142, 142
Cheltenham Festival 14, 77,
    141-144, 233
    specialists 143
Cheltenham Gold Cup 71,
    177
Chepstow 89
Chester 63, 63, 69, 70, 76,
    77, 89-90, 121, 137
Cheveley Park Stakes 80,
    134-135
Chiefs Crown 57
Choisir 247
Christie, Linford 74
Classic races 12-13, 134
    *see also 1,000/2,000
    Guineas; Derby; Oaks;
    St Leger*
Cochrane, Ray 84
Computer Timeform 40
contacts, useful 40
Coral 149-150, 168
Coton, Mark 188, 229
Cullinan, Mel 244-251
Cumani, Luca 75
Curtis, Paul 20, 24-31, 109,
    110-125

Danehill 53, 57
Danzig 56, 57
Darshaan mares 50, 54
dead heats 170
Delamere, Gerald 43, 58-63
Dench, Graham 43, 44-49
Denebola 55
Deportivo 141
Derby 13, 69, 136, 189,
    232 *see also Epsom*
    and breeding 57, 68-69
    and French horses 137
Derrinstown Derby Trial
    136
Desert Orchid 71, 142-143
Dettori, Frankie 98, 140,
    159
Dewhurst Stakes 105-106
disputes, betting 162-164,
    165
distance statistics 52
distances, specialist 249
Doncaster 72, 77, 90, 137,
    219
Dosage system 50, 53-54
    calculations 54
    the Derby 57

information 54
Double Trigger 139
draw 72-73, 73, 82
draw bias 46, 72-73, 82-85,
    241
    specific courses 85-103,
    140
Duffield, George 87
Dunlop, John 77, 137
each-way betting 155-156,
    175-176, 228-230
early prices 160-162, 176,
    177, 226, 242

Earth Summit 146
Eastern Purple 246
Easyodds.com 242
Emirates Racing Association
    32
Entrepreneur 67, 135
Enzeli 248
Epsom 63, 68, 69-70, 90-
    91, 136-137 *see also Derby*
Ezzoud 79

Fabre, Andre 247
Fairy King 57
Falbrav 246, 247
Fallon, Kieren 84, 189
Fasliyev 55, 56-57
favourites, avoiding 251
Favourites Index 202, 203-
    204, 205-206, 215
festivals, major 12-13, 14 *see
    also Cheltenham Festival;
    Chester; Goodwood; Grand
    National; Newmarket, July
    meeting; Royal Ascot*
First Gold 142
Flagship Uberalles 144
Flat racing 12-13
Folkestone 91
Fontwell 131
football matches, betting-
    exchange betting on 212-
    214
forecast betting 159
form 73-76
    French and German horses
    35
    insights into 245-246
    months, performance in 76
Form Book 39-40, 79
form ratings 20-22, 74 *see
    also Racing Post Ratings*
Fox, Nick 191, 195, 200,
    208-215

French form 35
French horses and the Derby 137

Galileo 57, 232, 245
Galtres Stakes 75
gambling activities, most popular 150-151
Gambling Bill (2003) 149
Gambling Review Group 148, 149, 150-151, 168, 180-181
Gaming Act (1845) 151
Garrison Savannah 147
Geos 21
Geraghty, Barry 143
German form 35
Gibson, Dale 84
Given, James 80-81
Godolphin 134, 136-137, 138
going 62-63, 64-66, 105
  reports 65, 66
Golan 135, 135, 136, 231-232, 245
Golden Apples 53
Golden Jubilee Stakes 139
Gone West 55, 56
Goodwood 69, 70, 71-72, 76-77, 91-92, 105
Gosden, John 77, 138, 139
Grand Lodge 57
Grand National 14, 17, 20, 136, 144-147, 145, 232
  see also Aintree
  narrowing the field 147
Great Commotion 57
Great Voltiguer Stakes 137
ground conditions see going

Hamilton 92-93
handicapping 17-19
  horse's position 78
  minimum weight ('out of the handicap') 20
  ratings see form ratings; Racing Post Ratings; ratings; speed ratings
  weight-for-age scale 19
  weights 19, 27
Hannon, Richard 75
Harefoot 55
Harrington, Jessica 143
Hawk Wing 249, 250
Haydock 63, 93

Hector Protector 55
Henderson, Nicky 77, 233
Hennessy Gold Cup 245
Hernando 54, 57
Hidden Dragon 99
High Chapparal 50, 54, 57, 71
High Estate 57
Hills, Barry 76, 77
Hobbs, Philip 233
horse, types of see also breeding
  chasers 14
  chefs-de-race sires 53
  'class' 251
  'drifters' 188
  foreign-trained 247
  front-runners 106
  hurdlers 14
  nicks 50, 54-55
  recently gelded 81
  'second string' 249
  seven-furlong specialists 248, 249
  'steamers' 188
  three-year-olds 12, 29, 246-247, 249
  two-year-olds 12, 43, 116-119
  what to look for 61
horseracing administration 11-12
horseracing structure 14, 16-19
horses see also breeding
  ability revealed 43
  to avoid 48
  body weight 81
  commitment 76-78
  equipment 38, 79, 80, 81, 248
  fitness 73-76
  genuineness 78-80
  improvers, spotting 46-49
  paddock inspection 49, 59
  performance, other factors affecting 80-81
  preparation for big handicaps 47
  revising assumptions about 249-250
  in season 60, 80-81
  stamina 52-53, 68
  surgery on 81

horses, preferences of 64
  combination 64-65
  distance 66-72
  draw 72 73
  going 46, 64-65
  racecourses 70-71
horses, what to look for 58-60, 59, 188
  action 62, 66
  coat 60
  sweating 60-61
  two-year-olds 61
Huntingdon 131
hurdling 13

If By Chance 96
If Paradise 95
in-running betting 196, 217, 218-219
In The Wings 52, 54, 56
Independent Betting Arbitration Service (IBAS) 162-164
Indian Haven 55
Indian Ridge 53, 55
Iris Royal 59
Irish 2,000 Guineas 55
Irish Derby 245
Irish domination of Classics 136
Isio 127
Island Sands 136
Islington 50
Istabraq 141, 143
Ivory's Joy 246

jockey booking 78
Jockey Club 11, 12, 79, 164
jockeys 106, 107, 139-140
  apprentice 15, 248
  conditional 16
  reading of draw and course bias ('draw jockeys') 84
  weight allowances 15
John Smith's Cup 84
Johnston, Brian 211
Johnston, Mark 75, 76-77, 138-139, 138, 141
jump racing 13-14

Kahyasi 57
Karminskey Park 96
Keen Leader 142
Kempton 63, 82-83, 93-94,

143-144
Key Of Luck 57
King George V Stakes 139
King Of Kings 67
Kingscliff 188
Knight, Henrietta 177
Kris Kin 13, 136, 137, 189
Kris S 57

La Landiere 188
Ladbrokes 149-150, 168,
  215
Lahan 135
Landseer 55
Langdon, Alfred 258, 259
laying-off bets 177, 192,
  194, 195
Leicester 94
Levy Board 185
Lincoln Handicap 72
Lingfield 23, 46, 72, 94-95,
  105, 249
Literary Digest (1936) 258-
  259
Little Polveir 20
Local Poet 99
Loder, David 251
Lord Gyllene 20
losers, unlucky 250-251
losing runs 225, 242-243
Lungo, Len 78

Machiavellian 53
Make A Stand 141
Malhub 139
Mamool 245, 246
market moves 188-189
Mason, Steve 76, 109, 126-
  133, 221, 223, 224, 228,
  233
Maxwell, Robert 187
May, Peter 252-266
McCoy, Tony 143
McKeown, Dean 84
Media Puzzle 67
Megahertz 53
Milan 137
Milk It Mick 106
Miller, Steve 53-54
Minnehoma 146
Mirror Group Newspapers
  186-187
Mister Baileys 136
Miswaki 55
Monopolies and Mergers

Commission 150
Monsignor 144
Monty's Pass 17, 144, 145,
  146, 147, 232
Moon Ballad 56
Mordin, Nick 20, 32-34, 36-
  37, 68
Mordin On Time (Aesculus)
  36, 68
Morris, Tony 78-79
Morshdi 245
Moscow Flyer 143
Moyanna 212
Mr Dinos 245, 246
Mr Prospector 55
Mtoto 57
Mullins, Willie 143
Murtagh, Johnny 140
Musical Bliss 135
Musselburgh 95, 131
Mutafaweq 137

Nad Al Sheba racetrack 32-
  33, 33
Namid 247
National Hunt racing 13-14
National Joint Pitch Council
  (NJPC) 165, 182, 185
National Press Challenge
  109, 110, 111
  jumps 126, 128
Nevison, Dave 222, 225,
  227, 228
New Seeker 84, 85
Newbury 21, 75, 95-96
Newcastle 96
Newmarket 69, 83, 84, 105-
  106, 134-135, 135 see also
  1,000/2,000 Guineas
  July course 63, 96-97
  July meeting 242
  Rowley Mile 97
Nicholls, David 75, 77, 79
Nicholls, Paul 233, 251
Nicholson, David 77
Nijinsky 56, 57
non-runners 170
Norse Dancer 251
Northern Dancer-line sires
  54-55, 56-57
Nottingham 97-98
Nureyev 55, 56-57

Oaks 136
O'Brien, Aidan 71, 75, 134,
  136, 138, 232, 247, 251

odds, conventional 153-154
odds, Tote and exchange
  154-155
odds, 'true' 173
odds as percentages 172
odds-on betting 155, 240
One Cool Cat 55
One Hundred Hints for
  Better Betting (Aesculus)
  188
1,000 Guineas 134-136,
  189, 231
overseas betting 35, 167-
  169
Oxx, John 139

P2P betting see betting-
  exchanges
Pagones, Rachel 43
Palarshan 143
Papillon 146, 147, 232
payouts, maximum 159
pedigree of horses see
  breeding
Persian Tack 79
Picking Winners (1979) 22,
  37
Pilar Chase 143
Pipe, Martin 60, 77, 143
Pivotal 53, 67, 75
Polar Falcon 57
Polish Precedent 55, 56-57
Pontefract 98
Potts, Alan 72-73, 184, 187-
  188, 220, 221, 224, 225,
  227, 229-230
Prescott, Sir Mark 75
Press Association 186, 187
prices, best value 176
prices, early 160-162, 176,
  177, 226, 242
Priest, David-Lee 65-66
Prime Recreation 83
Prix de l'Arc de Triomphe
  77
Prix Marcel Boussac 134-
  135
Prosser, Michael 96
psychology of punting 222-
  224, 242-243
publications, specialist 38-41
punters, on-course 187-188
punters, overview 150-152

Queen's Vase 139, 245, 246

Quinn, Richard 84

race, pace analysis of 104-107
  before the race 106-107
  front runners 106
  middle section 106
  speed maps 107
  three-part rule 105-106
  wind conditions 107
race, 'shape' of 221-222
race analysis 44-49
  draw bias 46
  making it pay 49
  spotting improvers 46-49
  unreliable form 46
  weighing up a race 44-46
race distance, horses' requirements 66-70
race distance, pedigree analysis 67
race times 66 see also timing, sectional
Racecourse Holdings Trust 12
racecourses
  all-weather tracks 13, 23, 37, 46, 72, 95, 100, 102, 105, 249
    as a profitable area 112
  to avoid 249
  bias 63, 85-103
  variety 69-71
  walking 62
  watering 62, 72, 102
Raceform 40
Raceform Interactive 40
Raceform Update 39
racehorses see horses
races, class structure 19
races, Flat, types of 15
  black-type 14, 16-17, 19, 75
  Group 14, 15, 16
  level-weights 14
  Listed 14, 15
  Pattern 15-16
races, foreign 35, 167-169
races, jump, types of 16
  bumper 13, 16
  Grade 16, 17
  Listed 17
  National Hunt flat 13, 16
  Pattern 17
races, profitable 109
races to avoid 248-249

Racing & Football Outlook 39, 82
Racing Post 38-39, 39, 40, 48, 78-79, 80-81, 83, 126, 183, 186, 187, 220, 232, 238
  analysis section 44
  'Mel's Maxims' 251
  Pricewise column 41, 84, 224, 226, 239
  Signposts section, Trainer Trace 80
  stamina index 52-53
  website 39, 226, 240-241
Racing Post Ratings 20, 21-22, 24-26, 27-29, 71, 74, 110, 111, 127
  areas covered 31
  compilation 25-26, 27-28
  tips 112
    by age restriction 115
    by class 120, 121
    by distance (3yo+) 121, 122
    by handicap/non handicap 116
    jumps 129, 130
    by month 113-115, 117, 125
    non-handicap hurdle 131, 132
    by odds 118, 124
Racing Post Smartbet service 39, 226
Racing Post Weekender 34, 39, 53
Rahy 53
Rainbow Quest 54, 55, 67
Rakti 247
ratings 18-19
  class factor 19, 29-31
  class gap 26
  edge 26-28
  private 19-20
  problem areas 28-29
  three-year-olds 29
ratings approach to jumps 126-133
  bet-provoking results 132-133
  continuity as the key 128, 130
  course study 130-132
  months to tread carefully 130
  non-handicap hurdle tips 131, 132, 133
ratings approach to the Flat 110-125
  class no guide to success 121
  consistency 111-112
  distances a confusing picture 121-122
  month by month 113-115, 122-123
  older horses in handicaps 119-121
  three-year-olds only events, avoiding 115-116
  two-year-olds, improved performance 116-119, 124
Ratio 85
Red Marauder 144, 145, 146, 147, 232
Redcar 98-99
Reed, George 243
Refuse To Bend 67, 136, 231, 250
Repertory 246
Rhyme 'N' Reason 146
Ripon 99
Roberts, Michael 84
Rock Of Gibraltar 136, 249
Rockfel Stakes 135
Roman, Steven 53-54
Ronaldo 157
Roosevelt, Franklin D 258
Rooster Booster 21, 141, 143, 233
Rough Quest 146
Royal Anthem 250
Royal Ascot 76, 83-84, 85, 137-141, 242
  see also Ascot
Royal Athlete 146
Royal Hunt Cup 45
Royal Predica 143, 144
Royal Rebel 138, 139, 248
Rules For Jokers 98
Rushcutter Bay 246
Russian Rhythm 55, 80, 134-135, 189, 231

Sadlers Wells 50, 51, 54, 55, 56, 57, 67, 134, 136
St Leger 77, 90, 137
Salisbury 63, 99-100
Sandown 63, 68-69, 70-71,

100
Satellite Information Services (SIS) 163, 186, 187, 199, 217
Seagram 146
Sedgefield 131
See More Business 248
Segal, Tom 41, 73-74, 109, 134-147, 222-224, 232-233, 234-237
Shirley Heights 55
Silver Hawk 57
Silver Patriarch 57, 137
Singspiel 56
Sinndar 247
Six Perfections 134-135
Smith, Kevin 110, 127
Song 54
Southwell 72, 100
SP Executive 186 *see also starting price*
specialising 223, 237, 241, 248
speed maps 107
speed ratings 20, 22-23, 33-37
  all-weather tracks 37
  compilation 34, 36-37
  favourite pick 36
  foreign races 35
Spinning World 55
splits, specific courses 85-103
Sporting Chronicle, The 186
Sporting Index 201
Sporting Life, The 163, 186, 187
Sportsman, The 186
spread betting 177-178, 191, 200-207
  advantages 204-205
  disadvantages 205
  Favourites Index 202, 203-204, 205-206, 215
  how it works 201
  the markets 201-204
  simple rules 202
  types of bet 205-207
staking plans 240
starting price 185-186
  best 226-227, 234-237
  history of 186-187
  rules 187
steeplechasing 13
Stewards' Cup 72

Storm Cat 55, 56
Storming Home 81
Stoute, Sir Michael 134, 135, 137, 138, 189, 233
strategy 238-242
Strensall 96
Suny Bay 147
Superform 40, 41
systems, horseracing 252-266
  data mining 254
  developing 254-255
    example using sensitivity analysis 255-258, 257, 258, 259
  implementing 265-266
  requirements 253-254
  underlying influences – hidden factors 258-261
  validating 262-265, 262, 263

Tattersalls' Committee 163, 164
Tattersalls Rule 4 (c) deductions 169
Taylor, Lawrence 107
telephone betting 168
television, racing coverage 41, 199, 217
The Wizard Mul 99
Theatrical 57
Thirsk 100-101
Thomas Pink Gold Cup 245
Timeform 40
timing, sectional 23, 74, 104, 107
tongue ties 38, 79, 81, 248
Topham Trophy 144, 145, 146
Torrent 229
Tote (Horserace Totalisator Board) 148, 164-167, 167, 183, 238
  odds 154-155
  pros and cons 179
  types of bet 165-167, 179
Tote Gold Trophy 21
trainers 74-75, 76-78, 79-80, 251
Trinity Mirror 163, 186
Turner, Simon 109, 112, 115, 222, 229
2,000 Guineas 135, 136, 231-232, 249

United States racetracks 69
value betting 224-226, 234-237, 239
Value Betting (Aesculus, 1990) 229
Victor Chandler Chase 127
Vinnie Roe 246

Walsh, Ruby 143
Warwick 101, 144
Weatherbys, Statistical Record Annual Issue 52
Weatherbys Super Sprint 75, 95
Webbon, Peter 80
weights carried 14, 261
Weld, Dermot 139
Wetherby 70
What's Up Boys 147
Wheldon, Graham 72, 82-103
William Hill 149, 150, 226
Williams, Freddie 171
Williams, Matt 191, 216-219
Willoughby, James 104-107
Wince 135
wind conditions 107
Windsor 63, 101-102
winners, backing big handicap, on the Flat 250
winners, picking 239
winners, wide-margin 250
winning distances, aggregate, betting on 196-197, 206, 207
Winston, Robert 84
Wolfhound 57
Wolverhampton 72, 102
Woodman 55
Wragg, Geoff 76
Wright, Howard 186

Xenophon 143

Yarmouth 102-103
Yesterday 50, 251
York 62-63, 70, 75, 77, 84, 103, 103, 137
Young Spartacus 143

Zafeen 55
Zafonic 55, 56
Zarfoot 55
Zero Tolerance 250
Zuhair 71-72